# SOMEONE YOU KNOW

# SOMEONE YOU KNOW

## AN UNFORGETTABLE COLLECTION OF CANADIAN TRUE CRIME STORIES

### CATHERINE FOGARTY

Collins

Published by Collins, an imprint of HarperCollins Publishers Ltd

First edition

HarperCollins Publishers Ltd
Bay Adelaide Centre, East Tower
22 Adelaide Street West, 41st Floor
Toronto, Ontario, Canada
M5H 4E3

*www.harpercollins.ca*

Library and Archives Canada Cataloguing in Publication

Title: Someone you know : an unforgettable collection of Canadian true crime stories / Catherine Fogarty.
Names: Fogarty, Catherine, author.
Description: Includes bibliographical references.
Identifiers: Canadiana (print) 20230202896 | Canadiana (ebook) 20230203035 | ISBN 9781443470001 (softcover) | ISBN 9781443470018 (EPUB)
Subjects: LCSH: Murder—Canada. | LCSH: Murderers—Canada.
Classification: LCC HV6535.C3 F64 2024 | DDC 364.152/30971—dc23

Printed and bound in the United States of America

23 24 25 26 27  LBC  5 4 3 2 1

FOR OLIVER

# CONTENTS

# SOMEONE YOU KNOW

# INTRODUCTION

W hy do you like telling stories about murder?"

"How do you sleep at night?"

These are questions I have been asked many times when I tell people I write and host a Canadian true crime podcast. And the answer is that writing about terrible crimes and cold-blooded killers *does* often keep me tossing and turning into the wee hours of the night.

But the reality is that bad stuff happens. We cannot escape crime; it happens all around us every day, regardless of who we are or where we live. Evil walks among us, yet it is something that has always fascinated us. Why? Is it a morbid curiosity about the worst of humankind, or does knowing who the monster is hiding under the bed somehow make us feel safer?

Prior to the twentieth century, newspapers went to war in the hope of getting the latest scoops on scandalous murder stories and local crimes. Criminals became famous villains who were either loved or loathed by the masses. Jack the Ripper terrorized the East End of London, while Lizzie Borden took a drastic disliking to her parents and Irish Canadian maid Grace Marks (made famous by Margaret Atwood) was convicted of a heinous double murder in Toronto. Simply put, salacious headlines sold newspapers.

Then radio broadcasting brought some of those same unforgettable crime stories alive. Families sat glued to their RCA or Zenith radios, listening to serialized true detective shows like *Ellery Queen*, *Sam Spade* or *Dick Tracy*. Everyone loved the amateur gumshoes and detectives chasing nasty criminals and solving crimes.

The invention of the moving picture and the rise of Hollywood film studios soon took us into dimmed movie houses to watch murder and mayhem play out on the big screen. The 1940s and 1950s gave us film noir, highly stylized crime dramas that introduced us to the often-disillusioned detective fighting gangsters, crooks and the mysterious femmes fatales.

Movie audiences couldn't get enough of the dark cinematic dramas, but soon the fedora-wearing private investigator was replaced by the terrifying psychopath. An entire generation of women, including my mother, stopped taking showers after Alfred Hitchcock's *Psycho* premiered in 1960.

Psychological thrillers and horror movies became popular entertainment because they exposed us to our worst fears and the scariest of monsters. But we all knew that Freddie Krueger was a Hollywood invention and that a guy named Jason wasn't likely coming after us on Halloween. Although I will admit, Hannibal Lecter and *Silence of the Lambs* did give me a few nightmares.

Fictional movie monsters give us an exhilarating, "jump out of your seat" form of entertainment. But what about the real ones? The 1960s introduced us to a real-life madman named Charles Manson who used compliant followers to butcher innocent people in their homes. The '70s and '80s presented us with a new kind of killer: the serial killer, lurking in the shadows and murdering out of compulsion—or just for the fun of it.

But what was perhaps more terrifying than the crimes was the fact that this new breed of killer wasn't necessarily the monster we had envisioned. He was the good-looking boy next door or the ordinary guy from our hometown. Soon, kids didn't play outside after dark and we started locking our doors at night. Crime wasn't just something that happened to other people. It was now in our communities, no matter where we lived.

Growing up in Toronto in the 1970s and 1980s, my first exposure to true crime came by the way of Max Haines and his weekly "Crime Flashback" column in the *Toronto Sun*. His lurid tales of murder and madness fascinated me. I also remember veteran crime reporter Jocko Thomas reporting "live from police headquarters" on CFRB radio, and what he was reporting was sometimes terrifying. In Toronto, children were going missing—Emanuel Jaques (1977), Lizzie Tomlinson (1980), Sharin Morningstar Keenan (1983), Christine Jessop (1984) and Alison Parrott (1986). Sadly, none of these children would be found alive, and my safe city, "Toronto the Good," was no more.

Years later, after studying sociology and criminology at university and becoming a social worker, I developed a further interest in exploring the darker side of human nature. My copies of Truman Capote's *In Cold Blood* (1966) and Vincent Bugliosi's *Helter Skelter* (1974) were dog-eared, and a TV newsmagazine show called *Dateline* became my new obsession. My Friday nights were dedicated to the latest real-life murder mystery, as traumatized families retold their harrowing stories to the ever-inquisitive Canadian newsman Keith Morrison. Soon, there was a plethora of similar programs like *48 Hours, 20/20, America's Most Wanted, Forensic Files* and *Unsolved Mysteries*. Clearly, I wasn't alone in my insatiable desire for crime stories. But who doesn't love a good whodunit?

Today, true crime has never been more popular, as evidenced by the growing number of books, podcasts and TV shows dedicated to the genre. Entire networks, like Investigative Discovery and A&E, now air murder and mystery 24/7, while Netflix has become the go-to place for true crime addicts to binge-watch gripping series based on shocking real-life events. Shows like *Making of a Murderer, Tiger King* and *Dahmer* have brought us into the minds of madmen. I know I'm not the only person who has stayed up until 4 a.m. watching . . . just one more episode!

But with true crime all the time, some have warned that we risk glamorizing killers and exploiting their victims with sensationalized coverage. Has our seemingly insatiable interest in violent and dangerous perpetrators meant that their victims are marginalized or overlooked? Where is their voice in these narratives?

When I began Story Hunter Podcasts in the summer of 2020, we were in the midst of an unprecedented event, a global pandemic that left many of us in fear. Suddenly, a mysterious virus became our bogeyman. It came without warning, and it was deadly. Life as we knew it changed in an instant. But we gradually adapted, and we ultimately prevailed because the human spirit will always be stronger than any bogeyman or monster.

And it is the strength of the human spirit that I want to honour in retelling twelve Canadian true crime stories. Beyond the often macabre and shocking details of many of these crimes is something else: the victims and their families; the ones lost and the ones left behind.

For the families of murder victims, their painful memories never go away despite the passage of time. Often their grief is exacerbated when the person who took their loved one away is someone they know. In this anthology, children are left without a father when their mother kills her husband; a family is betrayed by one of their own; and a mother is raising her newborn granddaughter after her own daughter is murdered by the man she loved.

Interpersonal and intimate partner violence accounts for most murders in our country. While we were all taught about "stranger danger" as young kids, the reality is that we are more likely to be sleeping with, socializing with, related to or married to our killer. And that is deeply disturbing. That is why police investigators start close to a murder victim. Who had the strongest reason for wanting that person dead? Motive is key to any murder investigation and can often fall under what is commonly referred to as the four Ls: lust, love, loathing and loot.

Husbands and wives will always be at the top of any list of suspects, and they are often the ones caught holding the proverbial smoking gun. And while love and marriage can be deadly, so too can friendships and family. In the stories that follow, people have been murdered by their best friend, a work colleague, mother-in-law and even a son. The victims had no idea of the lingering danger that was often right on their doorstep. Were there warning signs? In a few cases, yes, but still, most of us could never believe that someone so close would do us such harm.

But finding a motive for murder doesn't explain what makes some people commit such heinous acts. Anger, jealousy, hatred— these are all common human emotions. And who doesn't want more money? However, these emotions and desires, despite their intensity, will not drive most people to kill. But how can we begin to understand the actions of those who do? It is the ultimate betrayal of someone they once loved or cared for. Are they mad, or simply bad? That is the precise question asked in one of the following stories, and that is the question many victims' families are left with. Who was this person they let into their home? How could they not see them for who they really were?

While some of the stories in this anthology involve Canadian victims, others involve Canadian killers. A few of these killers have made headlines around the world, while others are lesser known but equally as diabolic. A Winnipeg woman transplanted to a sleepy Southern California suburb in the 1960s decides she wants a newer, wealthier husband; a Toronto trust fund baby uses his own graphic novel as a blueprint for a shocking murder in Los Angeles; a teenage son puts an end to his mother's nagging for good; and a Canadian reality TV star refuses to accept the reality of his own marriage.

These are all Canadian stories, and like it or not, they are part of our history and social conscience. But this anthology is by no means exhaustive, and you will undoubtedly notice some notorious names absent. Sadly, there are many more stories to be told, and tragically, none of us are immune to crime and violence. There are monsters among us. Some are strangers who live in the shadows, while others smile at us from our social media feeds, live in our homes or sleep beside us in our beds.

We are all potentially vulnerable, and perhaps this is why we have become voracious consumers of true crime. This particularly rings true for women, who account for the majority of true crime fans. It does not mean that we find pleasure in other people's tragedies. A murder is not entertainment. But perhaps our fascination is as fundamental as our basic need for human survival. If we know who the monster is, we can better protect ourselves.

But other people's trauma should not be overdramatized or sensationalized. What must remain in the retelling of true crime stories is the "true." Truth is storytelling and compassion towards the voices that have been silenced.

As the true crime genre remains a source of guilty escapism for many, killers old and new will emerge from the darkness and reappear on our screens and on the page. But we can never lose sight of their victims and the many lives forever altered by a single act of violence. And in the face of evil, we must remember our collective strength to overcome it.

# PART ONE

# FATAL FRIENDSHIPS

When your best friend turns out to be your worst enemy . . .

# MURDER IN THE MORGUE

## THE TWO FACES OF STEVEN TOUSSAINT

It was just after five o'clock on the morning of April 16, 1998, when the sirens and horns of emergency vehicles woke the sleepy residents of the Bloor and Ossington area in Toronto's leafy west end. The smell of black smoke filled the crisp spring air and flames could been seen for blocks shooting into the early-morning sky.

It didn't take long to discover the source of the fire. It was the historic Christ Church St. James on Shaw Street. But no sooner had the fire trucks arrived than they got word of another emergency: two nearby Catholic churches were also on fire. Police and fire crews dispersed to all three locations.

Later that same morning, a woman living in Etobicoke, a middle-class suburb farther west, awoke to reports of the church fires on the news, but she had something more pressing on her mind. Shirley Ivens was looking for her husband, who had failed to come home from work the night before. Bob Ivens was as regular as clockwork and never missed dinner with Shirley and their two kids, Meaghan and Michael. The couple had been married for twenty-two years, and family was Bob's priority. If something had come up at work, he would have called, as he always did.

Bob worked downtown, at the Medical Sciences Building on the University of Toronto campus. He was a technician in the morgue attached to the medical school, which was where human cadavers were stored for use by medical students. Bob had been at the university for over twenty-seven years, and he took great pride in his work. But lately he had been stressed more than usual. He had confided in Shirley that his long-time colleague, Stephen Toussaint, wasn't pulling his weight and often didn't show up for work. Stephen had a serious drinking problem, and Bob was getting tired of covering for his friend.

When Bob didn't arrive home on the evening of April 15, Shirley called the morgue office, but her calls went straight to voice mail. And the same thing happened when she tried Bob on his cellphone. Worried about the stress he had been under, Shirley decided to drive to the university lab.

When she got there, Shirley was relieved to see Bob's grey Jeep parked outside the Medical Arts Building. Maybe he had crashed on the couch in the lunchroom, thought Shirley, and would likely show up at home later that night. Shirley drove back to Etobicoke and had dinner with the couple's children alone. The following morning, she was awakened by a strange phone call. It was Norma Toussaint, the wife of Bob's co-worker. The two couples had known each other for years.

Norma said two police officers had been to her home in the east end at 6 a.m., looking for Stephen. According to the police, the church the Toussaints attended had caught fire and they needed to locate Stephen because he was a senior member of the church. Norma said she didn't know where he was—he hadn't come home the night before. Shirley told Norma she had heard about the church fires on the radio and that her husband had failed to come home from work, too.

‖‖‖‖‖‖‖

That same morning, a security guard working the overnight shift at the University of Toronto received two frantic phone calls from the wives of the men who worked in the morgue. Neither had returned home the previous evening, and the women were both very concerned. The guard knew Bob Ivens and Stephen Toussaint; like him, they were long-time employees of the university. He checked the morgue but saw no sign of either man, and it looked as though no one had been in that morning. The morgue, which was in the basement, was a secure area that few people had access to. He checked other areas in the building as well, thinking perhaps one or both were sleeping in the lunchroom, as some of the staff in the building were known to do after a long night. But there was no sign of Bob or Stephen anywhere.

Just before his shift ended at 10 a.m., the security guard decided to make another round of the building. Walking into the darkened morgue, there was still no sign of any activity, but this time he decided to check one of the backrooms. It was more of a closet where embalming and cleaning chemicals were kept. When he opened the door, he noticed something odd right away. In amongst the bottles and boxes on the shelves, there was a large black bag lying on the floor. It was a body bag, and it looked occupied.

The security guard usually didn't spend much time in the morgue—it creeped him out—but he knew bodies weren't supposed to be stored in that closet. Bending down, he unzipped the top of the bag and was immediately hit by a foul stench. He stumbled backwards, covering his mouth and gagging. Summoning all his nerve, he looked again. He could barely make out any facial features on the body. It was bloodied and swollen, and it looked fresh. Running from the closet, he was certain he had just found one of the missing morgue technicians.

When homicide investigators from the Metropolitan Toronto Police arrived later that morning, they were led to the battered body of a man they soon identified as Bob Ivens. It appeared that he had been murdered sometime the previous afternoon, as someone had reported seeing him just after 3 p.m. He was still wearing his hospital greens, meaning he hadn't changed to go home. An autopsy would later reveal that he had died from blunt force trauma to the head. His injuries were so severe that the pathologist deemed it overkill. The sheer brutality of the assault indicated a great deal of rage. But who would have wanted to do this do Bob Ivens?

Nothing was missing from the morgue, eliminating the possibility of a robbery gone wrong, and it wasn't the kind of place many people ventured into. And now the police had another mystery on their hands: where was Bob Iven's work colleague, Stephen Toussaint? His wife had reported him missing, and his church had burned to the ground, while two others had been set on fire. The police knew there had to be some connection between the bizarre series of events that had unfolded over the past twelve hours, but they weren't going to know much more until they found the missing man.

Stephen Toussaint was born on the West Indian island of Grenada in 1943 and immigrated to Canada in the early 1960s. He and his wife, Norma, whom he met at a square dance back in Grenada, had been married for thirty-one years and lived in a tidy bungalow in the eastern suburb of Scarborough, where they raised two daughters who were now young adults. Stephen had worked in the anatomy department at the University of Toronto Medical School since 1967. His job was to receive, prepare and store the donated bodies that were used by medical students in their anatomy lab work. He would also embalm and arrange transfer of the bodies once the medical work had been completed. Some of the bodies were returned to their families for burial, while others were simply cremated and buried in a mass grave.

Bob Ivens began working in the morgue in 1971 and reported to Stephen. For twenty-seven years, the men worked together, handling an average of 130 cadavers a year. But as the medical school grew and its enrolment expanded, more donor bodies were required for the anatomy classes and the workload in the morgue became more physically demanding and emotionally draining. Both men were adept at their job, but the constant handling of human remains did have an impact. They worked with cadavers but never lost sight of the fact that every one of the bodies they prepared had once been loved by someone.

In early 1996, Susan Hausmann joined the two-man team. A licensed mortician, Susan was hired to assist with the preparation of the bodies. Working alongside Stephen and Bob, she soon discovered that Bob was a quiet, hard-working perfectionist while Stephen was more gregarious and outgoing. But Stephen was hardly ever around. To Susan, it looked as though Bob was doing most of the work while Stephen would show up late most days, smelling of booze. It was no secret that he had a drinking problem and kept a whisky bottle in his desk and another behind some ceiling tiles in his office. Everyone in the anatomy department seemed to like Stephen, but Susan suspected he had a darker side. He would often talk about his dedication to his family and his church, but then he would also brag about the number of women he'd had sex with, including some he brought back to the morgue. He even had a little black book of his supposed conquests, where he wrote women's phone numbers backwards in case his wife ever found it.

Hausmann left the department in 1997, after only twelve months, but agreed to return in March 1998 to fill in for Stephen while he was on a three-week vacation. Susan was shocked to discover that the conditions in the morgue had gone from bad to worse. Bob told Susan that Stephen was rarely showing up for work, and when he did, he was usually drunk. When Susan opened a freezer originally meant to store a dozen donated bodies, she discovered over forty bodies as well as body parts. Bob said that Stephen didn't want to bother embalming the bodies after the medical work had been completed, so he just kept putting them in the freezer.

While Stephen was away, Susan and Bob cleaned up the backlog in the morgue and sent most of the unclaimed bodies to the local crematorium. Susan felt sorry for Bob and could see that the stress of the situation was wearing him down. He couldn't keep covering for Stephen, and she urged him to go to their supervisor to complain. Bob was reluctant to do so. After all, the two men had worked side by side for nearly thirty years. But he knew something had to change because his own health was suffering, and it was affecting his family life, too.

In early April, Toussaint returned from his vacation in good spirits. But he soon discovered that the morgue had been cleaned up and reorganized in his absence. He was not happy. Bob Ivens was his junior, and Stephen had not approved any changes. And then, within a few days of his return, the head of the anatomy department, Dr. Bernie Liebgott, issued him a letter of reprimand. It looked as if Toussaint's shoddy work and frequent absences had finally caught up with him. The letter did not address his drinking specifically, but advised him that the university would be forced to take further disciplinary action if his work performance did not improve within three months. It didn't take Stephen long to figure out who had complained about him. With just the two of them working full-time in the morgue, he knew that Bob had gone over his head and filed a complaint. Stephen was furious.

On Wednesday, April 15, ten days after Stephen Toussaint returned to work from his vacation, Bob Ivens did not come home for dinner. And while Bob's wife and kids waited for him to arrive, Toussaint had clocked out of work and was having drinks with

colleagues from the anatomy department. It was a regular thing—
the group would get together at the Elm Tavern on College Street,
across from the Medical Arts Building. Those in attendance that
night would later tell the police that Stephen was his regular, jovial
self and nothing seemed out of the ordinary. He had his usual shots
of vodka with a beer chaser and then left around 6:30 p.m., saying
he had something to do.

Hours later, the night sky over Toronto's Little Italy neighbourhood glowed red as flames danced above three local churches and
the two men who worked in the University of Toronto morgue
went missing.

On an overcast morning after news had spread about the church
fires, dozens of members of Christ Church St. James gathered
behind police barricades in front of their beloved house of worship. The stench of charred wood filled the air. Some of the congregants wept, while others stared in disbelief at the blackened pile
of bricks and broken glass. There was nothing left of their sacred
church, which had long been considered an important gathering
place for Toronto's West Indian community.

Built in 1924, the British Methodist Episcopal Church on Shaw
Street served the oldest Black congregation in Toronto, with more
than a thousand faithful followers. Some members of the congregation were descendants of American slaves who had escaped to
Canada via the Underground Railroad in the 1800s. The church was
a spiritual and cultural home to many, and a major renovation had
just been completed to update the kitchen and basement. Now it
was nothing but a burned-out shell, and it was going to cost millions
to rebuild.

The building was gone, but so too were the many historic photos
and documents that had chronicled the church's vital role in the
development of the city's Black community. Over two thousand

bibles and hymn books were destroyed, along with hundreds of memories and mementoes. But had anything else been lost in the unexplained church blaze? As the distraught parishioners looked on, the fire marshal's office began searching the rubble with specially trained cadaver dogs. A rumour was already circulating that one of the most respected church elders was missing.

Stephen Toussaint was seen as a pillar of Christ Church St. James, where he had been a member since his arrival in Canada. He was the Sunday school superintendent and treasurer of the church. He was even the captain of the church bowling team. Everyone loved Stephen. He was a hard-working family man with an effervescent personality and a great sense of humour. But beyond Sunday school and bowling nights, there was another side to Stephen Toussaint that neither his family nor church were aware of. He was a man with dark secrets.

In 1998, the corner of Bloor Street and Ossington Avenue was known for its seedy bars and booze cans. And Stephen Toussaint was a familiar face in most of them. At places like D & J Restaurant and Jankie's Bar, he was well known, and he never left sober. His drink of choice was vodka, straight up. And while Stephen had tried to keep his drinking life secret from his family and church, it didn't take long for people to start talking.

Nor was it long before Toronto police announced they were looking for Stephen Toussaint. The fifty-four-year-old was wanted for questioning in both crimes, but he had since disappeared.

The announcement caught the attention of a man named Terry Dinsmore, who told a *Toronto Star* newspaper reporter that he was a drinking buddy of Toussaint's and had been with him on the night of April 15. Terry, a former biker and ex-con, said he had known Stephen for fifteen years and considered him one of his closest friends. "He's always helping people," he said. "If he sees a guy on the street, he'll give him five dollars or buy him a sandwich. That's the kind of guy he is."

Terry told the reporter that, on the night of the church fires, he and Stephen had gone drinking at several establishments along Bloor Street. Later that evening, Stephen met an attractive woman and eventually ended up leaving with her. According to Terry, Stephen drove off in his red Toyota Tercel with the blonde around midnight. "He was so drunk he could hardly walk," said Terry. "I don't think he was running around starting fires," he added.

Terry said he met up with Stephen the following morning and the two shared a couple of glasses of Portuguese wine at another local dive bar. According to his drinking buddy, Stephen was nursing a bad hangover and talked about the blonde he had met the night before. Terry told the reporter he often met up with Stephen for a couple of drinks in the morning before Toussaint went to his job at the university. So, on the morning of April 16, he assumed that was where Stephen was heading when he left the bar, but no one had seen him since.

The police were not convinced of Terry Dinsmore's story. They had canvassed the bars around Bloor and Ossington, and no one remembered seeing Toussaint with Terry that evening. Nor did anyone recall seeing a mysterious blonde. The last confirmed sighting of Stephen Toussaint had been at 6:30 p.m. on Wednesday, April 15, when he left his work colleagues at the bar across the street from the Medical Sciences Building.

The police were anxious to speak to Toussaint, but he had not contacted his family or anyone else. His wife was distraught, fearing he, too, could be a victim of foul play. But the police had a different theory and were concerned that Toussaint could be on the run and might even try to flee the country. Investigators alerted customs and immigration officials at the airport and at border crossings to be on the lookout for Toussaint. Officials in Grenada were also contacted by the Toronto police. They agreed to interview Stephen's extended family, but no one on the island had heard from him.

"This is probably the most bizarre case I have ever worked on," said Detective Greg McLane, the lead homicide investigator on the case. Stephen Toussaint had simply vanished.

On Friday, April 17, two days after Toussaint was last seen, the police found his car. The red Tercel had been abandoned at the Scarborough Bluffs, a picturesque escarpment overlooking Lake Ontario in Toronto's east end, and not far from the Toussaint family home. The car was unlocked, but there was nothing in the vehicle that gave the police any further clues as to where Stephen might be. Soon after the discovery of the car, dozens of police with specially trained dogs, joined by officers on horseback, began searching the rugged area. The police marine unit was also called in to dredge the nearby shores of Lake Ontario. But there was still no sign of the man they were looking for. For investigators, it seemed that Toussaint had dumped his car and fled. But where he had gone remained a troubling mystery.

While the police continued their search for Toussaint, Bob Ivens's family mourned their sudden and unexplained loss. Four days after his bludgeoned body was discovered hidden in a closet at the university morgue, the forty-eight-year-old was laid to rest. The attack on the quiet lab technician had been so brutal that the service had to be held with a closed casket. Over three hundred people attended the funeral service, held at Christ the King Anglican Church in Etobicoke. Sitting in the front pew were Ivens's wife, Shirley, and their two children, fifteen-year-old Meaghan and ten-year-old Michael. Their grief was palpable to all those in attendance. They had lost a husband and father whom they adored, under extremely violent and bizarre circumstances.

Everyone was still reeling from the shock of what had happened.

Bob and Stephen were good friends. Stephen had introduced Bob to West Indian food, and Bob had taken Stephen ice fishing. But now one of them was dead and the other one was missing. It just didn't make any sense.

On Thursday, April 23, one week after the discovery of Bob Ivens's body, the Toronto police announced they were still looking for Stephen Toussaint, but now they were issuing an arrest warrant for him on a charge of second-degree murder. Investigators also announced that all three of the west end church fires had been classified as arson, and they believed there was a connection between the murder of Bob Ivens and the fires. That connection was Stephen Toussaint, and there was even speculation that the fires had been set to cover up additional crimes. The police were also investigating possible fraud. As treasurer, Toussaint had access to church funds, and police needed to know if any money was missing.

Back at the small bungalow in Toronto's east end, Toussaint's family did not want to believe that he was capable of the crimes he was being accused of. The past week had been a nightmare for Norma Toussaint and her two daughters. Stephen's picture was on the front of every Toronto newspaper, and the press had been camped out on their front lawn for days. They couldn't make sense of what had happened. Norma had known Stephen for over thirty years, and he had never been in any kind of trouble. Stephen's daughters adored their dad, and he had encouraged both of them to pursue musical careers.

The close-knit, private family retained criminal lawyer Scott Fenton to speak for them. "The family is concerned the police are overlooking the possibility that Mr. Toussaint may be a victim of a crime as opposed to being a principal suspect," Fenton told the press. "It does not appear to be a theory that has even been seriously considered," added the lawyer. He said the past few days had been extremely difficult for the family and that they had been given very little information about the investigation from the police. Now they just wanted Stephen found alive so that he could explain everything.

But while the Toussaint family maintained that the loving husband and father they knew could not be capable of such a heinous murder and arson, the police had a much different theory about the missing man and his bizarre crime spree. Investigators believed he returned to work after his vacation and became angry when he discovered that Bob Ivens and Susan Hausmann had straightened up the morgue without his permission. When Dr. Liebgott reprimanded him, directing him to clean up his act, it looked as though his days at U of T were numbered. His secret life, the one spent sitting in rundown bars drinking and picking up women, had been exposed, so he snapped. In a fit of rage, he bludgeoned Bob Ivens to death before stuffing him into a body bag and hiding him in the cleaning supply closet. The murder weapon was never found. Then, as the police later discovered, Stephen Toussaint did something else. At 5:18 p.m., likely not long after he had killed Ivens, he left a cryptic phone message for Dr. Liebgott. In an almost giddy tone, Toussaint said, "Hey doc, come on down to the morgue. I've got some bones to show you." After leaving the message, Stephen casually walked across the street to join other colleagues for a few after-work drinks . . . just as he always did.

As the weeks and months passed, investigators made no headway in their search for Stephen Toussaint. His passport and citizenship documents had been found in his home, so it didn't look as though he had left the country. But where was he?

While Toussaint's whereabouts remained a mystery, the story continued to make national and international news. Toussaint was added to Canada's most wanted list, and Ivens's murder was re-enacted on the crime-related television show *America's Most Wanted*, which portrayed Stephen Toussaint as a man living a double life. To many, he was a respected church elder and an upstanding family man, but in reality, he was a chronic alcoholic and philanderer who spent more time in bars than at his job. And when his two worlds collided, he killed his work colleague and friend. Then, for reasons unknown, he burned down his church and two others.

Because of the coverage, millions of people across North America had seen Stephen Toussaint's face, which meant he was going to have a much harder time hiding out. The Toronto police were confident they would eventually get their man. And while *America's Most Wanted* did generate renewed interest in the case and the police received hundreds of tips about potential sightings, none of the leads panned out. Months went by without any further developments, but Stephen's family continued to hope and pray he would be found alive.

On July 23, 1999, eighteen months after the murder of Bob Ivens and the mysterious church fires, Norma Toussaint received a disturbing phone call. It was a friend telling her that a body had been found, and local media were reporting that it was her husband, Stephen. Norma thought it must be a mistake since she had not heard anything from the police. If they had found Stephen, wouldn't they have notified her? Norma turned on the television.

Reporters and camera crews were gathered at the Scarborough Bluffs, where badly decomposed human remains had been found by a hiker in a heavily wooded area of the park. Discovered with the body were a decaying jacket, underpants, blue jeans and one shoe. The police said they believed the skeletal remains were those of the suspected murderer and arsonist Stephen Toussaint. The following day, the Toronto police confirmed their suspicions. An autopsy didn't reveal how he had died, but dental records verified his identity. The search for Stephen Toussaint was over.

For a man who was on Canada's most wanted list and had been the subject of an international manhunt, it turned out he hadn't gone very far at all. Toussaint's final resting place was less than five hundred metres from where the police had discovered his car two days after the murder and approximately three kilometres from his home. How had they missed him?

With the discovery of his remains, the police announced they were ending their investigation into the murder of Bob Ivens. They were confident that there were no other suspects to pursue. But while they were closing the books on one of Toronto's most bizarre murder stories, the people who knew Stephen Toussaint best still had many unresolved questions and feelings. Was it a case of Jekyll and Hyde? Who was Stephen Toussaint really, and how had he kept his darker side so well hidden for so long?

The congregation at Christ Church St. James had never stopped praying for Toussaint and his family. Many still didn't understand what could have driven the former Sunday school supervisor and church treasurer to commit such evil. And while rumours circulated that the fire had been set to cover possible theft, a thorough financial audit revealed that Toussaint had never stolen money from the church. There would be many questions left unanswered about that fateful night of April 16, 1998, but the congregants harboured no ill will towards their former fellow church member. Their house of worship was eventually rebuilt, and Norma Toussaint and her two daughters were always welcome.

For Bob Ivens's family, the discovery of Stephen Toussaint's remains left them without any answers as to why his long-time friend and colleague had brutally murdered him. Bob's sister, Marilyn Hodgkinson, believed that the university was partially to blame since it was aware of the overwhelming workload both men were working under. Cutbacks at the university had left the medical school morgue understaffed. A former University of Toronto employee herself, Hodgkinson claimed the university knew about the problems in the department for many years and hadn't done anything about them. Now her brother was dead, and sadly, the family would never get justice.

Today, a beautiful white chestnut tree flourishes outside the University of Toronto Medical Sciences Building in memory of Bob Ivens.

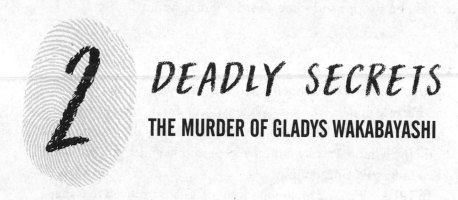

# DEADLY SECRETS

## THE MURDER OF GLADYS WAKABAYASHI

In 1992, *Murder, She Wrote* was one of the most popular shows on television. Every week, amateur detective Jessica Fletcher, played by famed actress Angela Lansbury, solved murder mysteries using good, old-fashioned logic and reasoning. The solution to every episode's whodunit usually involved the methodical unravelling of some character's secrets and lies. And no one was better at uncovering the truth than the inquisitive Mrs. Fletcher. But in real life, a murder can be notoriously difficult to solve, and police can spend years chasing down leads and frustrating dead ends.

When a real-life whodunit happened in a wealthy Vancouver suburb in 1992, the city's seasoned homicide detectives were initially perplexed. A quiet, middle-aged woman who taught music to children had been brutally murdered in her home, and the attack looked personal. Who would want to harm such a kind woman and mother? She didn't appear to have any enemies. But investigators soon found out she had a secret—a deadly one that led directly to her killer. And unlike a television drama series, investigators were going to need more than simple logic and reasoning to trap their

25

suspect. But very much like *Murder, She Wrote*, there would ultimately be a script and some award-winning acting.

Gladys Wakabayashi lived at 6868 Selkirk Street in Vancouver's
Shaughnessy neighbourhood, a wealthy enclave of gated mansions
and historic homes. The soft-spoken, petite forty-one-year-old was
the daughter of Taiwanese billionaire Y.S. Miao, the chairman of
both the Union Petrochemical Corporation and the giant Lien
Hwa Industrial Corporation.

In 1976, Feng Ling Miao, who went by Gladys, moved to Canada
from Taiwan to study piano. Not long after arriving in Vancouver,
Gladys met Shinji Wakabayashi, a manager for Japan Airlines. The
couple married in 1978 and had one daughter, Elisa, a few years
later.

In April of 1991, after thirteen years of marriage, Gladys and
Shinji amicably separated. Shinji moved out of their luxurious
property in the west end of the city, while Gladys remained in the
4,800-square-foot home with twelve-year-old Elisa. The couple
continued to have a civilized friendship and a supportive co-
parenting arrangement. At forty-one, Gladys was a good-looking
woman with a slim figure and long, curly black hair. And while
she hadn't dated in over fifteen years, she was excited about her
future.

Wednesday, June 24, 1992, was shaping up to be an unseasonably
warm summer day in Vancouver. At 8:45 a.m., as per her normal
routine, Gladys drove Elisa to school and then returned home. A
neighbour later reported seeing her pull into her garage around
9 a.m. At 10:30, Gladys had a regularly scheduled piano lesson
with her instructor, Edward Parker, but she failed to show up.
She was extremely punctual and had never missed a piano lesson.

Parker was concerned, so he phoned the Wakabayashi house but only got the answering machine.

Later that same afternoon, Gladys didn't arrive to pick up Elisa from school. This was very unusual, and Elisa couldn't reach her mother on the phone. She waited for two hours before finally calling her father to come and get her. He hadn't heard from Gladys, either.

When Elisa and Shinji arrived at Gladys's house around 5:30 p.m., Shinji found the back door ajar, which again was unusual. Gladys always kept her doors locked. Inside, the house was quiet and there were no signs of his ex-wife. Shinji decided to look upstairs. Maybe she was sleeping or ill in bed. When he entered the master bedroom, nothing seemed out of place and the bed was neatly made. On his way to the ensuite bathroom, Shinji was startled by a frightening sight. Gladys was lying face-up on the floor of her walk-in dressing room. A large pool of blood had soaked into the plush white carpeting close to her head and she wasn't moving. Shinji bent down to touch her. She was cold to the touch, and he could see a large gash on her neck. Rushing down the stairs, Shinji grabbed Elisa and ran next door to his brother-in-law's house. He was hysterical, saying something had happened to Gladys. The family dialled 911.

When Vancouver homicide detectives Murn MacLennan and Barry Peters arrived at 6868 Selkirk Street, they were presented with a gruesome scene. It was obvious that Gladys's throat had been slit by a sharp-bladed instrument and she had bled to death. She also had numerous slashes on her arms, legs and chest, and there were defensive wounds on her hands. The petite woman had tried desperately to shield herself from her attacker. The nature and extent of her injuries suggested the killer had acted in a violent rage. But no murder weapon was found and it didn't appear that a robbery had occurred. For the seasoned investigators it did not appear to be a random murder. It looked personal. Someone wanted Gladys Wakabayashi dead.

Whoever the killer was, they had been careful. There were few forensic clues such as fingerprints, and Gladys had not been sexually assaulted. But the police did discover one unique clue: a partial shoe print, left in blood, on the ceramic tile going into the master bathroom. MacLennan described the print as having a pointed toe, and a honeycomb pattern on the sole. It was obvious that the bloody shoe print had been made by a high-heeled shoe. The police didn't know if they were looking for one killer or more, but they were certain that a woman had been in that bedroom when Gladys Wakabayashi was murdered.

Based on the savagery of the attack, the police also believed the killer had to be someone close to Gladys, so they quickly turned their sights on her ex-husband, Shinji. But there appeared to be no animosity between them. They had remained friends after ending their marriage and were both focused on raising their daughter. Shinji was soon ruled out. The police began to dig deeper into Gladys's life, searching for other clues because someone clearly hated Gladys Wakabayashi enough to kill her.

As the police investigated Gladys's seemingly quiet life, nothing appeared out of the ordinary. They discovered that she had had a short-term relationship with a music teacher after her divorce, but that romance had also ended amicably. Then, just a few weeks into the murder investigation, investigators started hearing a strange rumour. It appeared that Gladys had a new man in her life—a secret romance with a married man. And apparently his wife had recently found out about their affair.

Derek and Jean Ann James were a middle-class couple who lived in a modest home on Bridge Street in the Vancouver suburb of Richmond. Derek was an air traffic controller. Jean, who was originally from England, had trained as a nurse, but after immigrating to Canada, she had worked as a flight attendant with

Vancouver-based Pacific Western Airlines. The couple had a son named Adam.

Derek and Jean met Gladys and Shinji Wakabayashi at a school event in 1985. Their children attended the same Montessori school. An unlikely friendship developed over their kids and their common careers—both husbands worked in the airline industry, as did Jean. The Jameses and Wakabayashis began spending time together at social events and dinner parties. But by 1991, Gladys and Shinji's marriage had collapsed, and they had decided to divorce. And by 1992, Jean's marriage with Derek was also troubled. Jean confided to another close friend that she believed Derek had been unfaithful.

But Jean wasn't prepared to give up on her marriage, so she began following Derek, trying to catch him in the act. Using a friend's car, she spied on Derek for a few months but couldn't confirm her suspicions about another woman. In June 1992, when Derek told Jean he had to go to Toronto on business, she suspected he was lying, so she asked a friend to get Derek's telephone records for the weekend he was supposedly in Toronto. The friend, who worked for a market research company, was able to surreptitiously obtain a copy of Derek's hotel bill. The bill confirmed that Derek had been in Toronto that weekend, and it included a list of the phone calls made and received from Derek's room during his stay. There was one number that appeared multiple times, and Jean recognized it right away. It was Gladys Wakabayashi's home phone number. Jean's suspicions about her husband were confirmed. He was having an affair, and the other woman was one of her closest friends. Two days later, Gladys Wakabayashi would be dead.

After Gladys's brutal murder, Jean reached out to Shinji Wakabayashi to express her shock and sorrow. Through her own tears, she wanted to assure the grieving widower that she and her husband were there for him. Two days later, she approached Shinji again, asking more questions about how Gladys had been killed. "Did she suffer?" asked Jean. Her concern seemed natural, since the couples had been close friends for seven years, but for Gladys's ex-husband, Jean's probing questions seemed morbid.

Shinji wasn't the only person who thought Jean's inquisitiveness was strange. When police discovered and confirmed Gladys's affair with Derek James, Jean became their number one suspect. Someone had left a bloodied high-heeled shoe print at the murder scene, and in a macabre version of *Cinderella*, they needed to find the shoe that had left that print. Find the shoe, find the foot that fits the shoe, find the murderer.

Two weeks after the murder of Gladys Wakabayashi, Vancouver police executed a search warrant on the home of Derek and Jean Ann James. Paying close attention to Jean's extensive shoe collection, they compared every pair to the imprint of the tread left at the crime scene but discovered no footwear that matched. The police also seized Jean's car, but found no evidence or traces of blood in the vehicle. The only evidence tying Jean to the crime scene were her fingerprints, but there was a logical explanation for why they would be in the Wakabayashi home: Jean and Derek had visited many times over the years, and Jean admitted to being in Gladys's bedroom just two days before the murder.

Jean's fingerprints in the house didn't prove she was connected to the murder, yet investigators remained certain she was involved. They interviewed friends and acquaintances of the couple, and soon discovered that Jean had told other people about her suspicion that Gladys and Derek were having an affair. A friend of Jean's told the police that Jean had confided in her and was very angry and upset that Gladys had betrayed her.

Having found no physical evidence in Jean's home or vehicle, investigators began to monitor her every move. They also decided to release details about Gladys's death to the media to see if they could rattle Jean or encourage any other witnesses to come forward. They disclosed how Gladys had been killed and that, based on the crime scene, they believed the murderer was known to her. The police also revealed that Gladys had been having an affair with a married man and evidence left at the scene pointed to a woman being involved in the slaying. They described the suspect as a white female in her mid-fifties, with blond hair, five feet four inches tall and weighing approximately 120 to 130 pounds. The police described Jean Ann James.

But the release of this information did not generate any new clues or additional information. Frustrated investigators still didn't have enough to charge Jean. While she had motive—an angry spouse betrayed by her husband and good friend—there was simply no forensic evidence tying her to the murder. And Derek James was standing by his wife, denying that he had ever had an affair with Gladys Wakabayashi.

The police were certain they knew who the killer was, but without further evidence, their investigation hit a brick wall and the case eventually went cold.

In 2007, fifteen years after Gladys Wakabayashi was murdered in her home, detectives from British Columbia's Unsolved Homicide Unit decided to re-examine the case. The evidence collected in 1992 was retested, and investigators hoped the passage of time, combined with more advanced forensic testing, might reveal something significant. Unfortunately, no new information came to light that could definitively put Jean Ann James in Gladys's bedroom on the day she was killed.

Once again, investigators were at a standstill. They had a prime suspect with a strong motive for wanting Gladys dead but no physical evidence tying her to the murder. If they had any hope of ever charging Jean with the crime, they were going to have to take a much different approach. Without DNA evidence, they needed something foolproof. What they needed was a confession from Jean Ann James. But how were they going to get the sixty-eight-year-old woman to confess to murder?

By 2007, a controversial investigative technique was being used by police departments in unique undercover cases. It was a covert sting operation known informally as a "Mr. Big," which became known as the "Canadian technique" by law enforcement agencies around the world. Originally developed by the Royal Canadian Mounted Police in British Columbia, the first documented use of the technique was in March of 1965, during an investigation into David Louis Harrison, a former Vancouver police constable who was tried and convicted for taking part in a $1.2 million robbery.

A Mr. Big operation is meticulously planned. The target is put under surveillance for an extended period of time so that the police can determine their habits, routines and lifestyle and create a customized strategy to approach the suspect. Once a game plan is established, an undercover officer befriends the suspect, who eventually learns their new friend is a member of a crime organization. The suspect is then offered opportunities to work for the criminal organization.

The suspect soon discovers that working for the organization brings serious financial rewards and learns that even bigger rewards are available if they advance within the organization. Undercover officers posing as criminals stress to the suspect that the organization values honesty and loyalty above all else. After the suspect is deeply enmeshed with the fake organization, they are finally introduced to the crime boss, Mr. Big, either as a reward for work accomplished or as an interview for a more trusted position within the organization. The clandestine meeting is secretly videotaped by undercover operatives, with the goal of getting the suspect to confess to their crime. Mr. Big may suggest that the organization needs details about the suspect's prior crime, as assurance of their loyalty to his organization, or that the suspect's advancement within the organization may depend on them confessing to a violent crime.

While the technique is extremely controversial, time-consuming and expensive, it has been used successfully in other difficult cases. Vancouver's cold case detectives knew a covert sting operation was their only hope of getting a full confession from their prime suspect in the 1992 murder of Gladys Wakabayashi. Sixteen years after the fact, the seduction of Jean Ann James was about to begin.

It was a cold, dreary day in January 2008 when retired homebody Jean Ann James received a surprise phone call. She had apparently won a day of luxurious treatments at a posh spa in downtown Vancouver. She didn't recall entering any contests, but who could say no to a free day at the spa, especially during a dull, depressing winter? A few days later, a stretch limousine picked Jean up at her home and drove her and another lucky winner to the spa. The two excited women started chatting in the back of the limo, and it turned out that Jean's new spa companion was the well-to-do wife of a Vancouver developer.

The ladies continued to get to know one another during their massages and pedicures, and by the end of their relaxing day, Jean had invited her new-found friend to join her and her husband, Derek, for a wine-tasting evening. Naturally, the woman accepted Jean's invitation. In fact, she couldn't wait.

Jean and her new friend were soon inseparable. Wine tastings, lunches, shopping, they seemed to have so much in common. Jean's friend was fun, carefree and loved spending money, which she seemed to have a lot of. And it was clear that Jean was a little envious. She would often admit to wanting a more lavish lifestyle. In fact, Jean said she dreamed of living in a big house in Shaughnessy, the same posh neighbourhood where her friend Gladys Wakabayashi had lived and died. But Jean never mentioned Gladys to her new friend.

Two months into their friendship, in March 2008, Jean's new friend began acting a little odd. On one social outing, she told Jean she had to deliver a package of money to someone at a downtown hotel, and on another occasion she showed Jean three giant bundles of cash totalling $75,000. Jean soon realized that her friend was involved in something shady and possibly criminal. But that didn't bother her. Whatever it was, Jean wanted in.

On one occasion, over a lunch date at Vancouver's Stanley Park, Jean's friend asked her to be a lookout while she met with someone. For keeping watch, Jean was paid $300, which she gladly accepted. The friend eventually confessed to Jean that she was part of an organized crime ring helping to launder money at Vancouver casinos and sell stolen credit cards. And if Jean wanted to make some money, her friend could introduce her to some people she knew. Jean didn't hesitate in accepting her friend's offer.

Soon, Jean was taking part in various small-time criminal transactions and meeting other members of the "crime syndicate" who lavished her with expensive dinners and flaunted the money they were making. But they warned Jean that sometimes their business dealings could get ugly. Was that something she was prepared to do? Jean said yes, she wasn't afraid of a little violence. Not long after, Jean's new associates took her to a secret location where they were holding a guy who apparently owed them $300,000. The guy had been kidnapped and badly beaten. He looked bad, but when Jean saw his battered face, she didn't flinch. In fact, the sixty-nine-year-old suburban wife and mother told her criminal friends that the deadbeat had gotten off lightly. She said she would have cut off his fingers, or burned his genitals with a curling iron, or put raw meat on his crotch and let dogs at him. Jean didn't look the part of a violent criminal, but she was certainly creative in her sinister machinations.

Jean had proven that she could handle herself, and she didn't shy away from the gritty stuff. She was ready to take on some more serious jobs. Her new associates offered her the chance to earn one-third of a $700,000 score, but first she would have to meet their boss. Nothing went on in the organization without his approval. A few weeks later, on November 27, 2008, Jean flew to Montreal for her meeting with the crime syndicate's boss. Looking more like a grandmother than a gangster, Jean knocked on the door of a suite at the InterContinental Hotel.

Inside the room were five men, including a good-looking middle-aged man who was impeccably dressed in an expensive suit and pricey shoes. He was clearly the boss. He eyed Jean up and down and said he wasn't happy that his associates had brought her in on an important deal without first discussing it with him. He didn't mince words and told Jean he didn't think she could cut it in their world. "It can get pretty sporty," he said referring to the need for violence sometimes.

Knowing she needed to convince the boss, Jean began reciting her work experience as a nurse and flight attendant. She assured him she wasn't squeamish when it came to blood and violence. But then the man pulled out a newspaper clipping from a file folder on his lap. It was an article about Gladys Wakabayashi's murder. He said that his people in Vancouver had heard rumours about the 1992 killing and that word on the street was that Jean was somehow involved. "Were you?" he asked point blank. Jean hesitated; it had been sixteen years since Gladys's murder, and as far as she was concerned, it was long forgotten—old news. But she really wanted to impress the crime boss. Admitting to her involvement in the murder would be her ticket to the lavish lifestyle she had always desired. "This is strictly between you and I," she cautioned before proudly revealing her darkest secret in a room full of strangers.

Confidently and calmly, she laid it all out: how she had discovered the love affair between her husband and her close friend. Gladys had betrayed her in the worst way, so according to Jean, she deserved to die. Jean described how she drove to Gladys's home on the morning of June 24, 1992. She parked a few blocks away and then walked through back alleys to the Wakabayashi house. She had called Gladys earlier that morning to tell her she had a present for her and would meet her at her house after the kids were dropped off at school.

Jean arrived shortly after Gladys returned home at 9 a.m. The two friends chatted over coffee in the kitchen before making their way up upstairs. Gladys was due at her piano lesson by 10:30, but Jean told Gladys she had bought her a new necklace and wanted her to try it on.

Gladys sat down on a chair in her dressing room while Jean stood behind her. But there was no necklace. Instead, Jean pulled out a box cutter and slit her friend's throat. Then, as Gladys lay bleeding to death on the carpeted floor, Jean slashed at her, demanding a confession. She wanted to know how long the affair had been going on. "I'll call an ambulance if you tell me," she taunted Gladys. But Jean had no intention of calling anyone. Gladys tried to push Jean away, but Jean kept slashing her. Finally, Gladys stopped moving. Jean stood over her, pleased with what she had done. Her husband's mistress was dead, and she was glad.

Continuing her chilling confession to the crime boss, Jean said that after she killed Gladys, she went downstairs, washed the coffee cups and left the house. She then tossed the bloodied murder weapon in a dumpster and burned all her clothing and shoes in the incinerator at her son's school. She also claimed to have traded in her car and bought a new one.

The crime boss listened intently to everything Jean was telling him. He said he was very impressed but was still concerned. Was there anything that could still link Jean to the murder? His contacts told him that the Vancouver police were reinvestigating the crime and retesting some DNA evidence. Jean assured him that the police would never be able to link her to Gladys's murder. Yes, her fingerprints were in the house, but the two women had been friends, so the police had nothing. Did anyone else know? asked Mr. Big. "No," said Jean. "My mother always told me that if you have secrets, keep them to yourself." It was the perfect crime, she bragged, and she had gotten away with it.

When Jean left the Montreal hotel room, she was certain of two things: she had impressed the crime boss, and soon she would have the wealthy lifestyle she had always desired.

Two weeks later on, December 12, Jean Ann James was putting the finishing touches on her Christmas decorations. Jean loved the holidays, and this year felt extra special because of her new role within a Vancouver crime family. She hadn't told her husband, Derek, about the secret meeting in Montreal, and she had set up a secret bank account for her earnings. What he didn't know wouldn't hurt him, and besides, it wasn't as if he had always been honest with *her*. If it hadn't been for his cheating and lies, her friend Gladys might still be alive. Oh well, thought Jean. That was a long time ago and it was all behind them now. But as the plump woman stood in her living room on that December afternoon, there was a knock at her front door. It was the Vancouver police, who wasted no time in telling her that she was under arrest for the 1982 murder of Gladys Wakabayashi.

||||||||

Jean soon discovered that she had been the target of an elaborate undercover sting operation and everything she had said in that Montreal hotel room had been secretly videotaped. There was no crime syndicate, no crime boss, and her new best friend from the surprise spa day was an undercover police officer. For sixteen years, Jean believed she had gotten away with the perfect crime. But then, desperate for the respect and riches she had long desired, she had been cleverly fooled into confessing to the cold-blooded murder of her good friend. Vancouver homicide investigators had always suspected Jean. She had the means and the motive, and now, with her confession on videotape, the police and prosecution were certain of a conviction.

The murder trial of Jean Ann James began on October 12, 2011, three years after her arrest and nineteen years after the vicious slaying of forty-one-year-old Gladys Wakabayashi. And while almost two decades had passed, the memory of what had happened on June 24, 1992, was still fresh in minds of the Wakabayashi family. The murder of Gladys at the hands of someone they had known and trusted was devastating. For long-time friends and neighbours of Jean and Derek James, it was hard to believe that the kind and generous older woman they knew could be a murderer. "She was an absolute sweetheart of a lady," said one neighbour to the press. She was an animal lover and a keen gardener. She couldn't be a killer.

Every day during the sensational murder trial, the Wakabayashi family arrived quietly, taking their seats on one side of the courtroom while Derek James and his son, Adam, sat across the aisle behind the defence table. For his part, Derek had always maintained that he had never had a physical affair with Gladys Wakabayashi, only an emotional one, and he believed Jean was innocent.

Jean, who always paid careful attention to her appearance, arrived to court each morning well dressed and perfectly groomed.

Her lawyer, Aseem Dosanjh, kept his opening statements brief, saying the main issue would be the reliability of Jean's videotaped confession to Mr. Big. Having tried and failed to get the taped confession excluded from the court proceedings, the defence lawyer knew his biggest challenge was to get the jury to focus on other aspects of the case. Dosanjh asked the jurors not to jump to any conclusions and to be critical about what they were about to hear. They needed to keep an open mind about the case and the ultimate guilt of his client. "Remember the presumption of innocence for the accused," he added.

During her opening statement, Crown prosecutor Jennifer Horneland told the court that Jean Ann James had gotten away with the vicious murder of her friend Gladys Wakabayashi for sixteen years. But she had been finally caught when she confessed to the killing during an elaborate undercover sting operation conducted by the Vancouver police.

Horneland told the jury that when they watched Jean's videotaped confession, they would see and hear the accused boast about the killing to the supposed crime boss, saying that she planned everything once she learned that her husband was having an affair with the victim. "You will hear her talk about how she cleverly fooled Mrs. Wakabayashi into believing she had bought her a necklace. But instead, she put on gloves and slit her friend's throat. Then she teased and tortured her friend, saying she would call an ambulance if Mrs. Wakabayashi told her what she wanted to know."

The prosecutor then advised the jury that she would be calling thirty-three witnesses, including several of Jean's friends, who would testify that she had learned of Derek's affair with Gladys prior to the murder. The prosecutor would also be calling Shinji Wakabayashi, Gladys's ex-husband, who found her body, and the couple's daughter, Elisa, who was twelve at the time of her mother's murder. "This was a premeditated, brutal slaying," added Horneland, and the Crown would prove that Jean Ann

James was the only person with enough hatred to murder Gladys Wakabayashi.

For the prosecution, motive was key to Gladys's murder, and her affair with Derek had sadly sealed her fate once Jean discovered what was going on. The first witness for the Crown, retired Vancouver homicide detective Larry Peters, testified that his initial observations of the crime scene indicated it was a crime of intense rage and hatred. There was a massive amount of blood in the master bedroom dressing area, and numerous slashes and gashes on the body of the victim, including a large wound to the neck. It was also obvious Gladys had tried to defend herself against her attacker, based on defensive wounds on her hands. To the seasoned detective, it appeared as though Gladys had been tortured before she bled to death.

Peters's former partner, Murn MacLennan, also described the murder scene as the most gruesome he had ever attended. Gladys was lying face-up in a pool of blood beside an overturned chair. There were smudged bloody footprints on the carpet, and a clearer partial footprint on the bathroom's ceramic floor that looked like it had been made by a high-heeled shoe. Based on the shoe print, the police were certain a woman had been in the room when Gladys was killed, and they theorized it had to have been someone Gladys trusted enough to let into her bedroom. Nothing else in the house had been disturbed.

During cross-examination, Jean's defence counsel asked the original investigating officers if they had ever considered other potential suspects, such as Gladys's ex-husband, Shinji. Naturally, the police had investigated Shinji, but quicky determined that he and Gladys were on very good terms as friends and co-parents, and he had no reason to kill her. In fact, Shinji told the police that Jean had contacted him twice shortly after the murder, wanting to know details about Gladys's injuries, which he found odd. Other potential suspects that the defence suggested, including the

Chinese mafia and a plumber who had worked in the Wakabayashi home, were quickly discounted. There was simply no evidence that pointed to a suspect other than the one who had confessed to the murder: Jean Ann James.

The defence also wanted the jury to ignore Jean's videotaped confession. Without the murder weapon or any other physical evidence linking Jean to the brutal slaying, her innocence or guilt rested heavily on the reliability of her confession to Mr. Big. The defence lawyer argued that the confession was elicited under duress, as Jean felt pressured to please the crime boss and wanted to appear worthy of membership in his criminal gang, so she had made up the story of killing Gladys to gain his respect and approval. Jean wanted the lavish lifestyle the crime syndicate was offering and, according to her lawyer, was even willing to lie about a murder to obtain it. Was it possible that a covert undercover operation such as the Mr. Big sting could induce a false confession? The defence referred to other cases where this had happened, but ultimately the jury would have to make up their own minds after they heard the secretly recorded tape.

On Wednesday, October 26, two weeks after the murder trial had begun, the jury was finally presented with Jean Ann James's confession, taped in the Montreal hotel room in 2008. Over the course of ninety minutes, the jury watched and listened to James talking to Mr. Big in what appeared to be a casual discussion about working for his crime syndicate. When told by the crime boss that things in their world could get "pretty sporty," referring to the occasional need for violence, Jean said she understood and was not afraid of violence. Then, when Mr. Big wanted to know about her involvement in the Gladys Wakabayashi murder, Jean barely missed a beat before confessing to the brutal killing and coolly adding that Gladys deserved what she got.

But as damaging as the taped confession appeared to be, the defence team was prepared to challenge its validity. Jean's lawyer argued that, on the tape, Jean did not reveal any information about the crime that hadn't been made public. "Holdback" evidence—information unknown to anyone but the suspect and the detectives investigating the murder—is one of the best tools in an undercover operation. If the suspect reveals the holdback evidence during their confession, it is a sure sign of their involvement in the crime. But while telling Mr. Big about Gladys's murder, Jean had not revealed any holdback evidence—and in fact, her lawyer argued, some of the details she had relayed did not match the evidence at all.

In her confession, Jean stated that she had not walked into the master bathroom after the murder, which contradicted the evidence found—the partial, bloodied print from a high-heeled shoe. But Crown counsel reminded the jury that the shoe impression was at the bathroom entrance, noting that if Jean started to go into the washroom and then backed away, it wasn't inconsistent with what she told the crime boss. And while the police never found a shoe belonging to Jean James that matched the impression left on the tile floor, the Crown contended that Mrs. James likely discarded the shoes along with all the clothing she had worn on that day. The police had not searched the James home until fifteen days after the murder, giving Jean plenty of time to get rid of any incriminating evidence.

In her videotaped confession, Jean admitted to burning her clothing in the incinerator at her son's school, but it was later discovered that the school did not have an incinerator. According to the defence, this was further proof that Jean was just making up a story to impress the crime boss. The Crown agreed that Jean James had likely embellished parts of her story to appear more criminally savvy to Mr. Big. Burning critical evidence that tied her to the murder sounded smarter than just throwing bloodied clothing into a dumpster, which is likely what she had done.

On Thursday, November 3, 2011, lawyers for the Crown and defence made their closing arguments. Crown prosecutor Kerr

Clark told the jury that Jean had motive for the brutal killing because she was filled with jealous rage over her friend's affair with her husband. "Jealous rage and betrayal are good reasons for someone to become very angry," Clark said. He pointed out that there was evidence that Jean's husband, Derek, had engaged in previous affairs, but suggested Jean's rage was intensified by the fact that Gladys was a friend rather than a stranger. "One thing that's clear is this was a very violent attack," he added. "It's a crime that was committed by someone with extreme anger and resentment." He also noted that Jean's taped confession to Mr. Big was irrefutable evidence of her guilt.

While there had been some discrepancies in her confession, it was obvious Jean had murdered Gladys and felt no remorse. Undercover officers had spent a year developing a relationship with Jean, and it did not appear that she was intimidated or scared into making a false confession. The Crown attorney also pointed out that the RCMP and other law enforcement agencies had used the Mr. Big technique many times with great success.

Jean's defence lawyer focused his closing argument on the videotaped confession, reminding the packed courtroom about the lack of physical evidence to incriminate his client. He told the jury that undercover police stings, like the Mr. Big operation that targeted Jean, are unreliable. "I want to be clear: this is not a DNA case," said the defence lawyer. "This is also not a fingerprint case. This is a false confession case." He also reminded the jury that the undercover investigation leading up to the apparent confession lacked reliable safeguards, such as holdback evidence. "Mrs. James's version of events in that video recording are just not reliable," he said. "It's not reliable because she did not do this crime."

On Thursday, November 3, 2011, Justice Catherine Bruce summarized the defence and prosecution positions on the case and advised the jurors to carefully review Jean's secretly videotaped confession, paying close attention to her behaviour and the details of her claims. She also reminded jurors that Jean's willingness to engage in illegal activities for the fake crime organization was not proof that she killed Gladys Wakabayashi. Ultimately, it would be up to them to take all of the points raised during the trial and determine the innocence or guilt of the accused.

The trial had lasted just over four weeks. Jean James had chosen not to testify in her own defence.

The next day, after deliberating for less than eight hours, the jury returned with their verdict. Jean Ann James was found guilty of first-degree murder in the brutal killing of Gladys Wakabayashi in her home on June 24, 1992. It was a bittersweet ending after a nineteen-year search for justice. Jean Ann James showed no emotion at the verdict. The seventy-two-year-old woman was sentenced to life in prison without the possibility of parole for twenty-five years.

Despite her stoic appearance, Jean had no plans of going quietly. She insisted she was innocent and denied any involvement in Gladys's murder. Her conviction was appealed. Her lawyer sought to have the verdict overturned and a new trial ordered on the grounds that the trial judge should have excluded the Mr. Big confession. But after reviewing the details of the original trial, the British Columbia appeal court upheld the conviction. Chief Justice Lance Finch stated: "The evidence of motive and opportunity, coupled with the detailed confession, formed an overwhelming foundation [on which] to base a conviction. I would affirm the verdict of guilt and dismiss the appeal." Justice Finch went on to note that Jean's confession to Mr. Big did contain key details about the murder and crime scene, which, when viewed as a whole, provided compelling evidence for the jury to conclude that her confession was reliable. Jean Ann James would not receive a new trial and would remain in federal prison.

|||||||||||

In 2015, four years after her conviction, Jean Ann James was back in the news. The seventy-six-year-old was petitioning the Federal Court to review the Fraser Valley Institution's refusal to allow private family visits with her husband, Derek, and thirty-five-year-old son, Adam, in a house on the prison grounds. The correctional facility had denied her request, stating that Jean posed too great of a risk of committing domestic violence. Their report stated: "Mrs. James can be volatile when angry and she has allegedly been observed throwing things at her husband in a state of rage." The correctional facility also alleged that the elderly inmate had once tampered with prison food and had tried to contract out an assault on another prisoner.

In her petition, Jean stated: "I have never been involved in violence towards my husband or my son. My husband and son are the most important people in my life. I love them deeply and would never do anything to compromise their safety, let alone intentionally hurt either of them."

After reviewing her appeal, the Federal Court noted that Jean wasn't addressing the biggest issue at the heart of her request, which was her refusal to seek help in prison regarding her volatile emotions. Therefore, the judge ruled that prison authorities were forced to consider her a high risk for violence. Her request for private visits with Derek and Adam was denied.

Jean Ann James remains imprisoned in British Columbia for the murder of Gladys Wakabayashi. She will be eligible for full parole in the year 2036, at the age of ninety-seven.

# LOST BOY

## THE MURDER OF NANCY EATON

**M**onday, January 21, 1985, would go down in the history books as one of the coldest days on record in the eastern United States and central Canada. US president Ronald Reagan's second inauguration was to take place that morning, and for only the second time in history, the ceremony had to be moved indoors because of the sub-zero temperatures.

Dubbed the "freeze of the century," the bitter winter storm that enveloped the eastern seaboard that weekend had caused 100 deaths and millions of dollars in damage. In Toronto, two feet of snow had fallen and the city was virtually shut down. The roads were a mess, and no one was getting anywhere fast.

When Nancy Eaton woke that morning, she had a strange, uneasy feeling. Looking out her front window, she saw the blizzard. "Damn weather," she mumbled. January was always such a depressing month in Toronto. But one thing that always cheered her up was talking to her daughter. Mrs. Eaton and her twenty-three-year-old daughter—also named Nancy but affectionately called "Tiger"—were very close. They would talk throughout the day, and their morning phone chats over tea were a daily ritual.

The mother and daughter had spoken the night before while Nancy and her friend Andrew were watching the Super Bowl. The San Francisco 49ers were favoured to win against the Miami Dolphins. Andrew was six years younger than Nancy, but the two got along well. They had known each other since childhood, spending summers together at their neighbouring Muskoka cottages. Andrew was an awkward teenager and had a lot of issues, but Nancy considered him her "little bro" and would let him sleep on her couch if he stayed late. Given the bad snowstorm, Mrs. Eaton assumed Andrew would probably spend the night at Nancy's.

Now, with the morning news saying that the storm was going to last all day, Mrs. Eaton wanted to check if Nancy planned to go into work. Better to stay home, thought the overly protective mother. But when she called Nancy, there was no answer. She left a message, and when her phone rang an hour later, she assumed it was her daughter calling back.

"Good morning, it's a beautiful day," said the voice on the line. It wasn't Nancy.

"Who is this?" asked Mrs. Eaton not recognizing the male voice.

"It's a beautiful day today," the man repeated before hanging up.

How strange, thought Mrs. Eaton before calling her daughter again. There was still no answer. It wasn't like Tiger not to call back. Mrs. Eaton left another message and carried on with her day. But when she had not heard back from her Nancy by later that afternoon, she called the real estate office where Nancy worked. No, she wasn't there, said the receptionist. She hadn't shown up for work and no one had heard from her all day.

Mrs. Eaton left several more phone messages, each one a little more frantic than the last, before finally deciding to drive over to Nancy's apartment on Farnham Avenue, near Yonge Street and St. Clair Avenue. It was 7:30 p.m. on a bitterly cold, snowy night. Using a spare key, Mrs. Eaton entered Nancy's apartment, which was in total darkness. A flashing red light illuminated the answering machine, and a single string of multicoloured bulbs hung off the dried-out Christmas tree. "Tiger?" she called out, but got no response. The apartment was eerily quiet.

Making her way through the apartment, she could barely see, but she noticed overturned furniture in the living room. The place looked a mess, which wasn't how Nancy kept her apartment. Mrs. Eaton moved towards the bedroom, again calling out for her daughter. The bedroom door was ajar. She noticed a large black stain on the carpet, and there was something on top of the bed. Moving closer, she realized it was a potted tropical plant. Then, suddenly, she stumbled over something on the floor. She fell, and her hand touched the dark stain on the carpet. It was wet. Struggling to see and struggling to get up, she spotted a comforter crumpled on the floor next to the bed. She lifted the blanket and screamed. It was her daughter, nude and smeared in blood. "Tiger!" she yelled. There was no response. She felt her daughter's leg. It was cold. Nancy Eaton was dead. Mrs. Eaton fumbled in the dark to find the phone. "Please, my daughter has been murdered," she gasped to the 911 operator before losing her grip on the phone receiver.

Nancy Alice Edward Eaton was born on May 28, 1961, to Nancy Leigh Gossage "Snubby" Eaton and Edward Young Eaton. Her birth made all the Toronto newspapers as the newest member of one of Canada's oldest family dynasties. Nancy was the great-great-granddaughter of Timothy Eaton, founder of Canada's largest privately owned department store chain. The Eaton name was synonymous with the Canadian establishment, a world of old money and privilege. On her mother's side, young Nancy was descended from the McCarthys, Campbells and Gossages, all affluent families in their own right, many of whom had contributed significantly to Canadian politics and law.

Shortly after her birth, Nancy's parents discovered she had a severe hearing impairment, with only 2 percent hearing in one ear and 1 percent in the other. Her family chose not to send her to a school for the hearing-impaired. Instead, she wore hearing aids and learned to lip read, but she never excelled academically and ended up attending eighteen different schools. Nancy had a difficult childhood. She was often teased by other children because of her hearing impairment, and when she was five years old, her parents divorced. Nancy and her mother were left with the Eaton name, but little of the family's wealth. Nancy's mother spent years fighting Edward in court for support, and as a result, young Nancy had a strained relationship with her distant father. At the age of eleven, she suffered an emotional breakdown that lasted into her teenage years. But with her mother's support, she eventually overcame her difficulties and blossomed into a sweet and caring young woman.

At seventeen, Nancy took a big step and moved out to live on her own. An inheritance from her maternal grandmother had given her the opportunity to spread her wings, while her overprotective mother was only a few blocks and a phone call away. Nancy loved her new apartment on Farnham Avenue. It was a decent-sized space on the top floor of a four-storey building and had a fake fireplace and lots of light. She even had a rooftop deck where she would go to read or listen to music on her Walkman. It wasn't long before Nancy's place became a favourite hangout for her friends.

By the time she was in her early twenties, Nancy had matured into a beautiful, independent young woman. She had a strong circle of friends and an exciting new career in real estate. After years of feeling self-conscious about her hearing impairment, she had become an expert lip reader and was more socially confident. She was working on her relationship with her father, and men were taking notice of the petite blonde with the beautiful smile. But now, at just twenty-three years old, she was gone.

|||||||||||

When the police arrived at 4 Farnham Avenue on the evening of Monday, January 21, 1985, they were met at the apartment building by a hysterical older woman. She was barefoot, standing in the snow, clutching at her mink fur coat.

The responding officers made their way up to the fourth-floor apartment. There they discovered the naked body of a woman who was identified as twenty-three-year-old Nancy Eaton. She was lying in a pool of blood on the carpeted floor of her bedroom. Her torn nightgown was wrapped around her neck. It appeared that she had been stabbed multiple times and possibly sexually assaulted. It was a grisly, violent scene with almost every surface in the bedroom splattered in Nancy's blood. Looking under the bed, the police discovered a bloodied knife with its long blade bent out of shape. Also cowering under the bed was a terrified cat. The crime scene had all the hallmarks of a vicious attack, but it also looked as though the killer had left some strange clues behind. There were two raw eggs, broken and left on the floor—one in the bedroom and one in the bathroom. And Nancy's attacker had placed a large potted palm tree on top of the blood-soaked bed. The apartment also appeared to have been ransacked. Nancy's purse was dumped out in the bedroom. Was this a robbery gone bad?

A crowd of curious onlookers had already gathered on Farnham Avenue, despite the cold, because word had already spread that Nancy Eaton, a member of the well-heeled Eaton family, had been murdered. Mrs. Eaton, the dead woman's mother, was inconsolable, but she told the police right away that she knew who had killed Nancy. "It was Andrew," she sobbed. "Andrew Leyshon-Hughes."

Andrew was a friend of Nancy's, explained her mother. In fact, the seventeen-year-old boy had been at Nancy's the night before. Mrs. Eaton had even spoken to him on the phone. She told the police that Andrew had a troubled past and had just recently spent a few days at a mental hospital in Penetanguishene, Ontario. Mrs. Eaton also told the police about the bizarre phone call she had received that morning. Now she was sure it was Andrew who had called her from Nancy's phone. The police soon discovered that Nancy's car, a gift from her father, was missing. A provincial all-points bulletin was issued for a white 1979 Buick Skylark, with distinctive licence plates that read TYGER. "Suspect could be armed and dangerous," read the alert. Andrew Leyshon-Hughes had to be caught before he attacked again.

Ernest John Andrew Leyshon-Hughes was born on July 14, 1967, in Montreal, Quebec. His parents, Sarah and Ernest, met while they were both attending McGill University. When twenty-year-old Sarah became pregnant in 1966, they decided to get married. The young couple were looking forward to becoming first-time parents, but Andrew's birth was traumatic for them. The new-born was what doctors called a "blue baby." The umbilical cord was wrapped around his neck, cutting off the flow of blood to his brain. After he was born, four agonizing minutes passed before he cried out. The neurological impact of those precious four minutes would be called into question many years later.

Sarah and Ernest moved to Toronto when Andrew was two, and by that time, he was already throwing explosive temper tantrums. With full-time careers, the Leyshon-Hugheses struggled to find childcare for their aggressive son. Later, when Andrew started attending school, he regularly acted out and was diagnosed with various reading and writing problems. While he was extremely bright, teachers believed he had an attention deficit disorder. By the age of eight, Andrew was seeing psychiatrists and psychologists on a regular basis, but no one could pinpoint a specific diagnosis for his actions and behaviours. Therapy didn't seem to help, and by his early teenage years, his parents were at their wits' end. Andrew was running away from home, stealing and becoming more aggressive. His academic progress continued to decline, and the expensive private schools he attended had little patience for his bullying. He was considered a threat to the other students and was eventually asked to leave. At thirteen, he stole his father's Volvo and drove to his grandmother's farmhouse in Pickering, Ontario. There, he smashed a window to get in and spent the night. He was quickly apprehended by the local police and returned to his parents, who didn't want any charges laid.

More psychiatric evaluations revealed that Andrew was intelligent but lacked self-confidence—typical teenage angst. But there was something else, something darker and more volatile lurking beneath the surface. At fifteen, Andrew swallowed a bottle of Tylenol pills in a suicide attempt. But when his cry for help didn't get the desired reaction from his parents, he trashed the family home. Then he stole his dad's car again and headed back to his grandmother's farmhouse in Pickering. The next morning, he robbed the owner of the local general store at knifepoint for a carton of cigarettes and $35 in cash. This time, his parents couldn't stop the police from charging him. After a few nights in a youth detention centre, Andrew was given a year's probation and returned to his parents. But by this point, the family dynamic had completely deteriorated. Andrew's dad was drinking heavily to cope, and his mother's nerves were shot. Sarah would often hit Andrew out of frustration, and Andrew would strike his mother back. After another physical altercation in which Ernest threw a screwdriver at Andrew, the Leyshon-Hugheses knew something had to be done before one of them ended up in the hospital.

Out of desperation, Sarah asked her younger sister, Amy Jephcott, to take Andrew. Andrew had always gotten along well with his aunt Amy and uncle Bill, and he seemed to settle in well with his younger cousins. But the happy family atmosphere would not last long. In December 1982, Andrew pointed a loaded gun at his aunt and threatened to shoot her if she didn't let him take his uncle's motorcycle. Amy would later describe how Andrew looked. "It was like the devil staring at me," she said. "Dr. Jekyll had turned into Mr. Hyde, and I was terrified." But Andrew did not shoot; instead, he quickly broke down into tears, which was his familiar pattern. He would explode in anger and then be instantly remorseful. But that was little comfort to his family, since Andrew's behaviour was becoming increasingly erratic and violent. One day, they feared, he might just go too far.

Andrew Leyshon-Hughes and Nancy Eaton had known each other since childhood, but it wasn't until the summer of 1983 that their friendship blossomed in Muskoka, a popular resort area 150 kilometres north of Toronto. Andrew was sixteen and Nancy was twenty-two. Despite their age difference, the two had a lot in common. Both were born into wealthy, well-established Canadian families—old money that came with a lot of power and prestige. Andrew's mother was a member of the wealthy Osler family, which boasted a long list of influential lawyers, bankers and politicians throughout the country's history. And Nancy was an Eaton, a name every Canadian was familiar with because it was the name of the country's most iconic retail business, the Eaton's department store chain. Andrew and Nancy spent the summer at their neighbouring family compounds on Lake Rosseau, the summer playground of Toronto's elite.

The Osler family cottage was a source of great joy for Andrew Leyshon-Hughes. The summers he spent in Muskoka as a young boy with his grandfather John G. Osler were an idyllic contrast to his turbulent city life. When Andrew met Nancy, he had found himself a friend he could talk to. As an only child herself, Nancy was happy to take on the role of a big sister to Andrew. "This is my little bro," Nancy would say. But Andrew's affections towards

Nancy were not necessarily ones of brotherly love. The maturing young man had other thoughts about the beautiful older woman— something he kept well hidden.

Nancy and Andrew spent lazy summer weekends lounging on the Eatons' sunny lakeside dock, talking for hours. Andrew had a difficult relationship with his parents, which Nancy could relate to. She was also no stranger to family conflict. Nancy had a fractured relationship with her father. Edward Eaton was a difficult man to get along with and took no interest in the family business. He preferred living a life without responsibilities and was said to have enjoyed a drink or two . . . or three. His main passions were managing his investments, skeet shooting and whisky.

That summer in Muskoka, Andrew was upset at all the medical and psychological testing his parents were putting him through. After threatening his aunt with a loaded gun, Andrew had been shipped off to the prestigious and expensive Institute of Living in Hartford, Connecticut. There, the doctors scanned his brain and discovered that he might have epilepsy. Could this explain his explosive violent outbursts? Was this related to his traumatic birth? The psychiatrists still weren't sure, but they prescribed anticonvulsant drugs to control what they called intermittent explosive disorder, which is characterized by a pattern of abnormal, episodic and frequently violent social behaviours in the absence of significant provocation. His doctors also suggested that Andrew remain in the treatment centre, away from his parents. One doctor noted in his records, "I am most concerned about the possibility that his behaviour might escalate in such a way that he will do serious harm to either himself or to others." But Andrew's parents were not happy with the doctor's recommendations and decided against giving their son anticonvulsant drugs.

Following his release from the Connecticut institution, Andrew was sent to more doctors for more tests. A neurologist at Toronto General Hospital found no brain abnormalities and described him as "a healthy young man in no acute distress." Another doctor, at Toronto Western Hospital, said that Andrew was exceptionally polite and cooperative during an endless battery of tests, which revealed no major disorder other than attention deficit disorder. Andrew was then sent to the C.M. Hincks Treatment Centre in Toronto. After another round of tests, the doctors there challenged the US diagnosis. They did not believe Andrew suffered from epilepsy or any brain abnormality. They felt he suffered from a conduct disorder, meaning an anti-social behavioural disorder. But they did agree with the Connecticut specialists' recommendations that Andrew should be treated away from his parents. They believed his problems were deeply rooted in his relationship with his family and his environment. The Hincks Treatment Centre recommended a residential treatment program for Andrew, along with family therapy. Andrew agreed to the treatment program. His parents did not.

For years, the Leyshon-Hugheses had sought a specific medical diagnosis to explain Andrew's behaviour, but after countless doctors and thousands of dollars, they still refused to believe much of what they had been told. And now his parents were left with the reality that, at age sixteen, Andrew wasn't getting any better; in fact, he was getting much worse. Even Andrew couldn't explain a lot of what he felt or did. He had outbursts of anger that would transform him into a different person. He was a hostage to his own dark moods and felt desperately lonely. That summer, it seemed there was only one person in the world he could confide in. Sitting on a sun-drenched dock in Muskoka with Nancy Eaton, all his troubles would melt away. But, sadly, summer always comes to an end.

For Andrew, life back in the city wasn't quite as tranquil as time spent at the family cottage. While Nancy had lots of girlfriends and no shortage of eligible bachelors hoping to date her, Andrew struggled to fit in anywhere. As a result, his friendship with Nancy had slowly morphed into more of a dependence. Whenever he ran into trouble, which he often did, he would end up at Nancy's apartment, which was only a five-minute walk from his parents' house on Alcorn Avenue. There, they would talk for hours, and then he would often fall asleep on her couch.

But Andrew didn't like it when Nancy was unavailable to him. One night, a neighbour encountered Andrew kicking and punching at Nancy's door in a rage because she wasn't home. The next day, the concerned neighbour told Nancy what she had witnessed, but Nancy brushed it off, saying that she knew Andrew could be volatile at times, but he would never do anything to harm her. Nancy was always protective of her "little bro" Andrew.

On June 15, 1984, just one month shy of his seventeenth birthday, Andrew was remanded to the Ontario Mental Health Centre in Penetanguishene on a warrant for breaking and entering and destruction of property. Andrew's aggressive outbursts and destructive behaviour had finally caught up with him, and the police arrested him for a string of offences—he had stolen his father's car again, broken into the family's Muskoka cottage, shot a neighbour's cottage full of bullet holes with a .22-calibre rifle and, in one memorable incident, had stolen three motorboats in one day. Andrew had also stolen Nancy's car once, along with her passport and some money, but she had forgiven him. Andrew was found guilty of breaking and entering and was given three years' probation and community service. He also had to report to a probation officer on a regular basis.

At the hospital in Penetanguishene, doctors reconfirmed his diagnosis of a conduct disorder—an anti-social behavioural disorder. A psychiatric report suggested that Andrew's actions could be seen as a "cry for help" in which he was trying to get his mother and father to pay attention to him. Andrew began group therapy and was encouraged to talk about confronting problems head-on. At first, the treatment seemed to be working. Andrew was calmer, made some new friends and was getting along with his parents when they visited. He finally seemed to be learning how to positively release his pent-up feelings of aggression that tended to create his problems. After a three-month stay, Andrew was discharged from Penetanguishene in September 1984.

During his hospitalization, the relationship between Andrew and his parents had improved, but his doctors decided it would be better for him to live independently. Andrew moved into a rooming house in the Annex area of the city, not too far from his parents' Summerhill home. He had quit high school, so he enrolled in a steelworkers' course and worked part-time. Life was tough, but he wanted to prove to his parents he could be independent and responsible.

That Christmas, Andrew spent the holidays with his parents at their farm east of the city and everything seemed fine. After Christmas, Ernest and Sarah Leyshon-Hughes informed Andrew they were going to Mexico for two weeks. The family had regularly vacationed in Mexico ever since Ernest's parents moved there. Andrew missed his grandparents and told a friend he was very hurt that his parents had not invited him on the trip. With his parents gone, the beginning of the new year was difficult for Andrew. Feeling like he was losing control again, he called his uncle and said he was scared and suicidal. His uncle Bill took him immediately to a psychiatrist at Toronto General, who diagnosed Andrew's feelings as the result of normal teenage hormonal changes. But Andrew knew this wasn't the case and told his uncle he needed help. Bill listened to what Andrew was saying and bought him a bus ticket to Penetanguishene.

Back at the hospital, Andrew told a staff psychologist and a psychiatrist that he felt like he was going to explode. His doctors were concerned about a possible relapse but didn't think Andrew was a danger to himself or others. One doctor suggested he get some exercise—play hockey to work off the tension he was feeling. Andrew took part in some group therapy, and a few days into his stay he indicated that he was seeing things more clearly and feeling better about himself. Three days later, on a frigid January night, Andrew was back at Nancy Eaton's apartment.

Just before midnight on January 21, approximately four hours after Nancy Eaton's bloodied body was discovered in her apartment, the Toronto police received a call from the Ontario Provincial Police in Bradford, Ontario, approximately fifty-five kilometres north of Toronto. Nancy's car had been spotted at the entrance to a Petro-Canada gas station. The car had stalled, and the driver had asked the gas station attendant to call a tow truck. But before the tow truck arrived, an OPP officer spotted the vehicle and realized the white Buick Skylark with the personalized TYGER plates was the car connected with a Toronto murder. The young driver was quickly apprehended.

When Toronto homicide detectives arrived at the OPP detachment in Bradford later that night, they arrested seventeen-year-old Andrew Leyshon-Hughes and drove him back to Toronto. Andrew slept all the way. Around the same time, Andrew's parents arrived home from their Mexican vacation. Apparently, they had had a wonderful holiday.

The following day, as the city dug out from the violent winter storm, Nancy Eaton's murder was front-page news. The beautiful heiress to the Eaton family dynasty had been killed in her own home in an upscale area of the city. The police announced that a suspect had already been arrested but did not name him. Then, two days later, a picture of her alleged killer was splashed across the front page of every major Canadian newspaper. The image was shocking. He was just a kid—a good-looking, baby-faced teenager with long chestnut-brown hair. How could he be a cold-blooded killer? Did the police have the right person? They did, because he had already confessed.

After his arrest, Andrew admitted to murdering Nancy Eaton. In a chilling account of the crime, he calmly told the police that, on the night of Sunday, January 20, he arrived at Nancy's apartment around 9 p.m. It was cold and snowing heavily outside, and he was looking for a sympathetic ear and a warm place to sleep. His parents were still away and the rooming house he was living in was a dump. Nancy's tidy apartment was his only refuge. He was feeling agitated, so he had taken fifty milligrams of Valium to try to calm down.

When he arrived, Nancy was already in bed, watching TV with her cat, Tinkerbell, nestled beside her. She had gone to bed early with a migraine. But Nancy could tell Andrew was upset, so she made time for him. The two friends watched the end of the Super Bowl game, drank Diet Coke and talked into the night about Andrew's many problems. He had no job and few friends, and his relationship with his parents had soured again. While they talked, Nancy answered the phone twice, and both times it was her mother. Nancy was very close to her mom, which made Andrew jealous. On the phone that night, Nancy told her mom about Andrew going back to Penetanguishene to seek further psychiatric help. "Congratulations," Mrs. Eaton told him over the phone. "Hang in there," she said, trying to reassure the teenager that one day his troubles would pass. At around 1 a.m. Nancy took out her hearing aids and went to sleep in her bedroom, while Andrew took his usual spot on the yellow couch in the living room. It was the last night Andrew would be sleeping at Nancy's.

The next morning, Andrew told the police, he was awakened by Nancy's TV in her bedroom. She had programmed it to come on at 8:10 a.m. He walked into the bedroom and saw that Nancy was still sleeping. Without her hearing aids in, she didn't hear him entering her bedroom. Andrew then proceeded to the kitchen, where he picked up a twenty-three-centimetre carving knife. He said the next thing he knew, he was standing over her, watching her. Then he plunged the knife into her head—once, twice, three times, four times. Nancy screamed out his name. She tried to fight back, but Andrew kept stabbing. Finally, she stopped moving. She was dead. Andrew, covered in her blood, stared down at what he had just done. He felt strangely excited. He then admitted to the police that he had sex with Nancy's dead body.

When asked why he had killed Nancy, Andrew had no explanation. When questioned about the broken eggs found at the crime scene, Andrew said that he was juggling some eggs that he got out of the fridge. "I dropped one in the bathroom, and I tossed the other. I was just juggling them," he said matter-of-factly. And the potted palm tree on the bed? Andrew had no recollection, but detectives theorized that it had probably been moved when he was ransacking the apartment. After he killed Nancy, Andrew said he made himself a cup of coffee, had a shower and put on a white tracksuit that belonged to her. When asked if he had called Mrs. Eaton that morning, Andrew said he had no recollection of making the call. He then rummaged through the apartment, looking for money. He dumped Nancy's purse out in the bedroom, taking $45 in cash and her car keys. Then in an ironic twist, he drove to the Eaton Centre, the Toronto shopping mall named after Nancy's great-great-grandfather Timothy Eaton. There Andrew said he hooked up with a friend and paid him back the $40 he owed him. He then returned to Nancy's apartment, where her dead body lay on the floor. He needed money, so he forged a cheque payable to himself for $191. At the bank, the fake signature fooled the teller, but the written and numerical amounts did not match. Andrew drove back to Nancy's apartment one more time, again ignoring the bloodied corpse of his dearest friend, to forge another cheque for $150. This time, the bank cashed the cheque. He then drove back to the Eaton Centre to hang out with his friend. He bought a couple of cassette tapes and managed to score a gram of cocaine off a dealer he knew. Later that evening, when he couldn't entice any of his friends to party with him, he decided to drive out of town. Andrew told the police that he was headed to Collingwood—Blue Mountain, a ski resort area two and a half hours northwest of Toronto. Andrew had skied there often as a kid with his dad and knew the area well. He admitted that his plan was to drive off a cliff in Nancy's white Buick because he felt bad about what he had done to her and wanted to die.

Andrew Leyshon-Hughes was charged with the first-degree murder of Nancy Eaton. For the homicide detectives, the investigation appeared to be an airtight case. They had the murder weapon and other physical evidence, and Andrew had given them a full confession. The Crown would have no trouble getting a conviction, and the teenaged killer would likely get life in prison. But Andrew's future was not so simply mapped out. His parents had hired one of Canada's foremost criminal defence lawyers, and he would argue that, regardless of the overwhelming evidence, Andrew was not guilty of killing Nancy—in fact, he wasn't guilty of anything.

In Canada, you cannot be convicted of a criminal offence if you are deemed insane. Under section 16 of the Criminal Code, "No person is criminally responsible for an act committed or an omission made while suffering from a mental disorder that rendered the person incapable of appreciating the nature and quality of the act or omission or of knowing that it was wrong." And while wrong can imply *moral* wrong, the courts are only interested in *legal* wrong: Did the offender know that the consequences of an act constituted an offence under the Criminal Code? Therefore, the most critical issue to be addressed at Andrew's murder trial would be his state of mind: At the time of the murder, did Andrew Leyshon-Hughes understand that what he was doing was wrong? The defence would argue that Andrew was insane at the time of Nancy Eaton's murder and therefore was not legally guilty of the crime.

Representing Andrew was Clayton Ruby, one of Canada's most prominent criminal lawyers and no stranger to high-profile cases. If the plea of not guilty by reason of insanity was to be put forward successfully, Ruby would have to show that, even if Andrew knew what he had done, he was unable to appreciate the nature of his actions and unable to fully comprehend the legal consequences.

Andrew Leyshon-Hughes's murder trial began on September 15, 1986, twenty months after he murdered Nancy Eaton as she slept. The trial attracted a great deal of media attention since the killer and the victim both belonged to prestigious Canadian families. Reporters and news photographers jostled for prime positions outside the courthouse on University Avenue in Toronto every day, trying to get a photograph or an interview from members of either of the devastated families.

Mrs. Nancy Eaton arrived every day in a chauffeur-driven black limousine. Frail yet composed, she was always elegantly dressed and made an effort to smile at those gathered. She wasn't going to allow the world to see her inner turmoil. Since her daughter's brutal murder, the elder Nancy had lost her will to live. For twenty-three years, her entire focus had been on her beautiful daughter, who had overcome a severe hearing impairment and a difficult childhood. But now Nancy was gone. Edward Eaton, her former husband and Nancy's father, had also recently died. While he and his daughter had never been particularly close, they had reconnected before he died and they had spent the Christmas holidays together, just three weeks before Nancy's murder. Her death had devastated him, and he died of a stroke just six months after Nancy was killed. Now Mrs. Eaton was truly alone and had to face the young man who had killed her beloved Tiger.

In his opening remarks, assistant Crown attorney Paul Chumak stated that the Crown would argue that Andrew Leyshon-Hughes murdered Nancy Eaton in the course of a sexual assault. At the time of the murder, the Crown believed, Andrew was of sound mind and knew exactly what he was doing on that cold winter morning. After recounting all of Andrew's actions that day, from killing Nancy to his capture at the gas station, Chumak said to the jury: "Are these the actions of an insane person? Andrew murdered Nancy Eaton and then committed a sexual assault. He knew exactly what he wanted and was determined to get it."

Chumak then presented numerous disturbing and graphic photographs of the crime scene—the victim lying on her back on the floor, the blood-splattered walls, the bent and bloodstained knife, and the victim's torn nightgown and panties. The jury was also shown autopsy photos that revealed that Nancy had been stabbed twenty-one times, including six times in the heart. And while it was obvious that jurors were having great difficulty looking at the images, Andrew sat slumped in his seat, showing no emotion.

It was now up to Clayton Ruby to prove to the jury that Andrew, at the time of the murder, did not appreciate the reality of what he had done. In his dramatic opening remarks, Ruby stated that the case before the jury was very much about mental disease and that it was clear that the Ontario health system had failed Andrew Leyshon-Hughes his entire life, including just three days before the murder, when Andrew sought help by telling his uncle he was feeling "uncontrollable surges of energy." But a doctor at Toronto General had dismissed his concerns as normal teenage hormonal problems. "Andrew knew something was wrong and felt like he was about to explode," continued his lawyer. Ruby then told the jury how Andrew had taken a bus to Penetanguishene Mental Health Centre, a place where he felt safe. There, a staff psychologist suggested group therapy and told him to play some hockey to relieve his stress. "The Ontario health system failed my client when he needed it the most," said Ruby. Concluding his remarks, the respected defence attorney said he would call several expert witnesses to support his theory that Andrew was legally insane when he stabbed and sexually assaulted Nancy Eaton on the morning of January 21, 1985. Ruby also promised that the psychiatric evidence would show that Andrew's seemingly normal behaviour after the murder was consistent with the kind of mental illness his client suffered from.

The first witness called by the Crown was Mrs. Nancy Eaton. Her voice was barely audible as she relived that horrible winter night when she discovered her daughter's body. She told the court that since Nancy's murder, her days were filled with overwhelming grief and her nights with fear. She was afraid to go to sleep, as the nightmare of what she saw would return and images of Nancy's bloody body would play over and over in her mind. "Good night, I love you" were Nancy's last words to her mom. Now, most days Mrs. Eaton said she would walk for hours, even in the freezing cold, often ending up at Nancy's grave in Mount Pleasant Cemetery. Her only solace was Tinkerbell, Nancy's poor cat.

When asked about Andrew Leyshon-Hughes, the grieving mother only had positive things to say about the teenager. "All I ever saw was this dear, patient, sweet child," said Mrs. Eaton, who met Andrew at their summer cottage. "He would take younger kids out water skiing, playing tennis and swimming. He never got angry," she said. "I'm sure if someone had known he had these mad rages, they would have warned us."

The next group of witnesses were various friends and acquaintances of Andrew's who had seen him on the day of the murder. Most testified that he seemed calm and normal. Nothing out of the ordinary.

As the trial continued, lawyers Ruby and Chumak soon became embattled in establishing the time of the sexual attack. Under Canadian law, a sex attack that results in death is automatically first-degree murder. The defence's tactic if the insanity plea failed, therefore, was to bring forward testimony that would distance the time between the killing and the sexual assault, resulting in a lesser charge. But pathologist Dr. Hans Sepp told the court that he had no way of telling whether Leyshon-Hughes had sex with Nancy Eaton before or after her death.

The defence's first witness was Andrew's mother, Sarah. She painfully described how she and her husband had spent years trying to get to the root of Andrew's bizarre behaviour. She referenced his difficult birth and his emotional difficulties that had manifested as early as two years of age. Cared for by a series of nannies and daycare facilities while both his parents worked, Andrew began having temper tantrums and would fly into uncontrollable rages. Nannies would quit and daycares would ask him to leave.

School became an ongoing battle between Andrew and his parents because he would refuse to do any homework and would often get into schoolyard fights. By the time he quit attending classes in Grade 10, his parents were at their wits' end. "Our home became a battlefield," said an emotional Sarah. "Verbal arguments became physical," she told the jury. "We dreaded coming home." As Andrew matured and began taking out his anger on other people and their property, the Leyshon-Hugheses were genuinely afraid of how far he might go. "We knew we couldn't control him," said Sarah.

After her testimony, Andrew's father, aunt and uncle and other relatives relayed their difficult encounters with Andrew and the family's ongoing attempts to get help. Andrew's aunt Amy relived the terrifying moment when he pointed a loaded gun at her. She told the jury that he seemed to be in some kind of trance and looked like the devil at the time.

On the third day of the trial, Dr. Basil Orchard, the first of several psychiatric witnesses called by the defence, told the jury that part of Leyshon-Hughes's mind "was shut off, unable to work" when he stabbed Nancy Eaton. Dr. Orchard, who had extensive experience working with the criminally insane, added that Andrew was responding to uncontrollable drives, which the doctor attributed to a psychosis produced by the combination of brain dysfunction and a borderline personality disorder. He believed that Andrew's brain had been damaged during his birth, and, even if he remembered what he had done to Nancy, he had no real conception of what had happened. In other words, surmised the doctor, the murder was mindless and motiveless.

During the Crown's cross-examination, Chumak returned to his key argument—that Nancy's murder had been a straightforward psychopathic sexual attack and Andrew knew what he was doing. Dr. Orchard could not be swayed from his medical opinion and insisted that Andrew lacked the mental capacity to appreciate that he was killing Nancy.

Dr. Lionel Solursh, a psychiatrist from Augusta, Georgia, who treated Andrew when he was fourteen, testified that he had referred the teenager to the Institute for Living in Hartford, where they had determined that Andrew had an electrical dysfunction in the brain. "It should have been picked up in Penetang," said the doctor, referring to when Andrew had been sent to the Ontario mental health facility. "It resulted in the death of a fine young woman," he concluded.

The next expert witness was Dr. Frank Ervin, chair of the department of psychiatry at McGill University in Montreal. He had trained at the Harvard Medical School, had written hundreds of peer-reviewed medical articles, and was the author of a 1970 book called *Violence and the Brain*. Although he had only met Andrew for one hour a few weeks before the trial, Dr. Ervin stated that, because of his brain dysfunction, Andrew was not responsible for his actions. He believed the teenager was in a dissociative state when he killed Nancy. Dr. Ervin said that the part of Andrew's brain that controls a person's basic drives, such as fear, anxiety and sexual arousal—the limbic system—was damaged. Then, to use a simple analogy, he said that Andrew had transformed into a "crocodile man" whose actions were controlled by the primitive limbic part of his brain. "That's all the brain a crocodile has." It was, Dr. Ervin believed, this poorly organized crocodile brain, unhindered by the higher part of the brain which regulates emotions and rational thought, that prompted Andrew's actions when he killed Nancy. Andrew was probably suffering from a limbic seizure at the time of the murder, which created electrical activity in the brain that cut off control and restraint. "He was on a roll downwards. He gets up, and this poorly organized crocodile man commits this heinous crime." In other words, according to the esteemed doctor, at the time of the murder, Andrew was a walking time bomb.

More psychiatrists, and their varied expert opinions, followed over the next few days, and in his summation, Clayton Ruby reiterated his original defence—that the murder of Nancy Eaton was not a crime, but a tragedy. Andrew Leyshon-Hughes had killed the one person he loved because the health system had failed him.

At 2:45 p.m. on the ninth day of the proceedings, the trial came to an abrupt halt when the Crown conceded that there was overwhelming evidence that Andrew was legally insane when he killed Nancy. (Crown attorney Paul Chumak later said his decision had been based on emotional family testimony and the overwhelming weight of the psychiatric opinions.) As a result, the jury did not have to resolve the question of intent or timing surrounding the murder and sexual assault. They only had to decide whether Andrew Leyshon-Hughes was guilty of murder, or not guilty by reason of insanity.

In a brief address to the jury before they retired to deliberate, Associate Chief Justice Frank Callaghan told them he was satisfied with the direction of the trial. "The accused at the time of the killing did not appreciate the quality or nature of his act," he said. "I'm satisfied he was criminally insane at the time." Justice Callaghan also reassured the jury that a finding of insanity would likely result in Andrew being detained indefinitely. "He may never go free," he said, "unless his illness is cured or controlled to the point where he is no longer a threat to society. And that may be never."

The jury of seven women and five men deliberated for only seven-teen minutes before finding nineteen-year-old Andrew Leyshon-Hughes not guilty by reason of insanity. Justice Callaghan ordered Andrew confined to Oak Ridge, the high-security forensic unit of the Ontario Mental Health Centre in Penetanguishene, Ontario. Andrew's tearful mother hugged Clayton Ruby. "Congratulations," said Mrs. Eaton to the defence lawyer before walking out of the courtroom.

Outside the courthouse, Ruby told waiting reporters that his client was pleased with the outcome of the trial. "After years of searching, Mr. Leyshon-Hughes has finally found out what's wrong with him."

For Mrs. Eaton, the trial had been a painful experience. "It was something that had to be done," she told the press. She was hope-ful that something good would come of the tragedy of losing her daughter. Speaking fondly of Nancy, Mrs. Eaton said, "Nancy would have been angry at Andrew for what he did because it hurt me. Then she would have forgiven him. She was always so forgiving."

The murder of Nancy Eaton was a crime that shook the coun-try. The beautiful heiress had been viciously stabbed and raped by her good friend, a seventeen-year-old kid whose family were also well-respected members of the Toronto establishment. And while shocking in its brutality, Nancy's senseless murder also exposed fail-ures in the country's mental health system. In 1989 a book about the murder, *A Question of Guilt*, was published, and five years later a made-for-television movie, *The Death and Life of Nancy Eaton*, was released.

In an interview in October 1986, one month after he was sen-tenced to a secure mental health facility, nineteen-year-old Andrew Leyshon-Hughes told a journalist, "I won't be in here for long, I know how to play the game. I don't even need to be here. All I need is a week up at my cottage and I'll be fine." But as it turned out, Andrew would have a great deal more time to reflect on the good times at his family's Muskoka cottage.

In 2006, twenty-one years after the murder of Nancy Eaton, thirty-nine-year-old Andrew Leyshon-Hughes was given a full discharge from the medium-security Royal Ottawa Mental Health Centre, where he had resided for several years and had attended classes at Algonquin College. In his request for freedom, Andrew said he was anxious to move on with his life and hoped to get married and have children one day.

In 2007, Mrs. Nancy Eaton passed away at the age of eighty-two. Those who knew her best said she never fully recovered from that fateful night in January 1985. Her final resting place is beside her much loved daughter, Tiger.

# PART TWO

# FAMILY TIES
# THAT BIND AND BREAK

*When family dysfunction turns deadly . . .*

# SINS OF THE SON

## THE DISAPPEARANCE OF MINNIE FORD

Sixteen-year-old Wayne Ford was looking forward to the May long weekend. It was the unofficial start to the summer after a long Canadian winter, and the official countdown to the end of the school year. The tenth-grade student at Earl Haig Secondary School in the middle-class suburb of Willowdale, Ontario, had already made plans to party with some friends. It was 1963 and downtown Toronto's Yorkville neighbourhood was the place to be. With its late-night coffee houses and bars, kids from the sleepy suburbs flocked to the area. Wayne was a familiar face in some of the local establishments. At six foot three and over two hundred pounds, the underage teenager had no problem passing for older and getting served alcohol.

It was the Thursday before the start of the long weekend and, as he did on most days, Wayne went home for lunch. Wayne lived with his mom, Minnie, at 21 Kingsdale Avenue, a few blocks from school. Wayne was an only child and grew up in comfortable surroundings. His father, Lorne, owned a gas station on Yonge Street and was the president of the Toronto Businessman's Association.

The Fords had a cottage on Lake Couchiching, north of Toronto, spent winter vacations in Florida and travelled to Europe in the summer.

But Wayne's family life had changed dramatically nine months earlier, when his fifty-two-year-old father suffered a fatal heart attack while they were in Florida. Now, with his father gone, it was just Wayne and his mother, and they didn't always get along. Minnie was still in a deep depression over the sudden loss of her husband, and she had little control over her son, who had become even more unruly since his father's death.

As the long weekend approached, Wayne was hoping his mother would head up to their cottage so he could hang out with friends in the city. And, like any typical teenage boy, Wayne wanted to borrow one of the family cars. But his mom said no, and for good reason. Her green 1959 Cadillac was just back from the repair shop after Wayne smashed it up a couple weeks earlier. After paying thousands to get it repaired, Minnie was not prepared to hand over the keys again. Wayne insisted, saying he needed the car to take some friends to a drive-in movie. Still, Minnie refused, and the argument between the two escalated. Minnie said she was sick of his poor attitude and his punky behaviour. "Go to hell, you old bitch," yelled Wayne. Minnie slapped Wayne in the face. Wayne, who towered over his petite mother, slapped her back. Minnie drew back in shock. Wayne had never struck her before. It would be the first and last time. A half-hour later Wayne was back at Earl Haig. He parked his mother's Cadillac in the school parking lot and headed to his first class.

Just after the Thanksgiving weekend in 1966, Julius Karu drove north to his cottage on Lake Couchiching, a popular boating and fishing lake 150 kilometres north of Toronto. It was a time of year that signalled the end of summer. The leaves were putting on a glorious show of colour, a blanket of frost glistened off the ground each morning and family cottages were being closed for the winter. Julius had a busy weekend ahead of him, but it was a small price to pay for his little piece of waterfront paradise.

It had been a particularly hot summer and a busy season on the lake. But the warmer weather had resulted in lower water levels and some of the cottagers had even gotten their powerboats stuck in the silty lake bottom. The conditions had also caused more garbage than usual to wash up on shore. On that October weekend, Julius Karu wasn't surprised to see some remnants of a busy summer on the beach: a few beer bottles, pop cans and the odd flip-flop. But he was surprised when he caught sight of what looked like a mannequin caught in some reeds close to the shore. Maybe someone was playing a silly prank, he thought. Getting closer to the greyish floating object, he noticed that one of its hands was missing and there was something around its neck. It was a plastic bag.

Moving closer, Julius suddenly realized it wasn't a store dummy. It was the body of a woman covered in some type of plaster or cement. Most of her face was missing, but he could see pieces of flesh and hair. As a long-time summer resident of the lake, Julius had heard about a few drownings over the years, but this bloated body looked like it had been in the water a long time. He wondered if it could it be related to the famous missing-person case he had read about. Three years earlier, a wealthy Toronto widow who owned a cottage not far from his had gone missing. Her sudden disappearance was front-page news, and initial reports suggested she was last seen heading to Lake Couchiching. The police dredged the lake looking for her but came up empty. Now it seemed the shallow murky waters had finally revealed their deadly secret.

||||||||

When Toronto homicide detectives learned of Julius Karu's discovery, they were certain of the woman's identity. Fifty-five-year-old Minnie Ford had disappeared three years earlier, during the May long weekend. Police searched the cottage area and had even travelled to Fort Myers, Florida, where the Fords had a winter home. But Minnie Ford had simply disappeared without a trace.

The plaster-coated body matched the age and description of Mrs. Ford, and divers later discovered parts of a plywood box that the police believed had been Minnie Ford's waterlogged make-shift coffin. The box was coated in the same white substance that had been found on the body. Dr. Fred Jaffe, a Toronto pathologist, later established that the fat in the woman's body had seeped out and formed a powdery, waxy-feeling substance called adipocere. This, he said, would look to a layman like plaster of paris. Dr. Jaffe also confirmed that the woman had likely been beaten and strangled. There was also a metal object embedded in her skull, which would eventually be identified as the sharp end of an ice pick. Most of the clothing was still on the body and the plaster coating had prevented decomposition. Only parts of her face and left hand were missing.

Minnie Ford's disappearance had been the talk of Toronto in spring of 1963. A middle-aged, recently widowed woman had vanished from her quiet neighbourhood. When newspapers reported that she had come into significant money after her husband's untimely death, rumours began to swirl that she might have taken off with a new man. But her concerned sister quickly put that gossip to rest, saying that Minnie loved her teenage son far too much and would never have left him.

As for Minnie's sixteen-year-old son, Wayne, at the time of her disappearance, he had told the police his mother was supposed to meet him at their cottage on the May long weekend but never arrived. He then suggested she might have gone to Florida without telling him. But as the police began their investigation, they discovered that Minnie did not pack a suitcase or take either of the family cars. Her bank accounts and credit cards remained unused, and she had not been in touch with any family members. Ironically, it was Minnie's sister who reported her missing a week after she was last heard from. Wayne, the dutiful son, had somehow forgotten to mention it.

With his mother gone, Wayne had no rules and no restrictions. One week after her disappearance, he quit school and the Fords' tidy suburban home turned into a party house for him and his friends. Wayne started dealing drugs and selling stolen guns. He thrived on pushing boundaries. But then again, Wayne had always been a troubled kid, stealing candy and toys since the age of eight. His father would discipline him, but Wayne continued to steal and act out. Now, with no parental supervision, his rebellious teenage behaviour was out of control.

By the age of eighteen, two years after his mother disappeared, Wayne had joined a biker gang and was robbing banks for the thrill of it. He then became a hired thug, breaking one man's legs, stabbing another and shooting someone—all for money. But Ford's reign of criminality was interrupted when he was charged with shooting another teenager during one of the parties at his house on Kingsdale Avenue. He spent three months in prison. Not long after his release, he was back in jail for possession of stolen goods. A year later he moved to California for a fresh start but was quickly deported. In late 1965, he was charged with breaking into storage lockers. This time he was sent to Ontario's Burwash Reformatory, near Sudbury, for a two-year sentence. But six months later, Wayne and another inmate escaped from the correctional facility and hitchhiked back to Toronto. Caught a few days later, an additional six months was added to his sentence. But he wasn't going back to Burwash. This time Wayne was headed to a much tougher prison.

||||||||||

While Wayne was incarcerated, the investigation into his mother's disappearance continued. The police were sure that Minnie Ford had met with foul play and they believed that Wayne knew more than he was telling them. Wayne and two friends had been spotted partying at the Fords' cottage that May long weekend, but no one saw Minnie. Now that her body had washed up on shore so close to the family cottage, the police were certain Wayne had killed his mother and then dumped her body in the lake. An arrest warrant was issued and the police knew exactly where to find the nineteen-year-old: he was residing in the notorious Kingston Penitentiary.

One month after the discovery of Minnie Ford's body, Wayne Ford was charged with capital murder. Wayne was accused of killing his mother in a planned and deliberate manner. If convicted, the teenager could face the death penalty. Investigators and Wayne's own lawyer suggested that he plead guilty to manslaughter and serve his time. But the cocky young man was certain the cops had nothing that could tie him to the murder. He didn't know that while he was in prison, investigators had returned to his former Willowdale home and found human blood in nine places, including the basement stairs. Wayne also didn't realize that two of his friends had turned on him and had admitted to helping him get rid of his mother's body.

Wayne Ford's murder trial began on May 17, 1967, four years almost to the day after Minnie Ford's killing. The 120-seat courtroom filled up quickly, and dozens of spectators stood outside. In Toronto, the sensational crime was front-page news. A handsome son stood accused of the brutal murder of his widowed mother.

On the opening day of the trial, Crown counsel Lloyd Graburn stated outright that he could not prove a capital murder case against Wayne Ford, meaning he could not prove the murder was planned and intentional. But he could prove non-capital murder, which came with a life sentence. Graburn then outlined his case to the all-male jury, saying that Wayne murdered his mother in May 1963 in their Willowdale home after a heated argument and then, with the help of two friends, dumped her body in Lake Couchiching, hoping it would never be found. But when Minnie Ford's body was discovered so close to the Ford family cottage, Wayne's friends finally revealed the horrible secrets they had been keeping for more than three years.

The first witness called by the prosecution was Ronald Walli, Wayne Ford's former best friend. As the young man began his testimony, those sitting in the packed courtroom listened intently to the ghastly details he revealed about Minnie Ford's murder. Wally testified that on the afternoon of May 16, he and Wayne were in class at Earl Haig Secondary School. After school, they drove to Wayne's house in Minnie's green Cadillac. In the car, Wayne told Ronald that he had killed his mother. Ronald said he was shocked and didn't know what to say. Then Wayne pulled out a gun from underneath the front seat of the car and told Ronald he needed to help get rid of the body. Ronald agreed, fearing what Wayne might do to him if he refused.

When they walked into the Fords' kitchen, Ronald said he saw a lifeless form underneath a bloodied bedsheet. Wayne pulled the sheet back to reveal his mother's body. Ronald told the jury that the woman had a grey patterned dress on, but he couldn't see the face because there was a blue plastic bag covering her head. The sight of the body made him sick and he threw up in the kitchen sink.

Then, according to Walli, Wayne told him they had to hide the body in the basement. As the two teenagers dragged the body down the stairs, Minnie's head thumped against every step, leaving a trail of blood. Ronald was sick again in the laundry sink. In the basement, they stuffed Minnie's body into a plywood box and wrapped it with an old garden hose. Then they proceeded to clean up the bloodstains on the stairs and in the kitchen. Wayne would later sand down and repaint the basement steps three times.

The following night, Walli said, they put the plywood box into the trunk of the Cadillac and drove to the Fords' cottage. He testified that when they arrived, Wayne suggested that they bury the box. They drove down a dark forested road and began digging, but the ground was too hard. They eventually gave up and drove back to the cottage. After a few hours of heavy drinking, Wayne described in sickening detail how he killed his mother. According to Walli, Wayne said he hit his mom over and over, but she wouldn't go down. He then began strangling her, but she was still fighting for her life. He then grabbed an ice pick off the kitchen counter and stabbed her in the head. When he tried to pull it out, the handle broke off.

After Wayne talked about how he killed his mother, he asked Ronald Walli to remove the ice pick, which was still embedded in his mother's head, and to smash Minnie's teeth to make any future identification of the body difficult. Ronald told the hushed courtroom that Wayne handed him a steel rod for the job. Afraid to refuse Wayne's request, Ronald went out to the garage, where the body was stored. He opened the lid but could not go through with it. Later, he told Wayne that he had done what he asked.

The next witness was nineteen-year-old Larry Metcalfe. He testified that he spent the 1963 May long weekend at the Ford family cottage with Wayne and Ronald. On the Saturday night, after he arrived and after a lot of drinking, Wayne confessed to him that he had murdered his mother and said her body was in the garage. Wayne then took him to the garage and opened a large wooden box that contained Winnie Ford's bloodied corpse. Wayne told his friends that they needed to get rid of the body. The three teenagers loaded the box onto a child's red wagon and pushed it down to the dock. Then they moved it onto a boat and rowed out to the middle of the lake, where they attempted to dump the box overboard. But the box was so heavy it ended up breaking part of the rowboat and all three teenagers ended up in the water. They finally tied an anchor to the box and managed to sink it. Then they went back to the cottage to party. Metcalfe said that Wayne swore them to secrecy and threatened to hurt them if they ever said anything.

Over the next few days of the trial, several other witnesses testified how Wayne joked about killing his mother and was giving away her clothing and jewellery to girlfriends. Two psychiatrists also testified that they would describe Wayne as an aggressive type of psychopath inclined towards outbursts of extreme anger or hostility. According to the medical professionals, Wayne was highly intelligent but lacked any sense of responsibility and was unable to experience guilt. He had a low regard for the rules of society and was preoccupied with his own wants and needs. In their professional opinions, Wayne Ford was a danger to society, would be difficult to rehabilitate and should be locked up indefinitely.


The courtroom was full on May 26, when defence attorney Donald Creighton called his final witness. Flanked by two police officers, Wayne Ford entered the witness box. The handsome, clean-shaven young man looked more like a movie star than a criminal accused of brutally murdering his own mother. Under oath, Wayne admitted to killing Minnie Ford but claimed it was in self-defence. Yes, he and his mother were fighting over the car that weekend, but then things got out of hand. She slapped him and he slapped her back. Then, according to Wayne, his mother picked up an ice pick from the kitchen counter and came at him. Wayne backed away and ran to his bedroom, where he grabbed the first thing he saw to defend himself: a miniature bat his father had given him. His mother followed him into the bedroom, swinging the ice pick.

Wayne said he ran back into the kitchen, trying to get away, but his mother caught up to him and slashed his arm. Wayne said he didn't remember swinging the bat, but the next thing he knew, his mother was on the floor, dead.

Wayne testified that after he killed his mother he put a plastic bag over her head and covered her body with a bedsheet. Then he changed out of his bloodied clothes and returned to school. Later, he asked his friend Ronald Walli to help him move the body to the basement, where they put it in a plywood box. Then they cleaned up the blood. That night, they went drinking and to a drive-in movie in Minnie's Cadillac. Wayne denied telling either of his friends that he had stabbed his mother in the head with an ice pick and he denied threatening his friends to stay quiet.

Under cross-examination, Crown attorney Lloyd Graburn challenged Wayne's claim of self-defence. He reminded Wayne that he never told anyone, including his friends who helped to dispose of his mother's body, that Minnie had attacked him with an ice pick.

"You are six foot three, 220 pounds; your mother was five feet five, 140 pounds," the prosecutor said. "If that were true, you could have grabbed it."

"I'm no judo expert," Wayne responded. Laughter broke out in the courtroom.


In his closing arguments, Creighton urged the jury to acquit Wayne Ford on the premise that he was simply defending himself against his ice pick–wielding mother. But if they rejected the self-defence argument, the lawyer said they should return with a verdict of manslaughter. "Wayne did not intend to kill his mother," said the lawyer. "He simply lost control." Referring to Walli and Metcalfe, who admitted to helping Wayne dispose of his mother's corpse, the attorney called them self-serving liars. He added that their testimony was so motivated by self-interest that it was worthless.

"They embellished everything to save their own skin," said Ford's lawyer.

Crown counsel Lloyd Graburn told the jurors that the evidence during the nine-day trial proved that Wayne had killed his mother and then tried to cover up his crime by burying her in the lake. But if they believed Wayne's story of self-defence, they should question why Wayne did not simply leave the house when his mother threatened him with the ice pick. He claimed he had done so on previous occasions, when his mother attacked him with a frying pan and a rolling pin. Graburn then reminded the jury that Wayne's friends who testified against him said that Wayne had told them he had killed his mother when she turned her back on him following her refusal to let him take the car. Wayne told his friends that he beat her repeatedly before strangling her and stabbing her in the head with the ice pick. Graburn concluded that the evidence justified a verdict of guilty of non-capital murder.

Seven hours later, the jury returned and announced their verdict: guilty of murder. Wayne was sentenced to life in prison and was returned to Kingston Penitentiary.

Inmate #2778 was already familiar with Canada's oldest penitentiary, but this time he was staying much longer. Faced with years behind bars, Wayne decided to go straight. He would do his time, however long that would be, and once he got out, he would make sure he never went to prison again. Wayne quickly adapted, taking classes to finish his high school degree and working at various jobs in the prison. But the day-to-day routine of the archaic prison was upended on April 14, 1971, when six inmates initiated a riot and kidnapped six unsuspecting guards.

Wayne, along with five hundred other inmates, suddenly found himself part of a deadly siege as prisoners ran wild, destroying everything they could inside the walls of the prison. No one was safe, and vulnerable inmates were soon rounded up and beaten. But Wayne was a respected con, and others knew better than to challenge him. Realizing the kidnapped guards were the prisoner's only insurance against an all-out military assault, Wayne armed himself with a three-foot length of lead pipe and moved the guards to a safe place within the prison. For the next four days, Wayne and several other prisoners protected the terrified guards against other inmates who were out for blood.

When the riot was finally quelled, all six guards were released unharmed. The infamous prison was a shambles, and two inmates were dead, having been tortured along with a dozen others. Ford's role in the riot was never formally recognized by prison authorities, but his actions and those of a few others likely saved the lives of the guards.

After the riot, Wayne Ford was transferred to the Millhaven Institution to serve out the remainder of his sentence. He was paroled in 1975 and began working with a prison outreach program to assist other inmates. In a 2013 interview for the *Toronto Star*, Wayne said he loved his mother and maintained that her death was an accident. Today, Wayne lives a quiet life in western Canada.

# 5 A MOTHER'S LOVE

## THE MA DUNCAN CASE

On the morning on November 17, 1958, Olga Duncan failed to show up for her early-morning shift at St. Francis Hospital in Santa Barbara, California. The thirty-year-old nurse had been working at the hospital since January, after graduating from nursing school in Vancouver and moving to California. Originally from Dauphin, Manitoba, Olga was recently married and expecting her first child in a few months.

The young nurse, who worked in acute care, was extremely dependable, so when she didn't come in to work or call, her co-workers became concerned. Adeline Curry, who was the chief surgical nurse at the hospital, decided to go to Olga's apartment on Garden Street to check on her. Adeline and Olga had become good friends over the past few months. When Adeline arrived at Olga's tidy one-bedroom flat, she discovered the front door to the apartment ajar. Inside, all the lights were on and the bed covers had been turned back, but the bed had not been slept in. A neatly pressed nurse's uniform hung in the bedroom closet, but there was no sign of Olga.

Adeline phoned Olga's husband, Frank Duncan, a successful Santa Barbara lawyer. Olga and Frank had only been married for five months, but Adeline knew there was already trouble in the new marriage. Olga confided in her that she had been repeatedly threatened and harassed by another woman who was very jealous of Olga's marriage to the attorney. When contacted by a concerned Adeline, Frank said he didn't know where Olga was and didn't seem too concerned that his pregnant wife was missing. Adeline feared the worst. Something was desperately wrong. Olga would not have just disappeared without telling her. What if something had happened to her or the baby? Adeline Curry decided to go straight to the local police station.

In 1958, Santa Barbara, California, was a wealthy coastal town famous for its colonial Spanish architecture and wide, sandy beaches. Dubbed the "American Rivera," it was a safe and respectable get-away for many fleeing the crime and grime of Los Angeles, 150 kilo-metres to the south. Nothing much happened in the sleepy enclave, so when the police were notified that an attractive, married nurse who was seven months pregnant had disappeared, they weren't ini-tially concerned. They suspected a lovers' quarrel between husband and wife, and assumed the missing woman would turn up very soon.

Looking into Olga Duncan's background, the Santa Barbara police discovered that the newly married woman was Canadian, and they contacted her parents, who lived in Benito, Manitoba. Olga Nettie Kupczyk was born on March 24, 1928, in Dauphin to Polish immigrants Elias and Justina Kupczyk. Elias, a section foreman on the Canadian Pacific railway, said that he and his wife had not heard from their daughter in a few weeks, but they told the police that Olga had written to them, saying she feared for her safety. Olga told her parents that her new mother-in-law, Elizabeth Ann Duncan, had threatened her on multiple occasions. In her letters home, Olga wrote that Mrs. Duncan had an unhealthy hold over her son that had led to constant quarrels between the couple, and they had separated just three weeks after getting married. According to Olga, Frank had returned to live with his mother. In one of her letters, Olga wrote:

> She came to the apartment and threatened to kill me and Frank . . . She cut up Frank's birth certificate and all of his baby pictures . . . She has not allowed Frank to live here. It was tragic at first, but now I don't even want him. Life is short and I want to enjoy the rest of it.

Olga was upset about the situation, but if Frank couldn't stand up to his mother, she knew they had no future. She told her parents not to worry about her because she was looking forward to having the baby despite her marital woes. But now she was missing and had not contacted her parents or anyone else. The police decided they needed to investigate Mrs. Elizabeth Duncan and her son Frank.

Elizabeth Ann Duncan was born Hazel Lucille Sinclara Nigh on April 16, 1904, in Kansas City, Missouri. One of four children, she quit school in the fourth grade and left home at fourteen. Married twice before her fifteenth birthday, Elizabeth eventually settled in San Francisco. In 1928 she married a travelling salesman named Frank Low, and four months later Frank Patrick Low Jr. was born. "Frankie," as she affectionately called him, was her fourth child, but the first three—two daughters and a son—lived with one of her previous husbands. Four years later, in 1932, Elizabeth married a man named Frank Duncan and changed young Frankie's last name. That same year, she gave birth to a daughter, Patricia "Patsy" Ann Duncan.

After several more failed marriages, and the sudden death of her fifteen-year-old daughter Patsy from a cerebral hemorrhage, Elizabeth moved to Santa Barbara in 1954 with the then twenty-six-year-old Frank, who had set up his own criminal law practice in the seaside city. "Pity the girl who marries Frank Duncan," said those who knew the young attorney. It was well known in Santa Barbara legal circles that Frank was an arrogant mama's boy who was not well liked among his peers. He suffered from a speech impediment, prompting colleagues to mock him behind his back, calling him a "wicked wascal wabbit."

But Elizabeth Duncan was very proud of her son. She had worked hard, doing whatever it took to support him through college and law school, and he had achieved the success and respectability she never could. Frankie was her world. But a few years after moving to Santa Barbara, Frank decided it was time to strike out on his own and move out of his mother's house. After all, he was a single, successful lawyer and he needed to live his own life. Elizabeth was devastated by Frank's declaration of independence. How could he leave her? She begged him to stay, but when that didn't work, on November 6, 1957, she overdosed on sleeping pills and was rushed to the hospital. It was the night before Frank's twenty-ninth birthday. The dutiful son stayed by his mother's side while she recovered from her attempted suicide, and he promised to continue living with her. But soon another woman caught the young bachelor's eye. During her stay in hospital, Elizabeth Duncan was attended by an attractive, auburn-haired nurse named Olga Kupczyk. Frank got to know the young Canadian nurse and was soon smitten.

Frank and Olga began dating, and Elizabeth took it badly. She called Olga every day, telling her to leave her Frankie alone. At one point, desperate to know where Frank was, Elizabeth snuck into Olga's apartment while Olga was at work. She wanted to see if any of Frank's clothes were there. On her way out of the building, it was later reported, she told the landlady: "She is not going to have him. I will kill her, if it is the last thing I do." But Elizabeth couldn't stop the blossoming romance between Frank and Olga and was furious when she found out that they had secretly married on June 20, 1958. She declared that she would never allow the couple to live together, but Olga was already pregnant. Elizabeth bombarded the newlyweds with threatening phone calls at all hours of the night and would show up unannounced at their door. She demanded that Olga get an abortion and insisted that Frank return to live with her. Three weeks after his wedding, Frank relented and moved back to his mother's house, but he would sneak away to visit Olga at her apartment a few nights a week. Elizabeth remained obsessed with losing Frank to his new wife, so she came up with another plan to destroy their marriage.

In August 1958, two months after Frank and Olga were married, Elizabeth talked an ex-con named Ralph Winterstein into impersonating Frank in a fraudulent scheme to get her son's marriage annulled. Elizabeth and Ralph, masquerading as Olga and Frank, presented themselves at the Ventura Superior Court. They said they did not live together as husband and wife, had not consummated the marriage and had no intention of doing so. The unhappy couple were granted an annulment. Elizabeth then began telling people around town that Frank and Olga weren't legally married. She returned to Olga's apartment and told the landlady that her son and Olga were living in sin—something frowned upon in respectable society in 1958. But when the landlady challenged her, Elizabeth snapped: "All you have to do is check with Ventura County. The marriage has been annulled." Three months later, when Olga disappeared, the landlady told the police about her strange encounters with Mrs. Duncan. She also told local reporters that Olga was deathly afraid of her mother-in-law.

Hearing that Elizabeth Duncan was telling people her son's marriage had been annulled, the police soon discovered that the annulment was a fraud perpetrated by Elizabeth and a mystery man. She was promptly arrested on charges of bribing a witness to influence testimony, falsifying a legal paper, and forgery with intent to defraud. A week later, she appeared in court, represented by her dutiful son Frank. In fact, the two walked into the court-room together hand in hand. Frank argued to have his mother's bail reduced from $50,000 to $5,000. Although he succeeded, neither of them could come up with the cash, so Elizabeth was stuck in the county jail while the police continued to investigate the disappearance of her pregnant daughter-in-law.

Since her arrest, the police had discovered many other inter-esting facts about the elder Mrs. Duncan. The fifty-four-year-old woman had been married at least a dozen times, sometimes moving on to the next husband before divorcing the last one. The petite grey-haired lady had a colourful past, including a criminal record. In 1953, undercover police in San Francisco had arrested a Betty Duncan Cogbill who was working as a madam in an illegal brothel and spent six months in prison. But regardless of any of her previ-ous transgressions, Frank Duncan was standing by his mother. After his mother's court appearance, Frank told reporters that he had no insight into why she had taken the drastic measure of faking an annulment of his marriage, but he was certain she had nothing to do with his wife's disappearance. "I know her, and she would not lie to me," said Frank. He then boldly declared that the Santa Barbara and Ventura County authorities needed to "put up or shut up" with their insinuations that his mother had anything to do with the mysterious disappearance of his wife. If they couldn't prove anything, they needed to release her. He wanted to take her home.

But while Elizabeth Duncan remained in jail on fraud charges, the police soon announced two other arrests in connection with the disappearance of Olga Duncan. Augustine (Gus) Baldonado and Luis Estrada Moya were two small-time criminals with extensive arrest records on theft and drug charges. During their investigation into Olga's disappearance, the police had uncovered an unusual link between the two men and Elizabeth Duncan. A Santa Barbara cafe owner had come forward to say she had introduced the two men to Elizabeth just days before Olga's disappearance. And the police had also found the car they believed had been used in the presumed abduction of the young nurse. The car belonged to a girl-friend of Baldonado's who told police he had rented it from her on the night of November 16. But when he returned it the following day, she discovered that the back seat covers had been removed.

On December 19, 1958, one month after the disappearance of her pregnant daughter-in-law, Elizabeth Duncan was formally charged with conspiracy to kidnap and murder Olga Duncan. Luis Moya and Gus Baldonado were also charged. Bail was set at $100,000 each (approximately $1 million today). Two days later, on December 21, the police made a public appeal to help them find Olga's body. The FBI and the Santa Barbara Coast Guard had joined in the search, but the appeal turned out to be unneces-sary when Baldonado finally confessed to murdering Olga and said he would take the police to where he and Moya had buried her. Later the same day, the battered remains of Olga Duncan were recovered from a shallow grave on Casitas Pass Road in Carpinte-ria, a small seaside town southeast of Santa Barbara. Her pregnant body was clothed in a nightgown and bathrobe, and she was still wearing the gold wedding band Frank had given her. After Olga's body was recovered, Luis Moya eventually confessed to his part in the slaying. Elizabeth Duncan, however, was adamant that she had nothing to do with her daughter-in-law's murder and said that Baldonado and Moya had tried to blackmail her.

In late December of 1958, while most people in Santa Barbara were finishing their last-minute Christmas shopping, a grand jury con-vened to determine whether there was enough evidence to move forward with murder indictments against Elizabeth Duncan and her two co-accused. The police had done their homework on Mrs. Duncan, and according to their investigation, she had approached at least four other people with diabolical plans to kill Olga. The first person to testify in front of the grand jury was Emma Short, a good friend and neighbour of Elizabeth's. The eighty-four-year-old woman stated that she had first heard about Olga when Elizabeth was confined to the hospital after taking an overdose of sleeping pills. According to Mrs. Short, Elizabeth was aware of the budding romance between the pretty nurse and her son, but Frank had vowed he would never marry Olga. After Elizabeth discovered that Frank had broken his promise, she told Mrs. Short she would make sure that Frank never lived with his new wife. "I will kill her first, destroy her," said Elizabeth to her friend. Then, according to the frail octogenarian, Elizabeth asked her to lure Olga to her apartment, where Elizabeth would be hiding in a closet. Once Olga was sitting down, Elizabeth would strangle her from behind and throw acid in her eyes. Then Elizabeth said she would pull Olga's hair out and hang her in the closet overnight. The next day, she would put a stone around Olga's neck and throw her into the ocean. In response to her friend's disturbing request, Mrs. Short told Elizabeth that her plan just wasn't possible. "I told her I didn't want a dead body in my apartment overnight," said the elderly lady. "I thought she had gone crazy."

When asked to describe the relationship between Elizabeth Duncan and her son, Emma Short said that Frank often called his mother "doll" and she had heard him say many times "I'll never leave you." And while no one had mentioned the possibility of an incestuous relationship directly, Short was asked about the sleeping arrangements in the apartment shared by Frank and his mother before and after his marriage. She told the grand jury she had seen Frank lying on his mother's bed on different occasions. "Liar," yelled Elizabeth Duncan, jumping from her seat. Her friend's comments had clearly touched a raw nerve. When asked if she had ever mentioned any of her disturbing conversations with Elizabeth to Frank, Emma Short said she did not like Frank Duncan and therefore had never approached him about his mother's plan to kill his wife.

The second person to testify in front of the grand jury was a woman named Diane Romero, who originally met Elizabeth when Frank was defending her husband, Rudolph Romero, on a drug possession charge. Diane said that Elizabeth Duncan talked incessantly about her hatred for her new daughter-in-law and how much she wanted to get rid of her. Finally, one day Elizabeth asked Diane to buy her some lye, which she said she planned to use on Olga. She said she was going to put Olga in the bathtub and pour lye all over her so that no one would recognize her. Diane said she refused to buy the lye. But then, she said, Elizabeth approached Rudolph to get rid of Olga. She offered him $1,500, and when he said he wasn't interested, she kept raising the price. Rudolph Romero later corroborated his wife's testimony.

The next witness was Mrs. Barbara Reed, a twenty-six-year-old waitress at the Blue Onion restaurant in Santa Barbara. She had known Elizabeth for ten years, as she had been a friend of Elizabeth's daughter, Patsy, who had died when she was fifteen. Reed testified that, in August 1958, Elizabeth told her that Olga had become pregnant by another man. She insisted it couldn't be Frank's because he had had mumps as a kid and was—according to his mother—impotent. She asked if Barbara would help get Olga out of the way because she was interfering with Frank's future. She wanted Barbara to go to Olga's apartment and throw acid in her face. Elizabeth said she would hide behind her, and as soon as Olga had a face full of acid, she would throw a blanket over her, drag her out to the car, drive her up to the mountains and push her over a cliff. Mrs. Reed was offered $1,500 for her troubles. She told the grand jury she was terrified by what

Elizabeth was suggesting and realized it wasn't just the ramblings of a crazy mother-in-law. Elizabeth was serious about her desire to get rid of Olga. Barbara said she was afraid of what would happen if she said no, so she told Elizabeth that she would think about the offer. But the following day, she phoned Frank Duncan and asked him to meet her at the restaurant. Barbara told Frank that his mother wanted Olga dead. She suggested that Frank take the threat seriously and get his pregnant wife out of town right away. She needed to be protected. Frank reluctantly agreed with her and said he would do what he could.

The final witness to appear before the grand jury was Frank Duncan himself. He testified that he had a loving relationship with his mother and that she had always been kind and thoughtful towards him and others. He explained that his mother relied on him and didn't want him to get married, so when she found out that he had wed Olga, she went crazy and threatened to kill herself. When asked if his mother tried to break up his marriage, he replied, "Let's just say she hindered its development."

Frank went on to describe his living arrangements following his marriage. He said that he lived part of the time with his mother and part of the time with Olga. When asked why he didn't stay with Olga continuously, he said that he and his wife had decided he would stay with his mother until shortly before the baby arrived. They were both hopeful that a grandchild would soften Elizabeth's hateful attitude towards their marriage. But then Olga had disappeared. Reiterating what he told the police at the time of her disappearance, Frank said that the last time he saw his wife was on November 7, the morning of his thirtieth birthday and ten days before she went missing. He recalled that the last thing she said to him was "Frank, when are you coming back?"

The testimony given during the grand jury hearing lasted seven hours, but the jury only took fifteen minutes to announce their decision. Elizabeth Ann Duncan and her co-conspirators, Luis

Moya and Gus Baldonado, were formally indicted on charges of kidnapping and first-degree murder in the slaying of Olga Duncan. Knowing they faced the death penalty if convicted, all three defendants immediately entered pleas of not guilty by reason of insanity. Later the same day, thirty-year-old Olga and her unborn child (a daughter) were cremated at the Ivy Lawn Cemetery in Ventura. A small, sombre ceremony was attended by her grief-stricken parents and some of her nursing colleagues. Frank was not in attendance; he spent the day at his mother's side. But as her next of kin, he had the authority to decide where Olga would be buried. Her ashes went unclaimed for months until they were eventually shipped back to her family in Manitoba.

On February 24, 1959, the trial of Elizabeth Ann Duncan began in Ventura. It was one of the most sensational cold-blooded murder cases the seaside town had ever experienced. The heinous crime captured national attention and was dubbed the "The Ma Duncan Case." Each day of the trial, spectators lined up before dawn, hoping to nab a spot inside the ninety-nine-seat courtroom, and places in line were sold for $5 a pop. Hamburgers and hot dogs were sold for fifty cents apiece to those in line who were craving a snack before they sat through the gruesome murder trial. The local press had been running front-page stories about the twisted murder-for-hire plot, and public sentiment towards Ma Duncan and her co-accused was not favourable. Jeers of "mama's boy" and "Frankie" greeted Frank Duncan as he made his way through the crowds every morning. Inside the courtroom, Elizabeth Duncan sat stoically, clutching rosary beads in her hand, even though she wasn't Roman Catholic. Seated beside her was her lawyer, Ward Sullivan, a well-respected criminal defence attorney from Los Angeles who liked to boast that none of his clients had ever ended up in the gas chamber.

One of the most difficult tasks at the start of the trial was to find jurors from within the county who could be fair and impartial. During interviews, many prospective jurors revealed that they had already made up their minds and felt that the defendant was guilty, and they wanted to see her put to death. It took five days to select a jury of eight women and four men.

As the trial got under way, District Attorney Roy Gustafson of Ventura County laid out a diabolical murder scheme, saying that Mrs. Duncan was intensely jealous of her pretty daughter-in-law and wanted her out of the way. She tried threats against Olga and even went as far as to have Olga and Frank's marriage fraudulently annulled, but when that didn't work, she decided that the new Mrs. Duncan had to die. The district attorney described Frank Duncan as a weak man dominated by a controlling and meddlesome mother he couldn't say no to. And because he hadn't taken the threats against his pregnant wife seriously, Olga was left alone and vulnerable.

Over the next four weeks, the jury heard from a parade of witnesses who testified that Elizabeth Duncan had approached them about killing her daughter-in-law. They all refused her request, but sadly, none of them had informed the police. Mrs. Duncan eventually stumbled on two petty thieves who were willing to do anything for money: twenty-one-year-old Luis Moya and twenty-six-year-old Gus Baldonado.

When Moya took the stand, he described meeting Elizabeth Duncan through a mutual friend, Mrs. Esperanza Esquivel, the owner the Tropical Cafe in Santa Barbara. At their first meeting, Elizabeth outlined her desire to get rid of her daughter-in-law. According to Moya, she told him she had acid, rope and sleeping pills for the job. The pills were to knock Olga out, the rope to tie her up and the acid to disfigure her face and fingerprints so police would not be able to identify her body. "I want you to kill the bitch," the middle-aged woman told the men. "I want you to throw acid in her face and burn her eyes out of her head! I want that woman cold in her grave!" According to Moya, Elizabeth even offered to tag along on the job if they needed her. Elizabeth agreed to pay them $3,000 once the deed was done, and then another $3,000 within three to six months. The plan Moya and Baldonado eventually came up with was to kidnap Olga and take some of her clothing to make it appear as though she had gone on vacation. Then they were going to kill her and dispose of her body near Tijuana, Mexico. Elizabeth Duncan pawned one of her many wedding rings to give Moya $175 for travel expenses.

On the evening of November 17, 1958, Moya and Baldonado rented a four-door 1948 Chevrolet from Baldonado's girlfriend for $25. They drove to Olga's apartment on Garden Street, and Moya rang the bell while Baldonado waited in the back seat of the car. When Olga came to the door, Moya told her he had met Frank in a bar where the two had enjoyed one too many drinks. Now Frank was drunk and passed out in his car. Could she help him bring him up to the apartment? Olga accompanied Moya out to the car wearing her pyjamas and bathrobe. Seeing a figure lying in the back seat, the pregnant woman reached into the car. At that moment, Moya bashed her over the head with a gun and Baldonado dragged her into the back seat. They quickly drove away from the apartment with Olga screaming in the back seat. They had a long drive ahead of them, but soon realized that the old Chevy wasn't up to a trip to Tijuana. Moya said he then drove south towards Ventura City. Olga was still yelling and struggling with Baldonado in the back seat, so he pulled over. "I stopped the car," Moya told the hushed courtroom. "Then I reached back and gave her a heavy blow on the head, which knocked her out. Baldonado then taped her mouth and hands." They drove for a little while longer before stopping on a dark and deserted road. The two men then dragged Olga out of the car and down a small embankment. They couldn't shoot her because the gun had broken when Moya hit her over the head, so they took turns strangling her and hitting her with a rock until Baldonado, who had been an army medic, decided she was dead. The hired hit men had neglected to bring shovels, so they dug a crude, shallow grave in the soft silt near a drainage ditch with their bare hands. Then they buried Olga and her unborn baby. "It was a pretty good place to bury her," said Moya matter-of-factly. "We didn't think she would be found." An autopsy later revealed dirt in Olga's lungs, indicating that she had not been dead when she was buried. The blows to the head had not killed her, and neither had the attempted strangulation. According to coroner Virgil Payton, Olga was unconscious but alive when Moya and Baldonado covered her in dirt. She had suffocated to death.

After they buried Olga, Moya said they returned to Santa Barbara. They removed the bloodied upholstery in the back seat of the car and burned their clothing. Then they went to see Mrs. Duncan to collect their payment, but she informed them that she couldn't get all the money. She owed them $6,000 but only gave them $360. Asked if he had anything else to say, Luis Moya told the court that he did not know Olga Duncan was pregnant when they kidnapped her. Mrs. Duncan had neglected to tell them that when she hired them. The father of three young children said if he had known, he would not have gone through with it.

On March 5, after forty-four prosecution witnesses had testified, Elizabeth Duncan finally took the stand in her own defence. The diminutive middle-aged woman with her grey hair tucked neatly into a bun and piercing blue eyes hidden behind her horn-rimmed glasses looked like a sweet grandmother, not a cold-blooded murderer.

On the stand, Elizabeth readily admitted that she did not want Frank living with Olga, but said that the only kidnapping plot she ever came up with was to kidnap her son Frank. She felt that if she got him away from Olga, he would snap to his senses. She also admitted to buying a gun, but said she planned to use it on herself.

"I just didn't want to lose Frankie," she said while dabbing at her tear-filled eyes. Although she was afraid her favourite son would leave her, she denied ever threatening Olga or having anything to do with her murder. She told the court that her co-accused were blackmailing her, saying they would kill her and Frank if she didn't pay them. According to her, the two Mexicans had a grudge against Frank because he had put one of their friends in jail. "I was scared to death of those men," she testified. But, while she portrayed herself as a weak woman afraid of two unsavoury characters, the prosecutor reminded Mrs. Duncan that she, too, had a rather unusual past—solicitation for prostitution, keeping a brothel, adultery, extortion, defrauding multiple landlords, forgery, grand theft, issuing bad cheques and bigamy, just to name a few of the charges on her lengthy rap sheet.

Unfazed, Elizabeth didn't seem too concerned about any of her prior run-ins with the law. She admitted to being married at least a dozen times and failing to get an annulment or divorce several times before remarrying. She acknowledged a few of her husbands but said she couldn't recall all of them. "I don't know why I married them," she laughed. "Because after I got them, I didn't want them." This included one of her son's law school classmates, whom she had married when she was fifty and he was twenty-seven. The district attorney also revealed that Elizabeth had three other children besides Frank. When asked if she loved Frank more than her other children, she replied, "Yes." When asked if she and Frank had ever slept together in the same bed, Mrs. Duncan angrily denied it, saying her relationship with Frank was one of a mother's pure love and devotion.

The final witness to take the stand during the sensational murder trial was the thirty-one-year-old object of Elizabeth's obsession, her darling son Frankie. Frank Duncan described meeting Olga Kupczyk when she was caring for his mother at St. Francis Hospital. They began dating, and six months later they married when they found out Olga was pregnant. Frank told the court that his mother was very upset when he returned to her home the morning after his wedding. "She was crying in uncontrollable hysteria," said Duncan. A few days later, she purchased a gun and told Frank she was going to use it on herself if he didn't return home to her. Frank said he succumbed to his mother's threats once again and left his pregnant wife. He then described how he went back and forth like a yo-yo between his wife and his mother, trying to appease both women in his life. "Mother was always proud of me," Duncan said. "I was the apple of her eye and she did not want to lose me." He admitted that the two women in his life did not get along, but he did not believe his mother would have arranged to have Olga killed. "I can never recall mother doing anything cruel," said Frank. "She couldn't even hurt an animal." When questioned about his current circumstances, Frank told the court he had moved to Los Angeles just ten days after Olga went missing, and now, four months later, he had already remarried.

Frank Duncan's emotionless testimony ended the four-week trial in which the many prosecution witnesses had painted a damning portrait of his mother—a woman so consumed with intense hatred for her daughter-in-law and extreme love for her son that she resorted to murder to keep them apart. In his closing statements, District Attorney Lloyd Gustafson had harsh words for Frank Duncan. "What is he, a man or a mouse?" the lawyer asked the jury. "He is a spineless jellyfish," he added. Gustafson accused the young lawyer of knowing that his mother had orchestrated the murder of his pregnant wife. Did Frank ever really care about Olga? "No," said the prosecutor. In fact, the police discovered that, just days after his pregnant wife went missing, he had been on a date with another woman in San Francisco. "Son of a bitch," yelled Elizabeth Duncan from her seat. Forever protective of her "Frankie," she wasn't going to let the lawyer disparage her son. It was the perfect ending to a dramatic trial that Gustafson said proved beyond any reasonable doubt that Elizabeth Duncan was responsible for the brutal death of her pregnant daughter-in-law. Pointing directly at the defendant, the district attorney asked the jury, "Have you ever seen anybody who showed less remorse or less regret over the death of someone, with all her preening, smiling, laughing and giggling? Does she show any concern for the victim? No, because she's glad Olga is gone." Gustafson then distributed disturbing and graphic pictures of Olga Duncan that showed the state of her badly beaten body lying in a shallow grave. Two of the female jurors gasped in horror. "This is the consequence of this beautiful woman crossing paths with Elizabeth Duncan," he said. "She is a mean and wicked woman."

In his final words to the jury, Gustafson said, "One of the pities of this case is that the girl who was so brutally murdered on the night of November 17 might have been any girl . . . anybody's sister, anybody's daughter. Any girl could have been Elizabeth Duncan's victim if she happened to marry her son Frank." Then, looking straight at the jury, the prosecutor added, "Please, for the sake of California, return a verdict of guilty."


On March 16, 1959, after less than five hours of deliberation, Elizabeth Duncan was found guilty of first-degree murder in the death of Olga Kupczyk Duncan. With her son Frank standing by her side, she showed no emotion when the verdict was read. "Don't worry too much," she said to Frank before being escorted out of the courtroom in handcuffs. Speaking to reporters, she claimed to have gotten a rotten deal by a biased jury. Defence lawyer Ward Sullivan called the verdict "the clearest case of a miscarriage of justice I have ever tried in more than thirty years as a lawyer." Frank Duncan was quick to tell the press that they would be launching an immediate appeal and that he was certain his mother would be vindicated.

One week later, Elizabeth Duncan was back in court for sentencing, Frank again standing loyally by her side. District Attorney Gustafson demanded the gas chamber for the convicted woman. A life sentence wasn't good enough, according to the prosecutor, because under California law she could eventually be paroled. "I would be afraid for my own safety if she ever got out of prison," he told the court. "Maybe she would pay someone $175 to end my life," he added.

Sullivan said his client did not deserve to die for her crime because she was mentally ill. If she was sentenced to life in prison, she would likely never get out, and if she was ever paroled, she would be an old woman.

In reviewing her insanity plea, the judge referred to reports from two court-appointed psychiatrists who stated that Mrs. Duncan was a maladjusted, impulsive, egocentric psychopath. "She has been a severe problem to herself and society for many years," noted Dr. Philip May, "but she is sane." Dr. Louis R. Nash, assistant director of Camarillo State Hospital, described Elizabeth Duncan as a "psychopathic personality" and a "pathological liar," but said she was mentally capable of knowing right from wrong.

One of Elizabeth's many former husbands also appeared at the sentencing hearing. George Satriano told the court that Elizabeth Duncan had bilked him out of money and a brand new car, but then he discovered that his bride of only a few months had tried to hire someone to throw acid into his face. He told the court he feared for his life and left the state.

For the first and only time in his long legal career, eighty-three-year-old Superior Court judge Charles F. Blackstock sentenced a convicted murderer to death. Elizabeth Duncan would be the fourth woman to die in California's gas chamber. The condemned woman showed little emotion upon hearing her fate and later remarked, "I'm not the least bit afraid," as she was led away to a waiting police car in handcuffs.

Luis Moya and Augustine Baldonado were also convicted of first-degree murder and found to be sane. Although they had testified against Elizabeth Duncan, they had not been offered any kind of plea deal in exchange for their testimony. Judge Blackstock also sentenced Moya and Baldonado to death.

After his mother was sentenced to death, Frank Duncan continued to support her and worked full-time on appealing her sentence. "I don't think my mother ever intended that my wife should be murdered," he said. "It was just unfortunate that she got mixed up with such mentally deficient people." After an appeal and two stays of execution, Governor Edmund G. "Pat" Brown refused clemency and the California State Supreme Court ordered her execution to go ahead.

Just before ten o'clock on the morning of August 8, 1962, fifty-eight-year-old Elizabeth Ann Duncan was escorted into the apple-green gas chamber at San Quentin State Prison. Scanning the faces of the fifty-seven witnesses present, the gaunt, ashen-faced woman was only looking for one person as she was strapped into the steel chair. Elizabeth Duncan's last recorded words were "I am innocent. Where's Frank?" Frank Duncan was not present at his mother's execution, having failed in his last-minute attempt to save her life. According to press reports at the time, he never claimed her body. It was later rumoured that he was working with a Hollywood producer on a movie about his mother's most unusual life.

On the same day, Moya and Baldonado, who were paid $360 to kill Olga Duncan and her unborn child, were executed together. "Be sure and close the door when you leave," Baldonado laughingly told guards as he was strapped into one of the two chairs in the octagonal death chamber.

Frank Duncan continued to practise law in Los Angeles and always maintained that his mother was not guilty of arranging to have his pregnant wife murdered. Elizabeth Duncan was the last woman to be executed in the state of California.

# ENEMY WITHIN

## THE MURDER OF GLEN DAVIS

Glen Davis was not your typical multi-millionaire. He rode the Toronto subway, spent months hiking and paddling through the Canadian wilderness, and was rarely seen without his trademark Tilley hat. He grew up surrounded by wealth, and then spent most of his life giving it away. He donated millions to hospitals, amateur sports organizations and environmental causes with no strings attached. He was a private man who shunned the spotlight and never sought fame or recognition for his generosity.

So, when he was viciously attacked by a baseball bat–wielding assailant in the parking lot of his Toronto office one night in 2005, he put it down to a random assault. But the police weren't so sure. Had the mild-mannered businessman and philanthropist made any enemies during his career? Did someone want to hurt him? Or, had their intentions been even more sinister? Glen refused to hire a personal bodyguard, as his family had suggested, and went about his daily life. He wasn't going to let the injuries he sustained in the attack slow him down. He was a man who embraced life and made it his personal mission to give back.

But sadly, not everyone believed in Glen's unique style of philanthropy and generosity. Glen Davis did have an enemy, someone who wanted a share of the family fortune for himself, and he was willing to do anything to get it. Even if it meant murder.

Glen White Davis was adopted as a baby by Toronto business tycoon Nelson Morgan Davis and his wife, Eloise, in 1941. The couple also adopted a baby girl named Elaine Morgan Davis. Nelson Davis was a self-made millionaire originally from Cleveland, Ohio, who had moved to Toronto in 1929. He made his fortune buying companies that were undervalued during the Depression, and by 1951 he was living in the twenty-nine-room Graydon Hall Manor, one of the city's largest estates, with a ten-car garage, nine-hole golf course, indoor swimming pool and horse stables.

As children, Glen and his sister were tended to by a legion of servants and were driven to school in a Rolls-Royce. They spent winters in Arizona and summers on a family-owned island in Muskoka.

Nelson Davis had convinced his younger brother Marshall to move from the United States to Toronto to work for him, and together they continued to acquire more companies and more wealth. Marshall Davis and his wife, Ruth, had two daughters, Marsha and Mary. Growing up, the girls would often spend time with their cousins Glen and Elaine at Graydon Hall Manor and on their island in Muskoka.

Davis was said to be a man who enjoyed spending money as much as making it. "Every time I make a dollar," he explained, "I spend a quarter of it on myself. There's nothing wrong with that." In 1964, he sold his ninety-six-acre estate and moved his family into a mansion overlooking the Rosedale Golf Club. The custom-built home reportedly featured a driveway made of dust-free meteorite rock, to prevent guests from tracking dirt into the house, and solid gold bathroom fittings. The location of the new house seemed perfect for Davis, who was a long-time member of the Rosedale Golf Club. But after a near miss with an errant golf ball, he decided to build his own eighteen-hole course on a 350-acre parcel of land north of Toronto. He called the course Box Grove and was the club's only member for many years. Much to his dismay, Glen never took to the sport. The course was later sold to housing developers and reduced to a nine-hole course called Markham Green.

In the early 1960s, Glen attended the University of Western Ontario, in London, where he studied political science. He was also a promising member of the school's swim team. A shy, unassuming young man, he was well liked, and he never bragged of his family's wealth. While at university, Glen met a young woman from Leamington, Ontario, named Mary Alice Setterington. Mary was the first woman Glen ever invited home to his parents' Toronto mansion. After graduating with a master's degree in political science, Glen married Mary Alice in a small civil ceremony in his parents' living room.

In 1965, the couple moved to Winnipeg, where Glen taught political economics at the University of Manitoba and coached hockey. A few years later, they returned to Toronto and Glen went to work for his father at N.M. Davis Corporation, a conglomerate of more than fifty transportation and manufacturing companies. While Glen worked at the family business, Mary Alice looked after their home and volunteered at the Canadian National Institute for the Blind.

Nelson and Marshall were close and had amassed a sizable fortune by the late 1960s. Still, regardless of their wealth, what the two brothers valued most was family and privacy. But then something happened that threatened both. In September 1969, Marshall's daughter Mary Davis Nelles—Glen's first cousin—was kidnapped. The pretty twenty-one-year-old had just returned from her European honeymoon when three masked men burst into the newly-weds' rural home and attacked Mary and her husband, Cliff Nelles. Within minutes, Cliff was tied up and Mary was gone. The kidnappers left one thing behind: a ransom note demanding $850,000 in cash. After Nelson Davis negotiated with the kidnappers, a $200,000 ransom was paid and Mary was released unharmed after three terrifying days. But the frightening ordeal shook the whole family. Nelson and Marshall were notoriously private and had kept their professional and personal lives out of the spotlight. When it was discovered that Mary had been betrayed by someone close— her former fiancé, Gary Adams, and five of his friends, including a Toronto police officer—the Davises were devastated. The family's millions had provided them with a luxurious lifestyle, but it had also brought greed and violence to their doorstep.

After the kidnapping, the clan became even more reclusive. They remained a close-knit family, wary of strangers and the press. But in 1979, tragedy struck again when the family's patriarch, seventy-two-year-old Nelson Davis, suffered a heart attack and drowned in his pool in Arizona. He left the bulk of his estate to his wife, Eloise, and when she died in 2001, Glen received three-quarters of the estate, estimated to be worth up to $100 million, while his sister was given one-quarter.

After his father's death, Glen took control of the family's trucking and transportation business. And, like his father, Glen avoided the media. He was painfully shy, and wealth did not dictate who he was. He preferred practical clothing and Tilley hats to expensive suits. He drove a GMC SUV and sported a Timex watch, not a Rolex. His favourite restaurant was Swiss Chalet, which he referred to as "The Club," and he could often be found at a Toronto Maple Leafs hockey game, enjoying a hot dog or two. Glen just didn't fit in with Canada's old-money establishment, and friends like Conrad Black were amused by his casual appearance and quiet nature.

Glen's wife, Mary Alice, was equally down to earth, and with no children of their own, Glen and Mary Alice spent time with the Davises' extended family, including Glen's cousin Mary, her husband, Cliff, and their two children. They would also spend holidays with Mary's older sister, Marsha. Marsha and her husband, Murray Ross, had two children, including a son named Marshall who had been named after his grandfather. Glen and Mary Alice were Marshall's godparents and they doted on him. Glen would often take the young Marshall on camping and hiking trips. Glen always preferred being outdoors, exploring the wilderness, over sitting in a stuffy boardroom. And while he didn't wear expensive suits or indulge in martini lunches with Bay Street's finest, he was a strong businessman like his father and the company continued to flourish under his direction. But, four years after his father's untimely death, something happened to Glen Davis that would change the trajectory of his entire life.

On June 2, 1983, Glen was returning from a business trip to Dallas when a fire broke out in one of the rear bathrooms of Air Canada Flight 797. The plane was forced to make an emergency landing at the Cincinnati, Ohio, airport and exploded on the runway ninety seconds after touching down. Glen was one of eighteen people who survived the explosion, while twenty-three other passengers died, including Canadian folk music legend Stan Rogers. The tragedy changed aviation rules forever, forcing the introduction of track lighting on the cabin floor and smoke detectors in the washrooms.

The near-death experience also changed Glen Davis. Not long after, he went from managing the vast fortune left to him by his father to donating a great deal of it to charity. He soon became the country's most generous wilderness philanthropist, giving substantial amounts to the World Wildlife Fund and the Sierra Club. Glen began spending even more time exploring the outdoors than sitting in his office. And his teenage godson, Marshall Ross, often came with him. Glen Davis and Marshall Ross were first cousins once removed, but their close relationship made them seem more like uncle and nephew. The two were inseparable and enjoyed various outdoor treks, such as camping in the Grand Canyon or skiing the Rocky Mountains.

After graduating from Lawrence Park Collegiate Institute in Toronto, Marshall attended Bishop's University in Quebec before enrolling in a master's program in business at the University of Victoria in 1994. University records show he did not receive a degree, though he would later claim he had.

In 2003, at age thirty-three, Marshall got married, and the following year, Glen Davis lent him $2.5 million to start Rosshire Enterprises, a development and luxury home renovation business. The loan came with a generous payback schedule and a rent-free office at N.M. Davis Corporation's head office near Bayview Avenue and York Mills Road in Toronto. Glen was very generous, but he believed in financial accountability and good management: if you take a loan, you pay it back. He had no intention of interfering with Marshall's company and assumed the loan would be eventually repaid in good faith.

While Glen was happy to help his godson, he was also donating millions of dollars to numerous environmental causes. Members of the Davis clan, however, were not necessarily impressed with Glen's philanthropy. The other side of the Davis family—Marshall Davis, his daughters, Mary and Marsha, and their children had all been cut out of the company after Nelson Davis died and Glen inherited almost everything. Stock options in N.M. Davis Corporation kept them comfortable, but most of their wealth was gone. There was even an unspoken resentment over the fact that Glen was adopted, yet he had inherited the family fortune. And now he was giving it away to conservation and wildlife charities. But Glen was not a man to get embroiled in family drama; he continued pursuing his passions. He was happiest when he was trekking through the wilderness or studying the natural habitats of native mammals. One of his favourite trips was to remote northern locations to watch the migration of caribou. "I don't think he was ever as happy as when he could look as far as the eye could see and see no trace of other people whatsoever," said former Green Party leader Elizabeth May, who counted Davis among her best friends. But while the eccentric multi-millionaire pursued his passions, another near-death experience would curtail his adventures.

On a dark winter evening in December 2005, as he was leaving his York Mills office, Glen was suddenly struck from behind and fell to the pavement in the parking lot. A masked man stood over him and hit him repeatedly with a baseball bat. Glen yelled out as he tried to fend off the blows. An employee in the office heard a loud commotion and ran outside to intervene. The attacker took off as Glen lay bleeding on the snow-covered pavement. The vicious assault left Glen in excruciating pain. He received numerous stitches and staples from the blows that had been inflicted, and his left arm was shattered. He eventually had to have a metal plate inserted into his elbow.

Was it a random attack, a robbery? Glen thought so. The police investigated, but no leads or suspects emerged. And while friends suggested that Glen needed to take the assault seriously, he refused to hire security. As soon as he recovered from his injuries, he eagerly resumed his philanthropic work and travel adventures. Mary Alice, while concerned about her husband's safety, continued to support his many endeavours. She admired and shared his guiding philosophy: "To whom much is given, much is expected."

On the afternoon of May 18, 2007, seventeen months after the baseball bat attack, Glen drove to the head office of the World Wildlife Federation at Eglinton Avenue East and Mount Pleasant

Road in Toronto. It was Friday of the Victoria Day weekend, the unofficial start to the Canadian summer. Glen, as usual, had a busy schedule ahead, with various trips and adventures planned, but on that particular afternoon he was meeting the director of the wildlife charity for lunch at the Granite Brewery to discuss the work of the organization and his continued support of their efforts. The restaurant was a regular haunt for Glen, who liked to stick with familiar fare. After lunch, around 1:45 p.m., Glen returned to the underground garage where he had parked his SUV. A security camera captured him as he opened the door to the parking garage stairwell. Moments later, two shots rang out. Glen Davis lay dead on the floor. He was sixty-six years old.

News of the shocking murder made front-page headlines across Canada. Davis, a relatively unknown multimillionaire philanthropist, had been gunned down in broad daylight in a busy area of the city. The police were calling it a brazen attack carried out with precision. They said they weren't ruling out robbery as a motive, since Davis's wallet was missing when they discovered his body. And they said they were not sure whether the attack on Glen two years earlier was connected to his murder.

Five days after the murder, the Toronto police released images of two male suspects caught on camera in the underground parking garage. Both men were white and in their mid-twenties. One was wearing dark sunglasses and a baseball cap and was carrying a backpack. Although the surveillance camera images were good quality, no one came forward to identify either suspect.

For the next year, a small team of homicide investigators interviewed dozens of friends, family members and business associates of Glen Davis. They pored over his bank records and phone records, looking for anything that stood out. They were digging for dirt, but Glen Davis simply had none. No blackmailers, secret lovers, gambling debts or offshore accounts. "So far, it appears the man had no enemies," said one of the detectives working on the case. But there were rumours. One Toronto newspaper columnist speculated on the "echo of a double life," adding that, historically, a baseball bat beating and murder do not happen to people without secrets.

A criminal profiler from Minnesota who was consulted on the case suggested Glen Davis had likely been killed by someone who knew him, and that the previous baseball bat attack two years earlier was probably linked to the same person. "That there would be two different people who went after him like that would be unusual," said Pat Brown. "I think he simply failed the first time and came back with a better weapon."

For police, the case was extremely frustrating. Dozens of people were interviewed, yet no one had a negative thing to say about the unassuming philanthropist. Eventually, the case went cold.

Then, on November 1, 2008, eighteen months after the murder, investigators got a lucky break. A small-time criminal, picked up on an unrelated charge and hoping to make a deal, told the cops he had a shocking story to tell them and it involved the assault and murder of Glen Davis.

Tyler Cawley, a roofer by trade who had been arrested in Toronto's east end, said he could tell them about the December 2005 baseball bat attack. He said that a tall Russian contractor named Dmitri had offered him and a friend $150,000 to kill Glen Davis. Cawley knew Dmitri because they had worked on some of the same home renovation contracts. Cawley admitted to agreeing to the murder for hire because he was in debt to drug dealers. He said he drove the getaway van to Glen's office, and an accomplice jumped out and attacked Davis with a baseball bat. But the attack was interrupted when an employee saw what was happening and ran towards Glen. Cawley and his accomplice took off. He said they ended up getting paid only a fraction of the agreed-upon price because Davis had survived. Cawley then told the detectives that he knew who had eventually killed Glen Davis. Dmitri had a friend named Eugene, who resembled one of the men in the surveillance video coming out of the underground parking garage at the time of the murder.

Homicide detectives working the case weren't sure if they should believe Cawley's story, but the petty thief did seem to know a lot of details about the very private millionaire, details that had been provided to him by Dmitri for the hit. On a ride around the city, Cawley showed the detectives where Glen Davis lived. He said that he and Dmitri had watched the middle-aged man walking a German shepherd down the driveway. "He was wearing a big, weird-looking hat," Cawley told the police. Cawley showed police where Glen parked his car when he went to hockey games, and pointed out his North York office, where Cawley and an accomplice had attacked him. But if a man named Dmitri had hired Cawley to kill Glen Davis, what was the Russian contractor's connection to the unassuming philanthropist? Cawley said he had been told that a business partner of Davis's was unhappy and wanted him killed, so he had hired Dmitri to find the men for the job. Cawley didn't know the name of the so-called business partner, but was sure he had worked on the man's house and knew where he lived. Cawley led the police to an address on Roselawn Avenue in Toronto's monied Forest Hill neighbourhood. The house was registered to Rosshire Enterprises. The man who owned that company was now their number one suspect in the murder of Glen Davis, and it turned out he had been right under their noses the whole time.

Three months later, in March 2009, after an intensive twenty-one-month investigation dubbed "Project Cincinnati" (a reference to Davis's near-fatal plane accident), Toronto police arrested Marshall Ross, Davis's thirty-seven-year-old godson. He and three other men were charged with first-degree murder. Ross's arrest was a stunning development in a case that had made headlines across the country. It was a high-profile murder mystery, and those who knew Glen Davis personally and professionally never believed he had any enemies . . . let alone one so close to him.

Police alleged that Ross hired two men—Dmitri Kossyrine and Jesse Smith—whom he knew through his home renovation business, as well as a third man, Ivgeny (Eugene) Vorobiov, who would act as their gun for hire. After the police received the critical lead from Cawley, they started to dig into Ross and his connection to Dmitri Kossyrine. Shortly after the investigation secretly began to focus on Ross, Glen's widow, Mary Alice Davis, approached investigators with her own concerns about her godson. He still owed Glen's company $2.7 million and had not made any attempt to repay the loan after Glen's murder. Yet he seemed to be enjoying an extravagant lifestyle. In the year following Glen's murder, Ross and his wife, Eva, had stayed close to Mary Alice to support her through her grieving. But Ross was also spending a lot of money. He rented a villa in Tuscany for his family and shipped back expensive bottles of rare wine that he stored in the wine cellar of his nicely appointed North Toronto home. According to Mary Alice, he also took frequent trips to Mexico and Cuba regarding development projects, but nothing ever seemed to pan out. Something just wasn't adding up, according to Glen's widow, but little did she know that the police already had their sights trained on Marshall Ross.

The detectives in charge of the murder investigation knew they needed to be careful. Ross couldn't know he was being watched. He had the means to flee the country, so they didn't want to spook him. They reinterviewed him about the case, but also spoke with other friends and relatives so that nothing looked unusually suspicious. Naturally, Ross had a solid alibi: he told police he had been at his cottage in Muskoka at the time of the murder. The police played along.

Then they held a press conference at which they offered a $50,000 reward for information regarding the murder of Glen

Davis, and they asked Ross to represent the family in front of the cameras. Of course, he was more than happy to help. But what he didn't know was that while he was helping the police with their investigation, every word he spoke was being recorded. Each time the investigators spoke with Ross, they wore bodypack recorders; they also wiretapped the cellphones and cars of Ross and his two Russian associates—Vorobiov and Dmitri Kossyrine. To get the three men talking, investigators began planting false information with Ross—telling him, for example, they had a suspect in custody whose DNA matched some evidence found at the scene of the 2005 baseball bat attack on Glen Davis. They also asked him for a list of workers from his renovation jobs—something he seemed reluctant to provide but discussed at length with his two accomplices. The police lies ultimately led to many nervous conversations between the three suspects, including one in which they implicated a fourth man, Smith, who was identified as one of the men caught on surveillance footage in the underground garage the day Glen was killed. The secret recordings finally gave investigators all they needed to make the arrests.

Upon learning of the arrest of her godson, Mary Alice Davis remarked "Those poor children," referring to Ross's two young kids. She and Glen had treated Marshall Ross like a son, and he had betrayed them. Now she could only think of his children.

On November 3, 2010, three and a half years after Glen Davis was shot to death in an underground parking garage, the first of the four accused murderers had his day in court. Jesse Smith pleaded guilty to the reduced offence of accessory after the fact for helping the man who shot Davis flee from the crime scene. Smith, a construction worker from Ajax, Ontario, said he first heard about Glen Davis when Dmitri Kossyrine told him that someone was willing to pay $100,000 to have him killed. A week before the murder, Smith met Eugene Vorobiov and Marshall Ross in a Home Depot parking lot, where they discussed the hit.

Ross told the two men that he wanted the murder to look like an accident, but if that wasn't possible, he still wanted it done as soon as possible.

According to Smith, Ross said he wanted to kill his godfather because he had been giving away the family money to charity. Smith also told the court that Ross was angry because he thought he should be the one controlling the family fortune, seeing as Glen Davis had been adopted. He was determined to get Davis out of the way, said Smith. "If you can't do it, get me a fucking gun and I'll do myself," an agitated Ross told Smith and Vorobiov.

Smith confessed to driving the getaway car after the murder. He said he and Vorobiov drove to Port Perry, about forty-five minutes northeast of Toronto, where Vorobiov threw the murder weapon into Lake Scugog. The next day, Smith said, he flew to Cuba. Then, six months after the murder, in November of 2007, Marshall Ross travelled to Cuba, where the two men met up. Smith testified that Ross assured him everyone was in the clear and that the hardest part of the entire situation was that Ross had had to give a eulogy at Davis's funeral.

Jesse Smith was arrested when he returned to Toronto from Cuba in 2009 and quickly agreed to plead guilty and testify against his three co-accused. He was sentenced to five years in prison for his part in the murder of Glen Davis.

After his arrest, Marshall Ross continued to protest his innocence. His family supported him and people began taking sides. Glen's widow, Mary Alice, suddenly found herself isolated from former friends and family members who had been by her side after Glen's murder. Then, in October 2011, only one week before his trial was to begin, Marshall Ross pleaded guilty to first-degree murder, a rare occurrence in a criminal trial, since a conviction would mean an automatic life sentence.

In front of a stunned courtroom filled with friends and associates of Glen Davis, Crown attorney Hank Goody read an eighty-six-page agreed statement of facts. The statement described in detail how Ross plotted the cold-blooded murder of his godfather, not once, but twice, using associates he had met in the renovation business. "Glen Davis trusted Marshall Ross implicitly," said the statement. In return for Davis's trust, Ross lied repeatedly to him. He cooked up falsified spreadsheets and invented addresses of buildings in which he pretended to be investing. It was also discovered that he had forged Glen's signature on a mortgage application to purchase his North Toronto house in 2004. Marshall Ross was in a deep financial hole and was in constant fear of being discovered, so he decided his only way out was to have Glen Davis killed. He assumed he would be in Glen's will and could eliminate his debt with his inheritance.

In 2005, Ross arranged the first attempt on Glen's life—the baseball bat attack outside his office. Petty thief Tyler Cawley admitted to the police that he had received $20,000 for that attack—a fraction of the agreed-upon price of $150,000, because Davis did not die.

After the assault, according to the agreed statement of facts, Ross continued to borrow heavily from Glen. Glen still believed the attack had been a random event and maintained his complete trust in Ross. When Ross's debts continued to grow with no hope of repayment, Ross renewed his plan to have Davis killed. He went back to the contractor Dmitri Kossyrine and asked him to recruit two more men—hired assassins who would finally get the job done.

On May 18, 2007, Glen Davis had just finished lunch at the Granite Brewery with a friend from the World Wildlife Fund, to which he was a generous donor. Just as he reached his vehicle in the underground garage, a man in a hood appeared from behind the parked car. He shot Glen in the back at close range. Glen fell to his knees. "Please don't kill me," he begged the stranger. The man fired again, right into Glen's heart. Then, as Glen Davis lay dying, the hooded man stole his wallet to make it look like a robbery and ran out of the Eglinton Avenue garage to his accomplice in a waiting getaway vehicle.

As Marshall Ross told police, he was at his cottage in Muskoka on the day of the killing. And just days later, he delivered a heartfelt eulogy at Glen Davis's funeral while wearing his godfather's trademark Tilley hat, and placed his uncle's ashes in the grave at Mount Pleasant Cemetery.

Now, four years after Glen's murder, Mary Alice Davis was in court to hear her godson's surprise guilty plea. Prosecutor Hank Goody read her victim impact statement, in which she described the anguish and despair she had felt since her husband's murder. What Marshall Ross had done was a disgusting betrayal, said the grieving widow.

Before sentencing, Ross did not personally address the court but had his lawyer, James Lockyer, read a statement. Lockyer, a Toronto defence lawyer best known for his work on cases exonerating the wrongfully accused, was able to convince Ross to plead guilty. In his signed statement, Ross admitted that he had been having financial difficulties and wrongly believed that hiring someone to kill Glen Davis would clear his debt. He also expected to be named in Glen's will. (He was not—Glen left everything to Mary Alice.) Ross also admitted resenting Glen because he was adopted and was giving away the family fortune to numerous charities. Marshall felt *he* should be running N.M. Davis Corporation. At the end of his statement to the court, he said: "I cannot do anything to change the terrible thing that I have done. I have devastated the lives of all those near and dear to me. I deserve the sentence I am getting." Marshall Ross was sentenced to life in prison without the possibility of parole for twenty-five years.

A few months later, the two Russian hit men who were hired to kill Glen Davis went on trial. Ross did not testify at the trial of Dmitri Kossyrine and Ivgeny (Eugene) Vorobiov, but the court heard that the three men had met in the home renovation business.

"It was a calculated fire for hire," said Crown attorney Hank Goody. "The death of Glen Davis had been in the works for a considerable period of time." For several days, the jury listened intently to the wiretap evidence the police had collected, including a series of calls in which Ross nervously tried to deflect police inquiries. The recordings also established Ross's familiarity with Kossyrine and Vorobiov. On the tapes, Ross was heard talking to Kossyrine, saying that the police didn't know Vorobiov and therefore wouldn't be able to make any connection back to them. A cocky Ross also told his accomplices that the video image of Vorobiov leaving the parking garage wasn't clear enough for the police to make a positive identification. When it came time for him to testify in his own defence, Eugene Vorobiov claimed that, although he had purchased a gun and a silencer, he had chickened out at the last minute and that it was Jesse Smith who had shot Glen Davis.

The trial lasted eight weeks. On December 20, 2011, Eugene Vorobiov, the man who fired two bullets into Glen Davis as he begged for his life, was convicted of first-degree murder and was sentenced to life imprisonment. But in a surprise outcome, the same jury failed to reach a consensus on whether Dmitri Kossyrine had arranged the murder of Glen Davis on behalf of Marshall Ross. A retrial was ordered, and a year later, Kossyrine was convicted of first-degree murder for his role as the middleman in the plot to kill Glen Davis. He was also sentenced to life in prison. Both men tried to appeal their convictions but were unsuccessful.

For Mary Alice Davis, the murder of her husband by their godson was an unforgivable betrayal that not only took the love of her life, but also ended her relationship with the Davis family—a family already divided by money and greed. Marsha Davis Ross—whose own sister, Mary Davis Nelles, had been kidnapped—refused to believe her son had engineered the murder of her cousin Glen, and cut all ties to Mary Alice. But as much as a mother would never want to believe that her son is a cold-blooded killer, it would have been hard for Mrs. Ross to ignore Marshall's alleged criminal activities behind bars.

In 2020, eleven years after admitting to arranging his godfather's murder, Marshall Ross was charged with four new counts of counsel to commit murder. According to court documents, he was trying to arrange the murders of four people from his prison cell. The names of his four intended victims were not released to the public at the time, but when his trial began in July 2022, it was revealed that one of his intended victims was his eighty-four-year-old godmother, Mary Alice.

After being convicted of the murder of Glen Davis, Marshall Ross was sued by N.M. Davis Corporation, the Davis family investment and holding company, for $3.2 million. Although the company won the lawsuit, it was unable to collect on the debt because Ross's only asset, a home in North Toronto, had been transferred to his ex-wife as part of their 2011 divorce settlement. In 2013, N.M. Davis Corporation sued Ross and his ex-wife, asking the court to declare the transfer of assets void because it had been done for the purpose of defrauding the company.

During Ross's trial on four counts of counsel to commit murder, the Crown alleged that he was feeling desperate and didn't want his ex-wife and children to lose their home, so he came up with another murder plot in which he tried to persuade a fellow inmate to help him find assassins who could eliminate Mary Alice Davis and three other unnamed persons. The former inmate, who testified under the pseudonym "Joe," claimed Ross wanted the four executed to wipe out the debt he owed to N.M. Davis Corporation. The Crown also presented a handwritten document written by the now fifty-one-year-old convicted murderer that included the names of the alleged targets and a map showing two of their Toronto addresses. She described the map as Ross's "hit list." The defence admitted that the note had been written by Ross but denied it was a "road map to murder." The trial lasted two weeks.

On August 24, 2022, Marshall Ross was acquitted on all four counts. While Superior Court Justice Graeme Mew considered the handwritten document listing names and addresses to be "a very troubling piece of paper," he ultimately believed that the purported scheme described by the Crown's main witness was too "fanciful and implausible" to pass a reality check. Moreover, the judge added, people do not commit a criminal offence "merely by talking about the possibility of committing some wrongful or unlawful act."

But friends and colleagues of Glen Davis sitting in the small courtroom in Napanee, Ontario, didn't agree with the judge's decision. They were painfully aware of exactly what Marshall Ross was capable of. "You're still a murderer, you scumbag. I hope you rot in hell," yelled Keith Jones, general manager of N.M. Davis Corporation and one of Ross's purported targets, according to press reports. Ross didn't look back at Jones as he was escorted out of the courtroom in handcuffs and leg irons.

Marshall Ross remains incarcerated in a federal penitentiary. He will be eligible to apply for early parole after serving fifteen years, in 2026. The lawsuit filed against him and his ex-wife was settled in 2021. The house in North Toronto that was originally purchased with money lent to him by Glen Davis was sold for $2.5 million. According to court documents, N.M. Davis Corporation received only 35 percent of the net proceeds of the sale.

Like his cousin Mary, who was kidnapped in 1969, Glen Davis was betrayed by someone very close to him. Someone he had loved and supported. But those who knew Davis did not want his violent and senseless murder to overshadow his legacy as one of the most committed conservationists Canada has ever known. To this day, he remains the single biggest individual donor to conservation groups in Canada. He gave more than $20 million over thirty years to various environmental causes, and his financial support led to the establishment of one thousand new parks and added millions of hectares of protected land in Canada. Ten years after his senseless murder, his friends and many of the charities he supported celebrated his life and legacy with the creation of a new $10,000 award named in his honour. The Glen Davis Conservation Leadership Prize is presented every year to a person who has demonstrated a personal passion and commitment to the conservation of Canadian spaces or species. "Think of any national park or provincial protected area that has been established in the past twenty years," said a close friend in 2007. "Glen Davis was probably involved in supporting it."

Glen Davis was a man adopted into great wealth. A shy, unassuming philanthropist who donated millions and never sought fame or recognition for his generosity. Those who knew him loved him, except for the one person hiding in plain sight—the enemy within.

# PART THREE

# IN THE NAME OF LOVE

*When obsession and jealousy lead to murder . . .*

# 7 BEHIND THE LAUGHTER

## THE PHIL HARTMAN STORY

It was just after six o'clock on the morning of May 28, 1998, in Encino, California, an upscale suburb of Los Angeles, when a 911 radio dispatcher received a frantic call saying there had been a shooting at 5065 Encino Avenue.

When the police arrived at the gated million-dollar property, they were met in the driveway by the distraught man who had placed the 911 call. He had a young boy with him. He said his name was Ron Douglas and he was a friend of the couple who lived at the address. The boy in pyjamas next to him was the couple's nine-year-old son. Douglas claimed that his friend, a woman by the name of Brynn Hartman, had arrived at his house at 3 a.m. in a drunk and agitated state, saying she had shot and killed her husband. He said he initially didn't believe her, but when the two of them returned to the Encino Avenue home, he discovered her husband's body in their bedroom.

Now the woman had locked herself in the master bedroom with her dead husband. Douglas had managed to get the couple's young son out of the house, but he told the police that their six-year-old daughter was still inside. The uniformed officers drew their guns and headed into the bungalow through the back door after loudly announcing themselves. It was an active situation and they needed to get the child out before they could ascertain exactly what they were dealing with. A few minutes later, a female officer emerged carrying the little girl, still half asleep and dressed in her night-gown. The policewoman raced down the driveway. Then a single gunshot rang out from inside the house.

The shocking news travelled like a California wildfire that sunny Thursday morning. Beloved forty-nine-year-old comedian Phil Hartman was dead. Shot to death by his wife, Brynn, who then took her own life, leaving their two young children orphaned. It didn't seem real. They were a Hollywood power couple who seemed to have it all. He was well known for his cast of many characters on *Saturday Night Live* and a starring role on an NBC sitcom. She was a beautiful former model. Together, they shared two young children and lived a million-dollar lifestyle with cars, boats and even a private airplane. But behind their perfect-looking family façade, there was trouble—tension, jealousy and addiction. Some long-simmering issues had resurfaced and their ten-year union was faltering. Those closest to them knew there were problems in the marriage, but no one could have foreshadowed its violent ending.

In the 1990s, Phil Hartman was one of the most famous comedi-ans in America. Nicknamed the "Man of a Thousand Voices" for the seemingly endless range of impressions he could do, he had entertained millions. From honing his craft in the small comedy clubs of Los Angeles to centre stage on *Saturday Night Live*, Hart-man had garnered a stellar reputation as a multifaceted performer and wonderful friend who supported those around him. But the comedian who was loved by so many had come from humble Canadian beginnings.

Philip Edward Hartmann was born on September 24, 1948, in Brantford, Ontario, to Doris and Rupert Hartmann (years later, he would drop the second *n* from his surname). Phil—or "Phippie," as he was called—was the fourth child born into the family, and four more would arrive after him, including a disabled sister who required full-time care. The family lived in a modest brick home that was busting at the seams, and money was always tight. Rupert was a deliveryman for Coca-Cola, and Doris ran a beauty parlour out of their house to supplement Rupert's income. Life was simple in the Hartmanns' small-town Ontario home. But Phil's parents always dreamed of making a fresh start in the United States, and in March 1957, when Phil was eight years old, the family finally packed up and moved south of the border. They spent a summer in Maine before relocating to Connecticut, where Rupert started selling roofing supplies and building materials. Travelling west, they eventually settled in Southern California in 1958, where Rupert took a sales job with Whirlpool.

The Hartmanns settled into a ranch-style bungalow in the middle-class suburb of Westchester, close to the Los Angeles airport. Phil and his siblings loved the California lifestyle, which included weekend surfing lessons and hanging out at the local beaches. Phil also developed a love for art and cartooning. According to friends, he could draw anything, and as his artistic creativity blossomed, so too did the shy Canadian teenager.

As the middle child in a big Catholic family, Phil always felt invisible, but he eventually found a way to get attention by being funny. He was the family jokester and the class clown. In high school, he joined the theatre group where he began honing his comedic talents. Sometimes he would give impromptu performances for friends where he would imitate popular comedians and actors of the day, including John Wayne, Jonathan Winters and Bob

Newhart. Phil enjoyed making people laugh but never assumed he could make a career out of it.

In 1966, Phil enrolled at Santa Monica City College, where he took courses in painting, drawing and public speaking. When he wasn't in class, Phil was either surfing the waves off of Malibu or skiing on the slopes at Mammoth Mountain, a six-hour drive from campus. He eventually dropped out of college to work as a roadie for a Malibu-based band called the Rockin' Foo that was managed by his brother John. But after a year on the road, Phil returned to school to study graphic arts, this time at California State University, Northridge. He then began designing album covers for rock bands, including the Foo's 1969 debut album. Working with his brother's music management company as a one-man art department, Phil went on to design album covers for Poco and America and a logo for Crosby, Stills and Nash. Phil also began supplementing his artistic work with voice work for radio commercials.

In 1970, while living in Malibu with his brother, Phil met a beautiful, free-spirited girl named Gretchen Lewis. Phil never had trouble hooking up with girls, but Gretchen was his first true love. A year later, the two were married at the Malibu courthouse. He was twenty-one and she was twenty. The young couple were excited about their future together. But according to friends, Phil had a habit of falling hard and then losing interest. Phil and Gretchen divorced two years later.

Single again, Phil decided to try his luck on national television and appeared on the popular 1970s game show *The Dating Game*. The funny, good-looking bachelor won the date, but ultimately got stood up. Regardless, he developed a taste for being in front of the camera and decided he wanted to pursue an acting career. In 1975, Phil joined a small improv group in Los Angeles called the Groundlings. For a $25 monthly fee, anyone could participate in weekly workshops and perform in front of small audiences on the weekends. Phil was finally in a place where he could explore comedy sketch ideas and develop his repertoire of characters. In the years that followed, for everyone at the Groundlings, the ultimate goal was to get on *Saturday Night Live*.

While performing and writing with the Groundlings, Phil became close friends with another comedian, Paul Reubens. Phil worked with Paul to help him create a unique character named Pee-Wee Herman. The quirky, childlike character was a huge success, and Phil was cast as Captain Carl on *The Pee-Wee Herman Show* and *Pee-Wee's Playhouse*. The two comedians also co-wrote the feature film *Pee-Wee's Big Adventure*, but eventually parted ways after creative disagreements.

In 1981, Phil began dating a twenty-three-year-old personal assistant named Lisa Strain. His career was finally beginning to take off with small movie roles and voice-over work. Phil and Lisa moved in together just a few weeks after meeting and were married in a small backyard ceremony in 1982. But the guy who could make people laugh proved to be elusive when it came to expressing his own emotions and contributing to a healthy marriage. In an interview years later, Lisa talked about the enigma of Phil Hartman. "My sense of Phil was that he was really two people," she said. "He was the guy who wanted to draw and write and think and create and come up with ideas. He was an actor and an entertainer, and then he was a recluse." The couple divorced after just three years.

Not long afterward, Phil met a beautiful blonde model named Brynn Omdahl, who was ten years younger than him. And true to his relationship pattern, he fell head over heels for her. Brynn, whose real given name was Vicki Jo, was a small-town girl from Thief River Falls, Minnesota. At sixteen, she dropped out of high school to pursue a modelling career. After a failed first marriage, she changed her name and moved to Los Angeles to pursue an acting career. Brynn was working as a swimsuit model and going to auditions by day, and hitting the Hollywood party circuit at night. But life in the fast lane had its dangers, and Brynn became addicted to alcohol and cocaine. Realizing she had a serious problem, Brynn checked herself into an addiction treatment and recovery centre and began attending Alcoholics Anonymous meetings in Beverly Hills. Not long after getting sober, she met a funny guy on a blind date. His name was Phil Hartman.

Phil and Brynn fell in love. She was beautiful and he was successful. They were both getting what they wanted. But only months into the relationship, Phil began to emotionally withdraw as he had in his previous relationships. It wasn't long before Brynn and Phil were locked into a destructive pattern of breaking up and then making up. Nonetheless, Brynn was determined to hang on to Phil because it was clear that his career was taking off.

In 1986, Phil got the chance of a lifetime: an audition for *Saturday Night Live*. The show had already made big stars of Chevy Chase, Eddie Murphy and Steve Martin, to name just a few. Lorne Michaels, the Canadian-born executive producer of *SNL*, liked what he saw in the fellow Canuck, and Phil was asked to join the cast for the twelfth season.

Phil was an instant success with the cast and audiences alike for his dry humour and perfect comedic timing. He was a master mimic, and could do imitations of more than fifty celebrities, including Frank Sinatra, Ronald Reagan, Bill Clinton, and even Jesus. Now living in New York, Phil's work schedule with *SNL* was all-consuming, but in the fall of 1987, he took time out to marry Brynn. It was his third marriage and her second. Close friends of Phil tried to talk him out of the marriage because they could already see that Brynn had some serious emotional issues, but Phil did not take their advice. Two years later, in 1989, Phil and Brynn welcomed their first child, a boy named Sean Edward.

When Phil's ex-wife Lisa Strain found out about the baby's birth, she sent a card of congratulations. She and Phil had remained friends, and she was thrilled for him and Brynn. But her well wishes were not kindly received. Brynn sent her a threatening four-page letter telling her in no uncertain terms to stay away from her family. Lisa called Phil to talk about the menacing letter, and Phil brushed it off, telling Lisa that Brynn was insecure and very intense. "You should have seen the letter she wanted to send you," said Phil. It would be years before Lisa ever spoke to her ex-husband again.

By 1989, Hartman was on top of the world. In the few short years that he had been on *Saturday Night Live*, he had established himself as one of the most important members of the comedy ensemble. Younger cast members like Chris Farley and Adam Sandler looked up to Phil and called him "the glue" that kept the group in sync. Years later, SNL creator Lorne Michaels explained Hartman's importance to the cast: "He kind of held the show together. He gave to everybody and demanded very little. He was very low-maintenance, and he was everybody's big brother."

As Phil's popularity on *Saturday Night Live* grew, he began getting other roles in commercials, TV and film, and the money started rolling in. With success came the toys—a Bentley, a Ferrari, a couple of boats and an airplane. But his growing stardom also meant he was often away from home, and his marriage began to suffer. Brynn, who had aspired to be an actress, became increasingly jealous of Phil and the attention he was getting. She would even get upset if he received fan mail. He was the star and she was the stay-at-home mom with two kids after their daughter, Birgen Anika, was born in 1992. While everything looked picture perfect on the outside, life inside the Hartman home was volatile. Confiding to a few close friends, Phil admitted that his third marriage was in trouble and that the way he coped was to stay away from home more and more.

In the early 1990s, Phil and Brynn decided to leave New York and return to live in Southern California. They moved into a four-thousand-square-foot dream home in Encino. Phil continued to commute between LA and New York. Then, in 1994, Phil left *Saturday Night Live* after eight seasons and 153 episodes. He would return twice to the famous stage at 30 Rockefeller Plaza to host the show.

After resettling in the Los Angeles area, Phil joined the cast of a new NBC comedy series called *NewsRadio*, portraying Bill McNeal, an arrogant and clueless radio news anchor. The cast included fellow Canadian Dave Foley, from *Kids in the Hall*, and comedians Andy Dick and Joe Rogan. Though the series received critical acclaim, ratings were inconsistent and the show was constantly under threat of cancellation. But Phil stuck with the series and kept busy with other projects. One of his favourite gigs was the Fox animated series *The Simpsons*. Phil was in fifty-two episodes and voiced numerous characters, including lawyer Lionel Hutz and actor Troy McClure. Phil's movie career was also taking off, with roles in such movies as *So I Married an Axe Murderer*, *Coneheads* and *Jingle All the Way*, with Arnold Schwarzenegger. He also appeared in numerous commercials.

But the more Phil achieved, the more Brynn seemed to resent it. She wanted an acting career and pestered Phil to get her roles in his projects, which put him in a difficult position professionally and increased the tension in their already unstable relationship. Feeling overshadowed by Phil's success, Brynn struggled to find her own identity, and as she got older she decided to undergo several cosmetic surgeries. She thought her breasts were too small, her face was too round and her jaw was too square. But although she continually altered her physical appearance, nothing seemed to alleviate her inner demons. Phil confided in his lawyer that Brynn had trouble controlling her anger and he had to physically restrain her at times. Work colleagues reported that Phil would sometimes show up on set with scratches on his face after fighting with Brynn the night before. Phil said he would end their disputes by withdrawing and going to sleep, hoping she would calm down by morning. This had become a long-established toxic pattern for the couple, who had been married at this point for more than ten years. But Phil was starting to grow impatient with his wife. He knew that Brynn had started using alcohol and drugs again after several years of sobriety.

At the beginning of 1998, just after turning forty, Brynn checked herself into an Arizona clinic but only stayed for five days before leaving. Her violent outbursts were becoming more frequent, and the couple's long-term housekeeper had quit after experiencing Brynn's rage once too often. Brynn was also taking an antidepressant and had been warned not to mix drugs or alcohol with the medication. She began telling friends that she wanted out of the marriage but said Phil would not agree to a divorce. Others said it was Phil who wanted out. Regardless, the Hartman household was not a happy one.

On the afternoon on May 27, 1998, Phil and a friend spent a leisurely day in Newport Beach, shopping for boat supplies. Phil was looking forward to spending more time on the water that summer. His favourite place to relax was on his Boston Whaler, which was moored off Emerald Bay on Catalina Island. He had also rented a house in Malibu for the summer. The kids loved the beach, and Phil was hopeful that he and Brynn could unwind and reconnect. He was trying to spend more quality time with his wife, and they had even instituted a weekly date night. But that evening, Phil had promised to watch the kids while Brynn went out with a girlfriend. He didn't mind. Of the many roles Phil had played over the years, his favourite was being a father to Sean and Birgen.

At 7:30 p.m., Brynn Hartman met her friend Christine Zander at Buca di Beppo, an Italian bistro in Encino where Phil and Brynn often dined together. The two women enjoyed a few vodka cocktails without ordering any dinner. Brynn, always conscious of her appearance, said she was concerned that she had put on a few pounds.

Nothing seemed amiss and Brynn was in a good state of mind, according to the restaurant manager, who knew her and stopped by that night to say hello. According to Christine, Brynn mentioned that Phil was thinking of retiring in a few years so they could spend more time with their children. While their marriage had been rocky due to Phil's hectic career, Brynn said they had sought marriage counselling and had even taken up hiking in recent months. She said she was looking forward to the upcoming weekend, as she had booked a full spa day for herself and Phil to enjoy.

After dinner, Brynn didn't go straight home. Instead, she dropped by to see an old boyfriend named Ron Douglas. Ron was a stuntman, and the two had known each other for more than fifteen years. According to Ron, they shared a couple beers while Brynn, as usual, complained about Phil. Close to midnight, Brynn left Ron's house and drove home. Given her intoxicated state, it has been speculated that she and Phil got into a heated argument. Phil would have known that she had been drinking and that she was possibly high on cocaine. According to close friends, Phil had warned Brynn several times that if she started using again, he would leave her and take the kids. He was sick of her violent outbursts. Phil hated arguing with his wife, but on that particular night, he wouldn't have been in any mood to deal with Brynn. His father, Rupert, had died just a few weeks earlier after a three-year battle with Alzheimer's disease. If they followed their usual pattern, Brynn probably ranted and raged, and Phil, being Phil, would have shut down and retreated to bed. They would deal with it in the morning.

At around 3:20 a.m., Ron Douglas was awoken by the phone. It was Brynn. She was hysterical, saying she wanted to drive back over to his place. She told Ron that Phil was out for the evening and had left her a note saying he would be back later, but she didn't want to be alone. Ron was confused by the frantic late-night call, but told her she couldn't leave the children alone in the house and that she should go to bed. "Drink a glass of milk, take some Aspirin and go to sleep," he told her. But Brynn ignored her friend's advice.

About twenty minutes later, Brynn showed up at Ron's house in Studio City. She was in her pyjamas and had no shoes on. She smelled of alcohol and was manic. "Don't yell at me," she said, sensing Ron was annoyed by the late-night visit. "Phil yells at me all the time." She collapsed on the living room floor, crying, and then ran to the bathroom to throw up. Ron had known Brynn a long time but had never seen her like this. She was acting erratically— yelling, muttering, shaking. He wondered if she was overdosing on something. But then she said something truly bizarre: "I killed Phil." Douglas was stunned. What was she talking about? Ron said he didn't believe her. Brynn then reached into her Prada purse and pulled out a Smith & Wesson .38-calibre handgun. But Ron still didn't think it could be true. He checked the barrel of the gun and thought it was fully loaded. He then put the gun into a plastic shopping bag. For the next two hours, he sat with Brynn, trying to console her while she sobered up. Maybe they'd had another big fight, thought Ron. There was no way Brynn would have killed Phil.

At approximately 5:45 a.m., Brynn said she wanted to go back to the house in case the kids woke up and insisted that Ron follow her in his car, which he agreed to do. She told him he should also bring the gun. On her way back to the house, driving erratically, Brynn called her friend Judy and told her she had killed Phil. Like Ron, Judy didn't know what to make of Brynn's bizarre confession but agreed to meet her at her home.

Brynn and Ron arrived at the house on Encino Avenue just as the sun was rising. It was going to be another beautiful day in Southern California. Walking into the Hartman home, all was quiet. The children were still asleep. Brynn led Ron towards the master bedroom at the back of the house. When Ron opened the bedroom door, he was confronted with a ghastly sight. Phil Hartman, clothed in a T-shirt and boxer shorts, was lying on the bed. He looked like he was asleep except for the blood splatter all over the wall and the bedding. Phil was dead, and there were obvious gunshot wounds to his face and head. "Oh my God!" yelled Brynn. "I killed him, I killed him. I don't know why!" Ron Douglas called 911.

When the police arrived minutes later, they were met by Douglas and a sleepy nine-year-old Sean Hartman, whom Douglas had carried out of the house. Douglas told the police that his friend Brynn Hartman had locked herself in the master bedroom with the body of her husband, whom she had admitted to shooting. Douglas said the couple's six-year-old daughter was still in the house. "Does Mrs. Hartman still have a gun?" asked the police officers. "No," said Douglas. It was in the trunk of his car. Quickly assessing the situation, the uniformed officers called for backup and then decided to enter the house. They needed to get Birgen to safety. Within a few minutes, a female officer came running outside, carrying the Hartmans' daughter.

Moments later, a single gunshot exploded from inside the house, followed by silence. Rushing back inside, the officers broke down the bedroom door and found the body of forty-nine-year-old Phil Hartman on the bed. Lying next to him was the body of Brynn. She had a single gunshot wound to her head, and a .38-calibre revolver was resting in her right hand. Brynn had put the gun in her mouth and pulled the trigger.

Police would later determine that Brynn had shot Phil three times while he slept—once between the eyes, once in the throat and once in the chest. "It was an execution," said one of the responding officers. The gunshots woke Sean, who later told the police he thought the sound was a slamming door. Although the gun she had used to kill Phil was locked in Ron Douglas's trunk, Brynn had used a second handgun taken from a lockbox inside the bedroom closet. The Hartmans had several firearms in the house, which friends had often tried to convince them to get rid of. Investigators would also learn that Brynn had called her sister Kathy in Wisconsin moments before shooting herself. "Take care of my children and tell them I love them very much," she said before hanging up the phone.

The Hartmans' murder-suicide was breaking news on that sunny spring morning. Even in a crazy town like Hollywood, it seemed unbelievable.

By midday, a media circus had descended on the quiet residential neighbourhood. News vans tried to get past the yellow police tape blocking the street and helicopters hovered overhead. Family and friends were in total disbelief, trying to come to terms with the shocking deaths. But while those who knew Phil and Brynn grieved for the once-loving couple, Hollywood tabloids were desperately trying dig up as much dirt as possible. Was there abuse in the marriage? Was there an affair? Who was Ron Douglas, the man who had called 911? Was he somehow involved? Rumours ran wild, and those closest to Phil and Brynn weren't speaking to the media. Their silence only fuelled further salacious gossip about the couple. Two days after their deaths, the families of Phil Hartman and Brynn Omdahl released a joint statement dismissing the rampant speculation offered in the media as completely unfounded. "Phil and Brynn were a loving couple, devoted to each other and their children," the statement said. "This tragedy is not indicative of who she was or who they were together." But, unfortunately, the family's heartfelt words did little to alleviate the ongoing morbid curiosity about what had happened in the Hartman home.

The rumours of a deeply fractured marriage had been tragically confirmed. The outwardly amiable Hartman, reclusive and introverted in private, and the combative Brynn, described as volatile and insecure about her husband's fame, were a toxic match.

Five days after their deaths, the Los Angeles Police Department confirmed that Brynn Hartman had acted alone. The police also released the 911 tapes from that morning to the press. There were no other lurid details, no secrets. It was just a tragic family story.

On June 5, 1998, a private memorial service was held for Phil and Brynn Hartman at Forest Lawn Memorial Park in Los Angeles. The intrusive media were kept away while both families came together to support the couple's young children, Sean and Birgen. During the service, Phil Hartman's older brother John urged everyone to be kind towards Brynn as they processed their grief. "They were victims of the same accident," he told mourners. "There is no one to hate and no blame to be laid. I beg you to forgive her." In accordance with his wishes, Phil's ashes were scattered in Emerald Bay off Catalina Island, the place he loved spending time on his boat.

When Phil Hartman was killed, he was at the pinnacle of his career. After many hard years, he had achieved stardom and was adored by all those who had worked with him—not an easy accomplishment in the cutthroat world of show business. In the wake of his unexpected death, NBC, the network behind *Saturday Night Live* and *NewsRadio*, issued a heartfelt statement saying that Phil Hartman had been blessed with a tremendous gift for creating characters that made people laugh. And everyone who had the pleasure of working with Phil knew that he was a man of tremendous warmth, a true professional and a loyal friend.

But as they say in the business, "the show must go on." Phil's character on *NewsRadio*, Bill McNeal, was said to have suffered a heart attack, and Phil's long-time friend and former SNL colleague Jon Lovitz filled in during the show's fifth and final season. A few months after his death, Phil was nominated for an Emmy for his work on *NewsRadio*.

For the close-knit cast of *NewsRadio*, continuing without Phil was extremely difficult, but there were other issues concerning Phil's death that were causing tension on the set. Lovitz accused *NewsRadio* co-star Andy Dick of reintroducing Brynn Hartman to cocaine, causing her to relapse and suffer a nervous breakdown. The two famous comedians even got into a physical altercation at a Los Angeles comedy club, where Lovitz smashed Dick's head into the bar. In an interview years later, Dick admitted to giving Brynn cocaine at a Christmas party six months before her death but claimed he knew nothing of her long-term drug addiction.

The reality of what had happened to Phil and Brynn Hartman was just too hard for their friends and family to accept. Yes, there were serious issues in the marriage, but that didn't explain why Brynn had shot Phil while he was asleep and then turned the gun on herself. Those closest to Brynn couldn't fathom how she could have left her young children without their parents. They believed something else had caused her to snap.

In 1999, a year after the double tragedy, Brynn's brother, Greg Omdahl, filed a wrongful death lawsuit against Pfizer, the manufacturer of Zoloft, and against Dr. Arthur Sorosky, the Los Angeles psychiatrist who had provided samples of the antidepressant to Brynn. According to court papers, Sorosky had given Brynn a manufacturer's sample of Zoloft on March 26, 1998, two months before the murder-suicide. The lawsuit claimed that Sorosky did not give her a physical examination or note her medical history of addiction, and did not have the traditional doctor–patient relationship with her because he was a children's psychiatrist who was working with nine-year-old Sean Hartman. The suit further alleged that Pfizer downplayed Zoloft's potential side effects, including violence or suicidal ideation in some people, while engaging in an aggressive marketing campaign to encourage physicians to dispense or prescribe the medication to patients. An autopsy conducted after Brynn's death confirmed that she had Zoloft, alcohol and cocaine in her system at the time of the shootings. The lawsuit was eventually settled out of court for a reported $100,000, which was put in trust for the Hartmans' children. Zoloft is still on the market as a prescription antidepressant.

In 2012, Phil Hartman was posthumously inducted into Canada's Walk of Fame, and two years later, a star bearing his name was unveiled on the legendary Hollywood Walk of Fame. In 2015, *Rolling Stone* magazine ranked Hartman as one of the ten greatest *Saturday Night Live* cast members throughout the show's forty-year history.

Brynn's sister Katharine Wright and her husband raised Sean and Birgen in Wisconsin. In an ABC News television special marking the twentieth anniversary of Phil Hartman's death, Greg Omdahl reported that Sean and Birgen, now adults in their twenties, were living successful, quiet lives. On the same show, John Hartman, Phil's older brother, reflected on Phil's death and his decision to forgive rather than hate Brynn for the murder, admitting that "it took a lot of hard work" to heal emotionally from the incident. As John recalled, when the coroner explained to him that Brynn was on Zoloft and drinking alcohol and did not know what she was doing, or why she was doing it, he didn't doubt it for a second. "I took that as true," he explained, "and I forgave her in that moment."

Phil Hartman, the shy kid from Brantford, Ontario, dedicated his life to making people laugh and smile. And in the years since his death, many famous friends and colleagues have struggled to make sense of what really happened on that early spring morning in May 1998. In an interview given shortly before his death, Phil spoke about how much he loved his life and how immensely delicate it was, too. "I think in my old age I've come to realize just how precious everything is," he said. "I try to value the many blessings that have been bestowed on me. But there's also this sense of vulnerability, if fortune took a turn for the worst. You live with the awareness that anything can happen in this world."

Phil Hartman's life came to an abrupt and tragic ending, but his legacy lives on in the many unforgettable characters he portrayed on screen, and to this day, he continues to make us laugh.

# *BACK TO REALITY*

## THE MURDER OF JASMINE FIORE

On the morning of Saturday, August 15, 2009, a disturbing 911 call came into the Buena Park police department located in Orange County, California, approximately thirty kilometres southeast of downtown Los Angeles. The unknown caller said he worked at a nearby apartment complex, and a homeless guy looking for recyclables in the dumpster had just discovered a body in a suitcase. And, he added, the man believed it was the body of a child. Officers on patrol nearby raced to the location. Climbing into the green industrial garbage bin behind the four-storey apartment building, they found a large grey suitcase amongst the other trash. Dark stains on the outside of the case appeared to be blood.

When police carefully opened the suitcase, they discovered a horrific sight. It wasn't a child, but it appeared to be the naked body of a petite woman lying in a fetal position. She was described as white, in her twenties or thirties, with dark hair. It looked as though she had been badly beaten and her face was very swollen. She didn't appear to have been dead very long, based on the lack of decomposition. But who was she? Right away, the police knew identifying her was going to be a challenge. There was nothing in the suitcase that indicated who she was, and forensic identification was also going to prove difficult because all of the woman's fingers below the first knuckle were missing and her teeth had been removed. Whoever killed her did not want her identified.

The body in the suitcase was taken to the Orange County coroner's office for an autopsy. The medical examiner determined that the unidentified woman had been dead less than twenty-four hours. She had been beaten and her nose was broken. The official cause of death was manual strangulation, and her teeth and finger joints had been removed post-mortem. The victim had no other defining characteristics, such as tattoos or scars, that could help to identify her, but she had had a breast augmentation. The coroner removed the silicone implants, hoping he could trace the woman's identity through the serial number on them.

Orange County homicide detectives were now on the case, but they still had little to go on. A thorough search of the isolated parking lot where the body had been dumped yielded no leads, and no one had filed a missing-person report. It looked as though they had another Jane Doe on their hands. Already in 2009, eight other unidentified females had been discovered in the area. Orange County was located on the outskirts of South Central LA, and it wasn't uncommon for bodies to be dumped there.

Following their instincts, the Buena Park detectives contacted the Los Angeles Police Department and were advised that, on the same day the body was discovered in the dumpster, a man in West Hollywood had reported his wife missing. The man, who identified himself as Ryan Jenkins, said his wife had left their penthouse apartment on the morning of August 14 to run errands but had never returned. He said they had just gotten back from a short trip to the San Diego area, where they had attended a poker tournament in Del Mar, the day before she went missing. He informed the police that his wife had taken off before, so he wasn't overly concerned, but he still wanted to file a missing-person report. When asked to describe his wife, Jenkins said she was a twenty-eight-year-old petite brunette. The last time he saw her, she was wearing a pink tank top, white pants and black flip-flops. But then he added two unique details: she had perfect teeth and had just had her nails done. He said his wife's name was Jasmine Fiore.

For Orange County homicide detectives, the missing woman from Los Angeles sounded like a good match for their Jane Doe. They contacted Jenkins and asked him to come in to speak with them as soon as he could, but he politely refused. He then told them he was going home to Calgary, Alberta, to deal with some family issues. This wasn't the response the police had expected from a man who had just reported his wife missing. Detectives knew they needed to find out more about Ryan Jenkins and his missing wife, Jasmine Fiore.

Jasmine Lapore was born on February 18, 1981, in Arizona, moving with her parents to California a few years later. Jasmine grew up in Bonny Doon, a small community outside Santa Cruz well known for lavender farms and wineries. After her parents' divorce when she was eight, Jasmine was raised by her mother, Lisa Lapore, a free-spirited ceramic artist. Growing up, young Jasmine had a lot of freedom. She grew into a tomboy who loved nature, animals and playing football with the guys. In high school she got her first job bagging groceries at the local supermarket and was well liked by everyone for her strong work ethic and bubbly personality. It wasn't long before the local boys started noticing the pretty teenager with piercing blue eyes and a beautiful smile. Jasmine had no shortage of admirers, but after her high school graduation she decided to leave small-town Bonny Doon and pursue an acting and modelling career.

In 1999, Jasmine moved to Las Vegas, Nevada, where she began working under a new name, Jasmine Fiore, which was the Italian word for "flower." Jasmine was ambitious and determined to make it big, but in a city like Vegas that was swarming with pretty girls, she soon discovered that lucrative modelling contracts were hard to come by. But she was resolute in her desire to break into show business, so she took gigs as a swimsuit model and supplemented her income by working as a waitress at various casinos along the strip. Life in Sin City for the aspiring model was very different than the sleepy town she had grown up in, but Jasmine embraced the high-adrenalin lifestyle. Anything was possible in Vegas as long as you looked good, and Jasmine made sure she always did. She worked out, dyed her hair blond and got breast implants. The now-voluptuous blonde turned heads wherever she went, but her true friends still saw her as a small-town girl with a big heart and a lot of insecurities. Vegas could be a lonely town, and Jasmine some-times drank and partied a bit too much to hide her vulnerabilities. But that's what the town did to a lot of women like Jasmine.

After seven years of chasing modelling gigs, she decided to pursue a more permanent career in real estate, and in 2007, she moved to Los Angeles. She obtained her real estate licence and made plans to open a gym and personal training business with a friend. With a new home and new career in LA, Jasmine was excited about the future, although she still yearned for one thing that had eluded her: true love.

Jasmine had no trouble attracting men who were eager to show off the buxom blonde on their arm, but few seemed to appreciate what was on the inside. In 2004, at twenty-three, Jasmine had got-ten married, but the relationship didn't last, and her ex-husband was now serving time in prison for dealing drugs. By the time she moved to Los Angeles, Jasmine was dating a wealthy real estate broker named Robert Hasman, but their relationship was rocky. After two years of an on-again, off-again relationship, they finally called it quits. They remained friends, and even talked about get-ting back together at some point in the future, but any poten-tial reconciliation plans the former couple might have made were thwarted when Jasmine announced in March 2009 that she had married a man she had only met three days prior to saying "I do."

On March 15, 2009, Jasmine Fiore met a guy named Ryan at a pool party in Las Vegas. The handsome and seemingly confident thirty-two-year-old was from Calgary, and said he was in Vegas to party after being a contestant on a reality dating show. Ryan Alexander Jenkins was the son of Dan Jenkins, an internationally renowned Canadian architect, and had grown up in an affluent Calgary neighbourhood. He attended boarding school in British Columbia and then began working with his father, selling high-end condominiums in Calgary. He was a well-known guy around town who liked the finer things in life, including pretty women.

Ryan bragged to Jasmine that he was a wealthy real estate developer back in his Canadian hometown but said his real passion was being in front of a camera. He talked about being on the VH1 reality series called *Megan Wants a Millionaire*. The show was one of the many dating programs that networks were cashing in on at the time. The genre had first taken hold with the Fox series *Who Wants to Marry a Multi-Millionaire?* in 2000. The show's producers quickly followed up with another winning format called *The Bachelor*. Suddenly, prime time television was dominated by catty contests that portrayed women as manipulative gold diggers in competition for rich men.

In *Megan Wants a Millionaire*, the show Ryan appeared on, wealthy bachelors competed for the love of a self-described materialistic blonde named Megan Hauserman, a former *Playboy* model. The winner of the show would get a trophy wife, and she would get their money. VH1's casting notice for the show called for "single men of the highest pedigree with a net worth of one million dollars or more." Casting directors placed ads on radio stations and threw wild casting parties in Los Angeles and Las Vegas nightclubs, looking for candidates. And it was in Vegas where they found a good-looking and charming Canadian.

Ryan Jenkins told the show's casting director he was a real estate developer and claimed to be worth $2.5 million. He exuded confidence and had just the right amount of cheeky cockiness the producers were looking for. On the first episode of the series, he described himself as "a little bit of a Prince Charming and a little bit of a bad boy." He said that he typically dated girls who turned a lot of heads. "I love the chase," he admitted. Nicknamed "Smooth Operator" by the other contestants on the show, Ryan said he could turn "player girls" into "princesses" and admitted to cheating on women only when he wanted to break up with them.

Ryan was competing with sixteen other rich bachelors for the affections of Megan Hauserman, and he quickly edged out most of the competition. Ultimately, Ryan was not chosen as the winning millionaire. Nonetheless, Megan liked the smooth-talking Canadian, and the two exchanged phone numbers off camera. She was upset when the producers asked her to pick one of the other bachelors. Megan did as she was told in front of the cameras, and then reached out to Ryan after the series wrapped. But, to her surprise, Ryan had already moved on. After being eliminated from the show, Ryan returned to Vegas, and it wasn't long before another beautiful blonde caught his eye, and this time he wasn't going to let her get away.

According to her friends and family, Jasmine was instantly attracted to the wannabe reality star. He was good-looking and charming, and he exuded an air of confidence that Jasmine found exciting. But those closest to Jasmine were shocked when she announced that she and Ryan had gotten married only three days after meeting. Friends assumed it was a rebound relationship, since she had just separated from her long-term boyfriend again. Photos from the twenty-four-hour Little White Wedding Chapel on the Vegas strip showed a beaming couple. But the ink had barely dried on their marriage licence before problems emerged.

Ryan Jenkins was not exactly the Prince Charming he had portrayed himself to be, and it turned out he had some dark secrets. Two years earlier, in January 2007, he had been convicted of assaulting his then girlfriend. In court, he admitted to punching her in the head and knocking her down when she attempted to leave his Calgary apartment. He was sentenced to fifteen months' probation, including counselling for sex addiction and domestic violence.

In her victim impact statement, Jenkins's former girlfriend stated that he would have temper tantrums when he didn't get his way, particularly when it came to sex. This came as no surprise to people in his inner circle back in Calgary who were familiar with Ryan's attitude towards women and sex. He was a well-known connoisseur of large breasts, blond hair and kinky sex. Friends around town still talked about his thirtieth birthday, when he hired two strippers to simulate sex in front of his guests. After his 2007 conviction, another former girlfriend came forward to say he had been abusive in their relationship eight years earlier.

Jasmine Fiore knew nothing about Ryan's violent past when she married him, but it didn't take long for him to show his true colours. Less than a month after their impromptu Vegas wedding, friends at a pool party saw Ryan punch Jasmine on her arm because he didn't like something she said. The blow pushed her off balance and she fell into the swimming pool fully dressed. Jasmine's friends were instantly concerned. If he was that aggressive in public, what was going on behind closed doors?

Jasmine quickly realized she had made a big mistake in marrying a man she barely knew, and two months after their wedding, she filed a domestic violence complaint against Ryan and left the marriage. She told her mother that she had gotten an annulment. Jasmine was anxious to put the whole impromptu wedding chapter behind her, and even reached out to her former boyfriend

Robert Hasman. They talked about rekindling their relationship and even took a romantic trip to Hawaii together. But moving on from her new husband wasn't going to be that easy.

Ryan Jenkins was not willing to give up on his marriage, and while his love life was in the gutter, his acting career was taking off. The producers of *Megan Wants a Millionaire* had been impressed with his on-camera charm and cast him in another dating reality series. While filming the new show in Mexico, Ryan couldn't get Jasmine out of his mind. He sent her love poems and letters, trying to convince her they should be together. In an email dated July 27, 2009, he wrote:

> *If you can come back to me and stop all this craziness, we can have a wonderful life . . . your forgiveness, trust and loyalty is all I need right now and when your love for me grows and our lives are heading in the right direction, I'll truly feel complete. I will never leave you. I only want you.*

For Jasmine—who, according to friends, had a heart of gold—Ryan's words of undying love wore her down, and she eventually returned to him. It was a pattern often seen in abusive relationships: violence and aggression, followed by an act of contrition, followed by a blissful honeymoon period. A month after reuniting, Jasmine and Ryan drove south to San Diego in her white Mercedes-Benz to attend a high-stakes poker tournament. On the afternoon of Thursday, August 13, the couple checked into L'Auberge Del Mar, a five-star oceanfront resort. The following day, only Ryan checked out, and twenty-four hours later, a mutilated body was discovered in a dumpster.

The Orange County police were almost certain that the remains found in the suitcase in Buena Park on August 15 were those of Jasmine Fiore, but the medical examiner's office had not made an official identification. Jenkins still refused to meet with police, so the detectives assigned to the case decided to retrace the couple's last known movements. They travelled south to L'Auberge Del Mar. The detectives wanted to talk with anyone at the hotel who might have interacted with the couple, and they wanted to look at the hotel's surveillance footage. Several of the staff at the luxury resort recalled seeing Jasmine and Ryan and reported nothing unusual. But the hotel's security cameras told a very different story.

At 3:28 p.m. on August 13, Ryan and Jasmine arrived at the hotel. An employee was seen helping them with their luggage, including a large grey suitcase. After they checked in, they were captured on camera walking to their room on the first floor of the hotel. Two hours later, Jasmine and Ryan were seen leaving their room. They were both dressed for an evening out and left the hotel. Police later learned that they attended a poker tournament at a Hilton hotel ten minutes away. Others at the tournament that night told police that Jasmine and Ryan had been arguing most of the evening.

Watching the security footage to determine when Jasmine and Ryan returned from their night out, detectives discovered that the camera closest to their room showed only Ryan returning at 2:30 a.m. Then, at 4:38 a.m., Ryan was captured running in the hallway, before disappearing back into their room. He appeared again a few minutes later, dressed in sweatpants and a tank top, carrying an ice bucket and another unidentified item. He wasn't seen on camera again until 6:24 a.m., when he walked down the hallway with his arms full of what looked like clothing and toiletries. Then, at 9:20 a.m., the footage showed Ryan checking out of the hotel. He was alone and did not appear to have the large grey suitcase the couple had arrived with.

The police searched Ryan and Jasmine's hotel room for any blood evidence, but it had already been thoroughly cleaned by hotel staff. The first-floor room had a small patio that backed onto the parking lot. Getting down on their hands and knees, investigators discovered a small spot of blood and one long, dark hair.

Orange County detectives were certain they had just found at least one of their crime scenes, and forensic tests later confirmed that the blood and hair belonged to Jasmine Fiore. Police were now confident that hers was the unidentified body found in the Buena Park dumpster and they needed to bring Ryan Jenkins in for questioning. But that was going to prove more difficult than expected. After reporting his wife missing, Jenkins had simply vanished.

Investigators travelled to West Hollywood to examine Ryan and Jasmine's penthouse apartment, but it looked as though the luxury suite had already been cleaned out. The police also discovered that Jasmine's white Mercedes and Ryan's black BMW SUV were missing. An all-points bulletin was issued on both cars. A few days later, investigators got a tip that Ryan had a storage unit in Las Vegas where he kept a speedboat called *The Night Ride Her*. They raced to Las Vegas, but by the time they got to the storage unit, the boat was gone—and so, too, was their prime suspect in the murder of Jasmine Fiore.

On Friday, August 21, five days after Ryan Jenkins reported his wife missing, his car and boat trailer were found at a marina in Blaine, Washington, a small city close to the Canadian border, approximately fifty kilometres from Vancouver. California authorities realized that Jenkins was likely heading back to Canada on water. The US and Canadian coast guards were immediately notified, and only a few hours into their search, the US Coast Guard spotted a speedboat matching the description they had been given. They gave chase, but the clunky coast guard vessel was no match for the powerful speedboat. A few hours later, police discovered Jenkins's boat abandoned in a marina in Point Roberts, Washington, a small peninsula community just south of the Canadian border. Ryan was familiar with the area because his stepmother and father had owned a home there. It looked as though Jenkins had eluded the American authorities and simply walked back into Canada. But his homeland had no intention of harbouring the suspected killer. The Royal Canadian Mounted Police began tracing his family members and any known acquaintances. They knew if Jenkins was hoping to disappear, he would need help.

On the same day that Ryan Jenkins escaped back into Canada, the Orange County District Attorney's office held a news conference to confirm that the disfigured body found in the dumpster in Buena Park had been identified as that of twenty-eight-year-old Jasmine Fiore. With her fingers and teeth missing, the coroner's office finally confirmed her identity by tracing the serial numbers on her breast implants. The district attorney announced that an arrest warrant for murder had been issued for Ryan, who they believed had fled back to Canada. The US Marshals Service offered a $25,000 reward for any American or Canadian citizen who aided in his capture.

The district attorney went on to speak of the brutality of the crime, saying it showed how dangerous her killer was. "Consider how much time it would take to pull out every tooth one by one," he said. In attendance at the news conference, listening to the horrific details of Jasmine's murder, were several of her close friends, including her ex-boyfriend Robert Hasman. But their grief paled in comparison to that of the visibly distraught middle-aged woman they were holding on to: Lisa Lapore, Jasmine's mother.

Speaking in front of the assembled news cameras, a tearful Lisa Lapore pleaded with Canadians not to shelter or assist Ryan. "I just want the people of Canada to help get him and not let him hide out," she said. She added that she was concerned he had access to financial resources, since he came from a wealthy family in Calgary. The district attorney concurred, saying that his office would seek bail in the amount of $10 million if he was captured and extradited back to the United States to stand trial. And, if a conviction was obtained, the DA would be seeking the death penalty.

When asked about her daughter, Lisa Lapore described Jasmine as an amazing woman. "She loved animals, especially horses," she said. "She had been riding since she was five years old. She also loved snowboarding and racing cars, high-adrenalin stuff . . . So many people loved her," she added before breaking down.

"Jenkins is a monster, and what he has done to Jasmine is unspeakable," said an angry and distraught Robert Hasman. Then he issued a direct message to Ryan Jenkins's family: "Bring Ryan in," he pleaded.

Ryan Jenkins had appeared on two reality dating shows and had dreams of making it big in television, and now his image was being splashed all over television news and social media because he was wanted for murder. His mother, Nada Antic, spoke to reporters from her home in Vancouver to say she was devastated by what had happened, but she was certain Ryan was not guilty of the grisly crime he was being accused of. "He's innocent as far as I'm concerned," she said. "I just want him found safe."

The RCMP knew Ryan had crossed the border into Canada on foot, but there was no sign of the fugitive. Using helicopters and tracking dogs, authorities searched the area where Ryan had abandoned his speedboat, but nothing turned up. The police theorized that someone had likely picked him up in a car, but if so, where was he going? Would he head back to his family in Calgary, or would he try to disappear into the vast British Columbia wilderness? He could be anywhere, and the media frenzy surrounding the manhunt attracted the attention of another reality TV celebrity: Duane Chapman, better known as Dog the Bounty Hunter, volunteered to join the search for Jenkins if asked by Canadian authorities.

The town of Hope, British Columbia, is in the Fraser Valley, about 150 kilometres from Vancouver. Originally established as a trading post for the Hudson's Bay Company in 1848, the town was also the epicentre of the Fraser Canyon gold rush in 1858, when gold was discovered in the Thompson River, a tributary of the Fraser River. Thirty thousand miners, many of them American, flocked to the area, and Britain responded by creating the colony of British Columbia so that British law and authority would be maintained in the region. Many years later, the area had become less populated and better known for its unspoiled nature. Described as a "woodsy" tourist town, Hope's heyday was long past, but it gained new popularity in 1982 when it was featured in the Sylvester Stallone movie *Rambo: First Blood*.

On the morning of Sunday, August 23, 2009, Kevin Walker, the manager of the Thunderbird Motel, was checking on his upcoming vacancies. Located off the Trans-Canada Highway, the one-star motel had seen better days. Most of the rooms were rented by the month to guys working in the local mining and logging camps, but the roadside motel did get the odd tourist as well. Checking his ledger, Walker realized that one of his guests who was due to check out that morning had not been by the front desk to turn in his key.

The guy in room 2 had arrived three days earlier. He and a pretty blonde had pulled up in a silver Chrysler PT Cruiser with Alberta licence plates. The woman registered and paid $140 cash for three nights while the guy stayed in the car. The couple checked in to their room, and then Walker noticed her driving away about twenty minutes later. Over the next few days, the hotel manager didn't see the attractive woman again but noticed the guy walk past his room a couple of times. The man looked dishevelled and depressed. Maybe he had just been dumped by the blonde, thought Walker.

Walker decided to check on room 2 to see if the guy had left. He knocked but got no response, so he used his master key to open the door. Right away, he noticed an open laptop and some other personal items scattered around the room. The guest obviously hadn't cleared out yet, and it was already an hour past checkout time. Typical, thought the frustrated hotel manager. Then, turning towards the bathroom, he saw the man. He hadn't checked out because he was dead.

Ryan Jenkins's flight from the law ended in a rundown motel in a secluded town named Hope, far from the bright lights of the Vegas strip and the Hollywood lifestyle he so desired. The thirty-two-year-old suspected murderer had used a belt to hang himself from the motel room coat rack.

In a note written on his laptop before his suicide, Ryan said he knew that he would be portrayed as a monster, but he claimed that the real monster was Jasmine. He said she was the love of his life, but he knew she was cheating on him when he discovered her texting her former boyfriend while they were in San Diego. He said that he had given her everything and loved her, but she had ruined their marriage. In his final words, he did not confess to killing Jasmine, but he apologized to his family for causing trouble.

With news of his death, it didn't take long for the tabloids to descend on the town of Hope. *Inside Edition*, *TMZ* and the *New York Post* rushed to the suicide scene, and a few industrious reporters even paid the hotel manager to film inside room 2, where Ryan had been found hanging. It was a tawdry tragedy. A reality TV contestant had murdered and mutilated his swimsuit model wife before instigating an international manhunt and then taking his own life in a seedy motel.

Soon, images of the couple in happier times were all over the internet. One video showed a bikini-clad Fiore gyrating to music and teasing the camera. "Wow," gasped a man's voice. "God, I love my life. And I love my wife." Then Jenkins turned the camera on himself. "Luckiest guy in the world," he said, pointing at his chest. But, within a few weeks, Fiore would be dead, savagely beaten, disfigured and tossed into the garbage, while Jenkins would be found hanging from his neck in a motel at the edge of the British Columbia interior.

With their number one suspect dead, the Orange County District Attorney's office declared the Jasmine Fiore murder investigation closed. They were confident that Ryan Jenkins was solely responsible for her death and that he had killed her on the night of August 13 when they were in the San Diego area. The police had obtained Jasmine's cellphone records, which helped piece together her whereabouts and actions before her death. Investigators learned that, just days before she was murdered, Jasmine had spent time with her ex-husband. She had picked him up from prison in the San Diego area and the two had spent the day at the beach to celebrate his release. She had also been texting ex-boyfriend Robert Hasman on the night she died. In her text to Robert, Jasmine said she was over her relationship with Ryan and wanted to return to him. Investigators believed that Ryan saw the texts to Robert and, in a jealous rage, strangled Jasmine to death.

It was a cold-blooded murder with a frustrating ending, but investigators still had some unanswered questions. They still didn't know where Jasmine had been killed and where her teeth and fingers had been discarded. Then, three days after Ryan Jenkins's suicide, the Los Angeles police received a tip about an abandoned car in a West Hollywood parking lot, approximately a kilometre and a half from Jasmine and Ryan's penthouse apartment. The white Mercedes-Benz turned out to be Jasmine's missing car, and when the police opened the car to process it, they finally discovered the gruesome crime scene they had been looking for. There was blood everywhere—on the door panels, in the carpet and on the dashboard. The windows were splattered with blood, and there was also a large stain on the back seat.

Homicide investigators theorized that there had been a violent struggle in the car and that Jasmine had been strangled to death. Then Ryan had removed her clothing and mutilated her body so that she could not be identified. It looked as though Ryan had placed the suitcase with Jasmine's body on the back seat. Blood had soaked through the case and into the car's upholstery. It also looked like Ryan had tried to clean up the blood. On the under-carriage of the car, crime scene technicians discovered grass and twigs. The police believed that Ryan had pulled off the road somewhere between San Diego and Los Angeles, a two-hundred-kilometre stretch, to dump Jasmine's fingers and teeth.

Back in Canada, the RCMP were trying to determine who had helped Ryan in his escape. Who was the attractive mystery woman who drove him to the Thunderbird Motel in Hope and paid cash for the room? They soon learned that the silver PT Cruiser that Ryan and the woman had arrived in was registered to Dan Jenkins, Ryan's father. A Vancouver news crew then discovered the same car parked in the underground garage of an upscale condo in Coal Harbour. The condo was registered under the name of Elena Jenkins, Ryan's twenty-year-old blonde stepsister. Aiding and abetting a known fugitive is a serious criminal offence, but the RCMP later announced that they would not be pressing charges against her.

Ryan Jenkins's suicide brought closure to the murder investigation, but the shocking crime also focused a much-needed spotlight on the "reality" of reality dating shows and how contestants were cast. How had a man with a prior conviction for domestic assault against an intimate partner become a contestant on a show about a woman finding a successful man to marry?

The production company responsible for *Megan Wants a Millionaire*, 51 Minds Entertainment, was suddenly in the news for all the wrong reasons. The company said it was unaware of Jenkins's criminal record when he was cast for the show, and claimed to have conducted thorough background checks on all potential contestants, including searching for any criminal convictions. But the production company was soon blaming a Canadian court clerk for not advising its investigative team that Jenkins had a criminal record in Canada. After Jenkins appeared on *Megan Wants a Millionaire* in March 2009, the company cast him in a second series called *I Love Money 3*. And even if his prior conviction in Canada had slipped through the cracks, he was charged again in June of that same year for assaulting Jasmine in Las Vegas. He was to appear in court that December.

Although 51 Minds Entertainment denied knowing anything about Jenkins's most recent assault charge, the damage was already done. VH1, the network that had paid for the series, abruptly pulled *Megan Wants a Millionaire* off the air after only three episodes. The second series, *I Love Money 3*, was never aired. The production company's reputation was in tatters and the network demanded its money back, to the tune of $12 million.

Jenkins's violent past, and his ability to be cast in two Hollywood reality dating shows, highlighted the exploitative truth about an industry that profited off of people's fragile egos, often casting dishonest and unstable individuals because it made for better TV. "Healthy, well-adjusted people are not interesting to watch," said Dr. Drew Pinsky, who became the host of another reality show called *Celebrity Rehab*.

Sadly, Ryan's story was not the only time reality contestants had been exposed. In 2000, Fox aired one of the first reality dating shows, *Who Wants to Marry a Multi-Millionaire?*, in which fifty women competed to marry a wealthy man named Rick Rockwell. The show was a ratings success, with twenty-two million people tuning in to watch Rick marry one of the lucky contestants. But it was later revealed that Rockwell was hardly a multi-millionaire, and it also emerged that a former girlfriend had obtained a restraining order against him in 1991.

Although *Who Wants to Marry a Multi-Millionaire?* was incredibly lucrative for Fox, the negative press associated with Rockwell prompted the network to cancel a planned rerun, as well as plans to produce further specials. But the controversy didn't stop other networks from cashing in on the fake romance genre. Nine years later, *Megan Wants a Millionaire* would premiere and Ryan Jenkins, a smooth-talking bachelor from Calgary, would get his fifteen minutes of fame before killing his wife and himself.

Today, fourteen years after the murder of Jasmine Fiore, many specialty television networks have faltered and the popularity of reality dating series has declined. But shows like *The Bachelor* and *The Bachelorette* still draw millions of viewers every season. People will always be attracted to the fantasy of a Prince Charming and the prospect of finding true love, even when it's completely contrived.

The shocking murder of Jasmine Fiore did ultimately change the way reality shows conducted their casting and background checks on potential contestants, but that came as a small consolation to Jasmine's family and friends. Those closest to Jasmine later wished they had stepped in when they suspected Ryan was being possessive and abusive. Jasmine's mother, Lisa Lepore, who appeared on NBC's *Today*, said she hoped the death of her daughter would shed light on the ongoing problem of violence towards women. She said that Jasmine was a smart, strong woman who could handle herself, yet she still fell victim to an obsessive, violent narcissist. With respect to Ryan Jenkins, Lepore said she had mixed emotions about his suicide. "It brings closure, and we don't have to worry about looking for him or be worried that he is a threat to other women. But he was a coward," she said. "He took the easy way out."

Despite the overwhelming evidence pointing to Ryan's guilt, his family refused to believe he was responsible for Jasmine's death. His father, Dan, hired a private investigator in Los Angeles to continue the investigation. Speaking to the media, Jenkins blamed the lure of Hollywood, and even Jasmine, for her own death. "He went to Hollywood and something happened down there in the last four months, including that girl," said the grieving dad. "It was hell on earth, and I advised him fifty times to get out of that relationship. It just destroyed him."

In an unusual move, the Buena Park police invited Dan Jenkins to Orange County to review the file of evidence they had gathered in the case. As far as they were concerned, there were no other suspects.

In the end, Jasmine's heartbroken mother did not want her only daughter to be remembered for how she died, but for how she lived. "She was a wonderful person," she said. "I wish with all my heart I could have my daughter back."

# HOLLYWOOD HORROR STORY

## THE MURDER OF IANA KASIAN

On the morning of Tuesday, May 24, 2016, Olga Kasian woke early to care for her newborn granddaughter, Diana. Olga had travelled from Ukraine to Los Angeles to help her daughter Iana, who had just given birth two weeks earlier. Thirty-year-old Iana Kasian was thrilled to be a first-time mother. Her little girl was perfect, and she was looking forward to getting married to Diana's father. But just days after bringing the baby home from the hospital, her fiancé began acting strange. Iana told her mother that he seemed jealous of the attention she was paying the baby and was demanding sex from her even though she was still recovering from a Caesarean. Then he was arrested after being accused of sexual assault by a former girlfriend. He had been cheating. Iana left their apartment with the baby and was staying with her mother temporarily.

The day before, Olga and her daughter had been out shopping for baby strollers when Iana got a series of frantic texts and calls from her fiancé. He denied the sexual assault accusation, begged for forgiveness and asked her to come back. Iana seemed resolute in her decision to leave him, but after several emotional phone calls her resolve softened. "I'm going to him," Iana told her mother. She asked Olga to mind Diana for a few hours. She would at least give him an opportunity to explain, and maybe they could work it out for the sake of their baby. Olga disagreed with her daughter and told her not to go. Iana told her mom she would only be a few hours. But a day later, when Olga had not heard from Iana, she began to get worried. Olga's phone calls went straight to voice mail, and she sensed that something was very wrong. Her daughter was breastfeeding and would not have left her newborn for so long.

When Iana still hadn't gotten in touch by that evening, Olga contacted the Los Angeles County Sheriff's Department. It was hard for Olga to relay her concerns because she spoke very little English. She wanted the police to check on her daughter at the apartment she shared with her fiancé. But the police refused her request and advised Olga to wait until her daughter contacted her. Olga waited a few more hours, but there was still no word from Iana. She then decided to go to the condo herself, but couldn't get into the gated property on Holloway Drive. Surveillance cameras showed her pacing back and forth in front of the metal gates. "Help me," she pleaded, calling the police multiple times from outside the condo complex. Still, the police refused to come.

The next morning, Olga was back in front of the condo, begging the police to show up. Finally, to appease the worried woman with the heavy Eastern European accent, a patrol car was sent over to do a welfare check on Iana Kasian. Forty-eight hours had elapsed since Olga had last seen her daughter.

When police officers knocked on the apartment door, there was no answer. They called out; still no answer. But they could hear movement inside. Someone was in there. Using a key obtained from the condo manager, the officers tried to open front door of the apartment, but something heavy was blocking it from the inside.

Using force, the police finally broke down the door. Olga was told to wait outside. Inside, they noticed the apartment was in total disarray, with overturned furniture, empty food containers and clothing scattered all over the floor. Walking down the hallway, they saw the first disturbing sign that something was wrong. There was blood smeared on the wall. They drew their guns. Then, moving towards the bedroom, the police encountered another locked and barricaded door. They could hear a man inside the bedroom, talking on the phone. They would later learn that on the other end of the call was a friend of the man, urging him to surrender. The police asked him to open the door. The man yelled out that he wasn't opening the door and that Iana was not home. The police asked again and waited. They called for backup.

Finally, a dishevelled, wild-eyed man opened the bedroom door wearing only boxer shorts. He had bruises under his eyes, cuts on his face and what looked like a bite mark on his arm. Behind him, the police could see what appeared to be another person in the bed, covered in a Mickey Mouse comforter. The figure wasn't moving. Moving past the man, one of the officers pulled back the comforter and discovered the lifeless and mutilated body of a woman. Olga Kasian's daughter Iana was dead, and the police had just discovered one of the most horrific murder scenes in the history of Hollywood.


Iana Kasian loved living in Hollywood, with its endless sunshine, nearby beaches and glamorous lifestyle. It was a dream come true for the petite brunette who was born in Estonia in 1986. When she was young, her family moved to Ukraine, where her father worked in the navy yards and her mother worked in health care. The family did not have much money, but they were very close. Iana excelled academically and eventually attended law school in Kyiv. After graduating, she worked for several years prosecuting tax crimes. Iana spoke fluent English and dreamed of travelling abroad to work as an interpreter and a model. Finally, her dream came true when she immigrated to Los Angeles in 2014.

Not long after arriving in California, Iana met an impressive up-and-coming Hollywood producer and publisher named Blake Leibel. The two instantly hit it off, and within two months of dating, Iana discovered she was pregnant. While unexpected, Iana was excited about the baby and Blake said he was, too. But the situation was complicated because Blake was still married.

Blake Leibel was born in Toronto on May 8, 1981, and was raised in the city's affluent Forest Hill neighbourhood. His father, Lorne, was a former Olympic sailor turned real estate developer who had made a fortune in the suburban building boom of the 1980s and 1990s, and his company was once described as the largest home builder in the country. The flamboyant billionaire real estate developer owned a fleet of Ferraris and was reportedly a well-known playboy about town.

Blake's mother, Eleanor, was the daughter of Paul Chitel, a wealthy businessman who had turned a plastic sheeting company into a multi-million-dollar enterprise called Polytarp Products. Blake's parents separated when he was young, but they never divorced. Blake lived with his mother, while his older brother, Cody, stayed with their father.

With money coming in from both sides of the family, Blake lived a life of privilege and hung out with the children of some of Toronto's wealthiest families. Around 2004, after graduating from the University of Western Ontario, Blake and a few of his rich friends decided to move to Los Angeles to try to make it big in the movie business. With trust funds and family money to burn, it wasn't difficult for the Canadian bachelors to start attracting a lot of attention in LA's party scene, particularly from women.

Blake's brother, Cody, was already living a glamorous Hollywood lifestyle, having founded a short-lived record label called C-Note Records and dabbling in real estate. By the age of twenty-three, he owned a $1.2 million Ferrari Enzo, one of only a few hundred in existence. Cody also had a reputation as a high-stakes gambler and was on the A-list of underground poker players, specifically in a circuit called Molly's Game, along with celebrities and well-known sports figures. Years later, Hollywood producer Aaron Sorkin would use Molly's Game as the subject for a film of the same name.

While his brother enjoyed the Hollywood playboy lifestyle, Blake considered himself to be more of a creative genius. As a kid, he was heavily into video games and comics, and now he wanted to turn some of his own story ideas into Hollywood blockbusters. Blake began networking and pitching ideas around town. He eventually founded a publishing house called Fantasy Prone with two of his friends from Toronto and worked with them on a television adaptation of *Spaceballs*, the 1987 Mel Brooks movie. Blake also wrote and directed a low-budget feature film, titled *Bald*, that went straight to DVD in 2009.

His most successful work turned out to be a graphic novel called *Syndrome*. Published in 2010, the book followed Dr. Wolfe Chitel, a neuropathologist who just happened to share Blake's grandfather's name. In the novel, the mysterious Dr. Chitel was on a quest to study a serial killer and find a cure for the disease that made men like him do terrible things. The cover of the graphic novel showed a disturbing photoshopped picture of a baby doll head with most of its skull removed to reveal a brain inside. Inside, the story included gory illustrations of a headless female body lying on a blood-soaked mattress, as well as two people hung from their feet, drained of their blood. Blake wrote a cryptic, two-page introduction to the story, where he asked, "If you loved hurting things, what would you do?" Blake was hopeful he could turn the graphic novel into a screenplay, but there was little interest. Even by Holly-wood standards, the story was a little too macabre.

In 2011, Blake's sixty-one-year-old mother, Eleanor, died of brain cancer in Toronto. Blake did not attend the funeral; instead, he sued to have her will overturned because it left only half of her estate to him and the other half to Lorne and Cody. Eleanor's estate was worth over $12 million, and Blake wanted it all. He was living large in Los Angeles and didn't want anything disrupting his lavish lifestyle. That same year, he had married Amanda Braun, a former model, and one month later she gave birth to their first son. The couple lived in an impressive 1926 Tudor-inspired Bev-erly Hills home, drove luxury cars, and Blake was a regular at the Soho House, a private club on Sunset Boulevard.

But in documents from the civil lawsuit against his mother's estate, Blake confessed to having almost no income of his own. After his mother died, he told the court, he had to rely on his father to pay his credit card bills. His father told the court that he and Blake's mother had supported their son's extravagant LA life-style, buying him a home and giving him close to $2 million cash since he moved to California. But Blake's father was done. There would be no more family money. Blake lost the lawsuit in 2013 and was sued by the law firm that represented him in the case, claiming he owed $400,000 in unpaid legal fees.

The rich kid from Toronto's Hollywood fantasy was beginning to collapse. And according to those who knew him, there were already signs that all was not well with Blake Leibel. He had a heavy marijuana habit and seemed to be getting more paranoid. He told friends he was concerned that Cody, through his gambling, owed money to potentially dangerous characters who might come after him or his family. He began cutting ties with most of his

Toronto friends in LA, and then, in July 2015, he unexpectantly walked out on his wife and their young son. Amanda was eight months pregnant with their second child.

It wasn't long before Blake was seen around Hollywood nightclubs with a new girlfriend on his arm. Her name was Iana Kasian, an attractive twenty-nine-year-old former lawyer from Ukraine. Two months later, Iana was pregnant, too. The couple moved into an upscale apartment in West Hollywood, and Blake bought Iana a Mercedes-Benz SUV.

On May 3, 2016, Iana gave birth to a daughter they named Diana. Then, just a few weeks later, on May 20, Blake was arrested on suspicion of sexual assault. It turned out that Blake was seeing another woman he had met several years before. After an argument, the woman called police to report a sexual assault she alleged had taken place months earlier. Blake spent fifteen hours in jail before posting $100,000 bail.

When Iana learned of the arrest, she left the condo the two were sharing and moved in with her mother, Olga, who was staying in another apartment close by, which Blake had rented for her. But just four days later, Iana went to see Blake after he begged her to meet with him, and now she was dead.


When homicide investigators were called to the upscale condo in West Hollywood, they were initially told that a woman had been discovered dead in the apartment with her estranged fiancé. Sadly, it sounded all too familiar. Domestic homicides were a common occurrence. But for veteran detectives William Cotter and Robert Martindale, nothing could have prepared them for what they encountered when they arrived at the scene. Iana's pale, nude body lay on the blood-soaked bed. It looked like she had been dead for a while, but her cause of death was not readily apparent. In fact, it was likely going to be difficult to determine her cause of death because it was clear that Iana had been brutally tortured and mutilated before she died.

As the police led a handcuffed Blake Leibel out of the apartment and into a police car, a crowd of curious onlookers had gathered. But standing alone, away from the crowd, was a middle-aged woman anxiously waiting to find out about the welfare of her daughter. Moments later, homicide detectives Cotter and Martindale approached her. They were about to inform Olga Kasian of the worst news she would ever hear in her life.

On June 3, 2016, one week after the discovery of Iana's body, Blake Leibel walked into a Los Angeles courtroom in a padded suicide prevention vest, with his hands cuffed in front of him and a thick chain around his waist. The former Hollywood wannabe looked unkept and vacant. From the glass-walled prisoner's box, he looked around the almost empty room for a familiar face. But no one was there—none of his former Toronto friends, his brother or his estranged wife. Leibel was charged with first-degree murder, torture and mayhem in the death of Iana Kasian. The elements of torture included the intent to cause cruel and extreme pain and suffering for revenge, extortion or sadistic purposes. If found guilty, he was facing the California death penalty.

Blake pleaded not guilty to all counts. His court-appointed lawyer then suggested he might not be fit to stand trial. The judge agreed. Blake would undergo a psychiatric assessment. Two weeks later, when he was due back in court for a competency hearing, Blake refused to leave his jail cell. Regardless, he was eventually found mentally fit to stand trial.

||||||||

Blake's trial began on June 11, 2018, two years after Iana's brutal murder. In her opening statement, Deputy District Attorney Tannaz Mokayef told jurors that it was the most sadistic and gruesome murder she had ever prosecuted. "This case reads like a bad Hollywood movie script," she said. "But there is nothing cinematic about what you will see in photos of the victim." She described Blake Leibel as a spoiled rich kid from Toronto, living a lavish LA lifestyle as a film producer and graphic novelist. "Now he is accused of a brutal murder that in some ways mirrored his art," she continued. She said that she would prove that Blake had planned and choreographed Iana's murder, acting out details he took from his graphic novel, *Syndrome*.

The first witness called to testify was Olga Kasian, Iana's mother, who had travelled back to Los Angeles from Kyiv for the trial. Using a court-appointed Russian interpreter, the sixty-two-year-old grandmother recounted her desperate pleas to the sheriff's department to check on her daughter after she had gone to see Blake at the apartment they shared. She knew something was terribly wrong. But by the time the police finally agreed to do a welfare check on her daughter, it was too late. Iana was already dead. "They could have saved her," she cried.

On the second day of the trial, Detective William Cotter took the stand to testify about the horrific crime scene he had encountered in Leibel's apartment. But before his testimony started, the prosecutor leaned over and spoke to Olga Kasian to warn her about what was to come. But Olga refused to leave. She sat stoically while Sergeant Cotter referred to the graphic images displayed on the courtroom monitor. In photo after photo, the detective described the apartment where Iana was found dead. Cotter pointed out smudged bloodstains on the drapes, on a headboard in the guestroom and on a lamp. He said it was obvious Blake had tried to clean up the stains. Then he described the photo of Iana's lifeless, naked body sprawled on the bloodstained mattress in the master bedroom, with trauma to her head so severe it rendered her unrecognizable. "I stood there for a while," Cotter said, referring to the first time he entered the bedroom. Nothing in his thirty-year police career had prepared him for what he was looking at. "The injuries she suffered were horrific and unspeakable." Iana had been scalped, and her body was eerily and unusually pale. "It wasn't simply the killing of somebody," the detective said, "it was sadistic torture."

The detective went on to tell the jury that, when they arrested Blake at the scene, he had scratches and bruises on his face and a bite mark on his arm. "She fought hard," said a clearly emotional Cotter. He said that they also discovered $4,000 in cash and Blake's passport in the pocket of his pants. It looked like he was planning on cleaning up the apartment, disposing of the body and taking off, probably back to Canada.

After his arrest, according to the detective, Blake seemed surprised when he was told Iana was dead and refused to acknowledge any involvement in the brutal crime. Blake told the homicide detectives that "science would tell them who did it." It turned out Blake was right. Science would help explain exactly what had happened in that apartment. The next witness to testify for the prosecution was a forensic pathologist who explained that blood evidence had been collected from all over the apartment, including the kitchen drainpipe. The DNA found at the crime scene belonged to both Iana Kasian and Blake Leibel. Crime scene specialists also found pieces of flesh from Kasian's mutilated body in the bed, underneath the mattress and in the bathroom. The bedsheet also bore distinctive bloody handprints that matched Leibel's right hand, which was missing part of its pinky finger. Noticing a garbage chute outside the apartment door, crime scene specialists went to the basement of the condominium to see if any other evidence could be located. There they found eleven trash bags, many of which contained bloody sheets and clothes. But some of the bags also contained body parts belonging to Iana, pieces of her hair and scalp. And in one bag, they discovered her ear.

Next on the stand was Dr. James Ribe of the Los Angeles County coroner's office, who, in calm, clinical detail, described Iana's wounds. Iana's entire scalp was absent except for a few parts at the back of her neck. It appeared that the scalp had been cut by a sharp object, like a paring knife or razor, and then torn from her head by hand. Portions of her face were missing, including her eyebrows and her right ear. Ribe added that there were also a number of bruises and abrasions on Iana's face, including a bite mark.

As the pathologist spoke, graphic images from the autopsy appeared on a monitor for all to see. There was complete silence in the courtroom. Then a woman in the audience fainted and had to be helped out of the courtroom. Olga Kasian stared at the violent imagery intently, forcing herself to look at the images of her daughter, before crying softly and burying her head in her hands. How much more could she handle? But Dr. Ribe wasn't finished.

In addition to the obvious torture inflicted, there was another disturbing detail. Dr. Ribe said that when he examined Iana Kasian's body, he discovered that it contained almost no blood. "The average human body contains about five litres of blood," he explained to the jury. "But the victim had less than a teaspoon," adding that "a dead body cannot bleed out." Which meant the victim had likely been alive for the duration. Defensive wounds on her hands also indicated she was alive while she was being tortured. Dr. Ribe concluded that Iana had likely suffered, for up to eight hours, before she finally succumbed. "I have never seen this before," said the pathologist. "And I doubt if hardly any forensic pathologists in this country or abroad have ever seen this. It is extremely rare." Iana Kasian died from exsanguination, explained the doctor. All the blood in her body had been drained.

By the last day of the trial, the prosecution had called thirteen witnesses to the stand; the defence had called none. In her closing remarks, Deputy District Attorney Beth Silverman asked the question that had hung heavily over the case from the beginning: Why?

"I'm sure you've asked yourself the question of why?" she said to the jury. "Why would a human being do anything close to this to another human being, and why do that to someone he supposedly loved, someone he just had a baby with?" She conceded that motive was often difficult to discern, but then offered clues as to what might have driven Leibel to such extremes. "Power, jealousy and anger were likely at play," she said, suggesting that Leibel was jealous that Iana's attention had been diverted away from him and towards the newborn. "Blake Leibel was a privileged narcissist who was used to getting what he wanted, and he controlled those around him with money," said Silverman. "So, when Iana left him, he decided that she would have to pay with her life."

"This was pure evil," Silverman said bluntly. "Ms. Kasian died a slow and painful death as he continued to mutilate her bit by bit." She explained how the police and the medical pathologist theorized that Leibel had dragged Iana into the bathroom and submerged her under water in the bathtub. The running water would have stopped her blood from clotting. "And we know that the defendant had ample time to stop and change his mind," Silverman added. Security footage from the condo showed that Blake managed to have food delivered several times in the two days he was alone with Iana.

Silverman also reminded the jury that it appeared that Leibel used *Syndrome*, the graphic novel he had funded and created, as a reference for his torture. The novel that depicted a baby doll with a partly removed scalp on its cover also included illustrations of torture and bloodletting. "The defendant basically handed us a blueprint, a case of life imitating art," the prosecutor said.

Wrapping up her closing arguments, Silverman said there were no words to describe Leibel's crimes. "What happened," she said, "is beyond anybody's worst nightmare." She then asked jurors to recall a quote written by Blake in his graphic novel: "'In the end, we all become monsters.'"

Leibel's attorney, Deputy Public Defender Haydeh Takasugi, began her closing arguments by acknowledging the sadness and anger she had witnessed in the jurors' eyes during the trial. But regardless of the horrific nature of the crime, the defence attorney asked the jurors to review all the evidence critically. If they did that, she said, they would no doubt acquit her client. Takasugi stressed that Leibel didn't write or illustrate *Syndrome*, adding that the cover image of the scalped baby was someone else's idea. "We're reaching for something that is simply not there," she said. And while Takasugi did not offer another potential suspect, she attempted to poke holes in the idea that her client was the perpetrator by asking jurors to think about the trash bags found in the condo's dumpster, which contained some of Kasian's body parts, as well as a T-shirt that belonged to Leibel. DNA samples retrieved from the drawstrings of three of the bags, the defence attorney noted, did not match her client's, but revealed genetic evidence of an unknown male.

The trial had lasted six days. On June 20, 2018, the jury of eight men and four women returned with a verdict. After deliberating for less than four hours, they found thirty-five-year-old Blake Leibel guilty of first-degree murder, aggravated mayhem and torture. Dressed in a blue blazer and white shirt, Leibel remained motionless, staring straight ahead. His brother, Cody, who sat behind Blake every day of the trial, also showed little emotion. But on the other side of the courtroom, Iana's mother, Olga Kasian, broke into tears. Family and friends, many of whom had flown in from Ukraine to offer support, hugged one another. Their nightmare was over and Blake Leibel would pay for what he had done to Iana.

One week later, Olga addressed the court. Her hands trembled as she read from her prepared text. With the assistance of a Russian interpreter, she said that since her daughter's murder, her life had turned into a hell of endless suffering. She described how her mind would often race with thoughts of Iana's dying hours and the slow torture she endured. And she now lived with the agonizing reality that the man who murdered her daughter was the father of her beloved granddaughter. "The life of this little angel began with the fact that her father massacred her mother," she said, as she glared at Leibel. She ended her impassioned statement with a plea that everyone go home and hug their children.

Dressed in a standard yellow jail uniform, a bloated, balding Blake Leibel remained expressionless. Superior Court Judge Mark Windham addressed the court saying that the case was most unusual in its savagery and that the defendant had exhibited "inconceivable cruelty" in his actions. He then praised the jury, saying he couldn't imagine a more difficult case. He sentenced Blake Leibel to life in prison without the possibility of parole. The state had not sought the death penalty.

Outside the courthouse, an emotional Olga Kasian hugged Detective William Cotter, who had told her of her daughter's death outside the West Hollywood apartment two years earlier. The seasoned police officer crumpled into her arms and wept.

In March 2019, Iana's family won a wrongful death suit against Blake Leibel. A Los Angeles court ordered Leibel to pay $41.6 million to the family. "This murder didn't just kill one person, it shattered the entire family," said an attorney representing the Kasians. The lawyer added that the payout would help Olga Kasian raise her granddaughter, a little girl who will never know her mother and who, one day, will find out about her father's heinous crime.

## PART FOUR

# 'TIL DEATH DO US PART

When matrimonial bliss turns into the kiss of death . . .

# 10 MURDER IN THE SUBURBS

## THE CASE OF LUCILLE MILLER

**F**amed American writer Joan Didion was well known for her intimate essays, political writings and non-fiction books. The diminutive novelist wrote about the realities of American life in the 1960s and '70s through an honest and personal lens. She helped establish a new kind of journalism that captured the divisive mood of the times. In later life, she wrote more about her own personal struggles, including her enduring loves and her most profound losses.

As a fifth-generation Californian, she wrote about the state often. In 1966, in a rundown rented house in Hollywood, she penned a story for the *Saturday Evening Post* titled "How Can I Tell Them There's Nothing Left?" It was the story of a murder trial in San Bernardino County, a sleepy enclave of subdivisions and middle-class families about an hour east of Los Angeles. On the surface, the facts of the case read like a tawdry tabloid tale of sex, jealousy and murder, but for Didion, it was so much more. It was a story about love, loss and death in the golden land of opportunity. This is that story.

||||||||||

On the night of October 7, 1964, at approximately 1:50 a.m., the fire department and California Highway Patrol were notified of a car fire on Banyan Street in Alta Loma. Alta Loma, Spanish for "tall hill," is nestled in the foothills of the San Gabriel Mountains in San Bernardino County, one hour's drive east of Los Angeles. For years, the area had been home to old citrus groves, vineyards and peeling eucalyptus trees before the creeping urban sprawl of Los Angeles County pushed middle-class families higher up into the hills to build their suburban dream homes. Banyan Street was well known to locals for its steep inclines and dangerous corners. The reported car fire wasn't the first accident emergency crews had been called to on the treacherous gravel roadway.

When the first responders arrived at the fiery scene on that particular moonless night, a small car at the edge of the roadway was engulfed in flames. Standing not far from the blazing inferno was a frantic woman and a man who was trying to console her. The slender brunette said something had gone wrong with her car, a 1964 black Volkswagen Beetle. She said she was on her way home from picking up milk at an all-night market when the car had suddenly veered to the side of the road as if a tire had blown, and then it had burst into flames. Luckily, she had managed to get out, but her husband was still trapped in the burning car. The woman told the officers she had tried to reach him, but his door was locked, so she ran to a nearby residence to ask for help. There, she had asked the homeowner to call the fire department and the family friend who was now standing with her at the side of the road while the Volkswagen continued to burn. Moving quickly, the firefighters worked to get the flames under control, but they already knew it was too late to save the life of the man trapped inside the car. Fortunately, it looked like the woman had escaped without a single burn or scratch.

The distraught lady identified herself as Lucille Miller. She lived at 8488 Bella Vista Drive, just five kilometres from the accident. Mrs. Miller said that she and her husband had three children. And now she would have to go home and break the news to them about their father. "What will I tell the children, when there's nothing left, nothing left in the casket?" she sobbed. "How can I tell them there's nothing left?"

Mrs. Miller was taken home by her friend while firefighters continued to extinguish the fire. Inside the car, slumped across the passenger's seat, they found the badly burned remains of a man who would later be identified as thirty-nine-year-old Gordon Eugene Miller, a local dentist. It was a gruesome scene. The car fire had burned Gordon's body beyond recognition. But in examining the charred wreckage, the firefighters noticed that the car did not appear to have been in an accident of any sort and its gas tank had not ruptured. What had caused the car to burst into flames? Peering into what was left of the back seat, the fire crew discovered a portable gasoline can tipped over and missing its cap. The highway patrol asked the San Bernadino County Sheriff's office to investigate.

What was initially thought to be a tragic accident was beginning to look more suspicious. The police needed to talk to Mrs. Miller. But that wasn't going to happen any time soon because the distraught housewife had already contacted her attorney, Harold Lance. In fact, he was the family friend who had been standing with her at the accident scene, and he was going to make sure that Lucille Miller didn't talk to anyone.

Lucille Marie Maxwell was born on January 17, 1930, in Winnipeg, Manitoba. She was the only child of Gordon and Lily Maxwell, who were both teachers and members of the Seventh-day Adventist Church, whose members did not drink, smoke, wear makeup or jewellery and observed the Sabbath on Saturday. When Lucille was eighteen she enrolled at Walla Walla College in Washington State, the Seventh-day Adventist school where her parents were teaching. While at college Lucille met Gordon Eugene Miller, a handsome, twenty-four-year-old dental student whom everyone called Cork. According to their families, it was love at first sight.

In 1949, Lucille and Gordon were married while he was stationed at Fort Lewis as a medical officer in the US Army. After he was discharged, Gordon set up a private dental practice in Oregon while Lucille stayed home to raise the couple's two young children. In 1957, the Millers moved to Southern California so that Gordon could pursue further education. Though he followed his father and brother into dentistry, he wanted to switch to general medicine and was hoping to attend medical school at Loma Linda University, operated by the Seventh-day Adventists. The family relocated to the newly developed suburb of Alta Loma, where Gordon set up a new dental practice. They moved into a modest home and eventually became a well-liked and respected couple in the growing community.

By 1964, the Millers had three children: fourteen-year-old Debra, ten-year-old Guy and eight-year-old Ronnie. Dr. Miller's dental practice was successful, and it looked as though the family was doing well financially. They had just moved into a brand new custom-built California bungalow on a one-acre lot. This house was twice as big as their last one, and the kids had plenty of room to play. But despite their upward mobility, trouble was brewing in the Millers' fifteen-year marriage.

Gordon was a quiet, introverted man with a good career, nice home and loving family, but he was terribly unhappy. His dreams of becoming a doctor had never materialized, and he told his accountant he was sick of looking into open mouths all day. He had recently been hospitalized with a bleeding ulcer and suffered from bouts of depression and migraine headaches. He was taking drugs that he prescribed to himself and, according to his wife, he had even threatened suicide.

In July of 1964, Lucille had had enough of her husband's mood swings and filed for divorce on the grounds of cruelty. Their suburban California dream had imploded, and the couple were thousands of dollars in debt. But one month later, the Millers reconciled. They started seeing a marriage counsellor and even talked about having a fourth child. By October of that same year, Lucille and Gordon seemed to be back to their normal domestic routine. Gordon was still looking into open mouths and Lucille busied herself with the children's activities and household duties.

Wednesday, October 7, 1964, was just another ordinary day for the Millers in sunny Alta Loma. The temperature reached 102 degrees in San Bernardino County that afternoon, and Lucille spent the day running errands and dealing with the children, who were off school. When Gordon arrived home from work in the late afternoon he was upset because he had hit and killed a German shepherd with the family's Volkswagen. The troubling accident had left a small dent in the front bumper of the car and had triggered another one of Gordon's debilitating migraines. He told Lucille that his head felt "like it had a Mack truck on it." Fortunately for Gordon, Lucille had picked up a refill of his prescription that afternoon, a sedative called Nembutal.

According to Lucille, that evening the couple watched a movie, and when the film ended, around eleven, Gordon asked for some hot chocolate. They were out of milk, so Lucille suggested they drive to the all-night market. Gordon, who was still feeling unwell and groggy from his medication, took a blanket and pillow from the couch and climbed into the passenger seat of the Volkswagen, leaning his head against the window. Lucille reached over to lock his door as she slowly backed down the driveway. It was just after midnight and Gordon Miller would soon be dead.

Three hours later, the fire crew had finally extinguished the car fire on Banyan Street. Photographs were taken of Gordon Miller's charred remains and what was left of the vehicle, including the open gas canister on the back seat. Sheriff Frank Bland sent three homicide detectives to question Lucille, but by the time they arrived at the Miller home they were told that she had been given a sedative by a doctor called in by her attorney. The detectives were told that she had suffered an awful shock and needed to rest. She would not be able to speak with them.

The following morning, the fiery crash that had claimed the life of a local dentist was front-page news across San Bernardino County. Dr. Miller had been well liked by many. How devastating for Mrs. Miller and the couple's three young children. Everyone in the close-knit community was talking about the tragedy, and many felt sorry for the young widow. But it wasn't long before words of sympathy turned into whispers of suspicion when, twelve hours after the car fire, Lucille Miller was arrested.

The police had a lot of questions for Lucille because the evidence at the scene just wasn't matching her original story. After their initial investigation, the police were certain of two things: the Millers' car had not been in an accident, and it had not exploded. The skid marks on the road were much shorter than they normally would be in a loss of control, as Lucille had reported. The car was still in low gear—unusual for a crash—and was dug into the soft shoulder, implying that someone had tried to push the car the rest of the way over the embankment. Also, the empty can of gasoline was lying sideways on the back seat of the car, while two charred milk cartons were still standing upright. Wouldn't they all have fallen over when the car veered and suddenly stopped? A Polaroid camera box also lay undisturbed on the back seat.

To investigators it looked as though the fire had been deliberately set—and if that was true, it meant Dr. Miller had been murdered. The police wanted to know exactly what had happened between approximately 12:30 a.m., when the fire broke out, and 1:50 a.m., when it was reported. But questioning the newly widowed housewife would prove difficult. In an unprecedented move, her newly hired lawyer, Edward Foley, and his team of nine associates had set up camp in the women's section of the county jail, where Lucille was being held. Sitting on a chair outside her cell, each lawyer was taking a four-hour shift because they did not want their client interrogated by the police without a lawyer present. When Lucille finally spoke with investigators the following day, she repeated the story she had told the highway patrol, with a few additional details.

Lucille Miller told the police that she and her husband had been watching TV on the night of October 7 when her husband asked for a hot chocolate. They were out of milk, so they decided to drive to the all-night grocery store to pick some up. Lucille was afraid of the dark, so Gordon agreed to come with her. They left their three children at home, sleeping. Lucille stated that her husband was taking drugs for his migraines, which made him groggy, so she decided to drive. When they were driving back from the store, Lucille said her husband was asleep in the passenger seat, wrapped up in a blanket. She said she was going approximately fifty-five kilometres per hour when the car suddenly pulled sharply to the right. It bounded over a curb and stopped on the soft shoulder. Lucille said she heard her husband groan. He wasn't moving and she assumed he had hit his head when the car jumped the curb—no one wore seat belts in those days. Then the car suddenly burst into flames. She said the flames were coming from the back of the car, which was where the Volkswagen's engine was located. "I jumped out and ran to the passenger door," Lucille said. "But it was locked from inside." She said she broke the window with a rock but was pushed back because of the flames. She said she then tried to wake her husband by poking him with a stick, but he wasn't moving.

Realizing she needed help, she ran approximately a kilometre and a half along the dark gravel road, yelling for anyone, but there were no houses in the deserted neighbourhood and no other cars passed by. She then ran back past the burning car and said she could see her husband engulfed in flames. "He was just black," she said. Then she ran in the other direction until she spotted a house and banged on the door, waking the residents of the home. "Cork is on fire!" she screamed. She asked the couple to call the fire department and then asked them to call a family friend who just happened to be a lawyer.

By the time the emergency crews arrived at the scene of the accident, almost an hour and a half had gone by. It was way too late to save Dr. Miller, and it took the fire crew another hour to extinguish the flames and remove the badly burned body. When asked about the gas canister in the back seat of the car, Lucille said that her husband always insisted on carrying extra fuel as they lived eight kilometres from the nearest service station and he had run out of gas on a few occasions. She and her daughter, Debbie, had purchased the gas just a few days before the accident.

It was a plausible explanation, but the police still weren't convinced of Mrs. Miller's story. An autopsy on Gordon Miller's charred corpse revealed an usually high level of barbiturates in his blood, and it did not appear that he had sustained any other injuries from the supposed car crash.

On Tuesday, October 13, thirty-four-year-old Lucille Marie Miller was formally charged with the murder of her husband, Gordon. For her arraignment, Lucille arrived at the courthouse with a team of nine lawyers, but the bizarre display of legal might did not impress the court. She was denied bail and was barred from attending her husband's funeral later that same day.

|||||||||||

Across town, at the Draper Mortuary Chapel, more than two hundred mourners gathered to pay their final respects to Dr. Gordon Miller, including his three children. A tape recording of the service was made for his imprisoned widow.

While Lucille sat in prison for the next two months, her legal team tried desperately to get the charges dropped and get her home to her children. At the same time, investigators were learning much more about the soft-spoken suburban housewife and mother. The rumour around town was that Mrs. Miller had been having an affair with a prominent local attorney named Arthwell Hayton. In fact, she had bragged about it. But in a strange twist of fate, just six months before Gordon Miller's untimely death, Arthwell's wife had also died suddenly. At the time, it had been reported in the local press that family friend Lucille Miller was the last person to see her alive.

The police were now looking into a second suspicious death related to the unassuming housewife, but Hayton, a strict Seventh-day Adventist, denied any extramarital wrongdoing. Hayton, a former member of the district attorney's office, even held a televised press conference at his San Bernadino law office to publicly deny any romantic link to Lucille Miller, saying she and her husband had just been family friends.

"Would you deny that you were having an affair with Mrs. Miller?" a reporter asked.

"I would deny that there was any romance on my part whatsoever," said the handsome attorney, choosing his words carefully. The widower went on to say that he was shocked and stunned that the police were looking into a possible link between Lucille Miller and his wife's death.

Things were going from bad to worse for Lucille Miller. She had been charged with her husband's murder, and now reports of her suspected infidelity were front-page news all over Southern California. But just before her trial was set to begin, her lawyer had some new information that he hoped would positively impact his client's future: Lucille was three and a half months pregnant with her fourth child. She claimed the child was her deceased husband's. Lucille's lawyer, Edward Foley, was confident that her delicate condition would sway the court into granting her bail and allowing her to be home for Christmas with her other children. But the judge was not won over. The expectant mother would remain behind bars until her trial.

Lucille Miller's trial began on January 11, 1965. It was a typical bright, sunny California day. The line of mostly women outside the San Bernardino courthouse had begun forming before sunrise that morning. It was the most sensational trial to ever take place in the county, and everyone wanted to catch a glimpse of the pretty brunette accused of burning her husband alive. For the modest suburban city, it was hard to believe that one of their own was on trial for a cold-blooded murder. But the small courtroom only had enough room for forty-three spectators, leaving many disappointed. And it wasn't just the people of San Bernardino who were interested in the sensational murder trial—the story had gained attention across the state, and many of Southern California's seasoned crime reporters had set up camp in the town for the duration. Lucille's parents travelled from Oregon to California to support their only child, and seated behind Lucille in the courtroom was Debra Miller, her fourteen-year-old daughter. Debra's brothers were too young to attend.

Flanked by her team of lawyers, Lucille, who had just turned thirty-five, appeared relaxed and composed. Her lawyer had arranged for a hairdresser and a new maternity dress to conceal the growing baby bump on her petite frame. Local newspapers announced that the expectant mother had gained twenty-five pounds in prison. But regardless of her well-coiffed, stoic appearance, Lucille was struggling. She knew that the stakes were very high. The prosecutor had already indicated during a preliminary hearing that he would be seeking the death penalty if she were found guilty.

In his opening remarks, prosecutor Don Turner told the jury that thirty-nine-year-old Gordon "Cork" Miller had been burned alive. The well-liked dentist was murdered in the early hours of October 8, and the person responsible for his death was the defendant sitting in the courtroom, Mrs. Lucille Marie Miller. But why did the pretty housewife want her husband dead? The state would argue that she had been having an affair and wanted out of her troubled marriage. The Millers were heavily in debt and had previously discussed divorce. According to the prosecutor, Lucille Miller wanted more than just her freedom and an alimony cheque. She wanted a higher status in life, which Arthwell Hayton, her lover, could provide. "This is a woman motivated by love and greed," said the prosecutor. It was later discovered that Lucille had even forged her husband's signature on the mortgage documents for their new home. It was a home they couldn't really afford and one that had created more stress for her overwhelmed husband, who suffered from debilitating migraines and depression.

"She wanted more than her husband was providing with his $30,000 yearly salary," said the prosecutor. "And her ticket out was his life insurance." If Dr. Miller died, Lucille would receive $70,000, but if his death appeared to be accidental, under a double indemnity clause in the policy, his widow would receive $140,000. "That's why she had to make his death look like an accident," declared the prosecutor.

It was the state's contention that, on the night in question, Lucille secretly gave her husband an overdose of sedatives in hot chocolate to make him extra drowsy. Then she suggested that they drive to the store to buy more milk. After picking up the milk,

Lucille pulled the family Volkswagen over to the side of Banyan Street. She stopped the car at the highest point in the road. And it was there, the prosecutor said, that Mrs. Miller attempted to push the car over the embankment into a lemon grove below, hoping it would catch on fire. But when she couldn't move the car, she poured gasoline all over the inside of the vehicle and ignited it. Dr. Miller in his drugged state was unable to get out of the car and was burned alive while his pregnant wife watched. "Gordon Miller's death was a cold, calculated, premeditated murder," said the prosecutor, and the state would prove it beyond any reasonable doubt.

In his opening statement, defence attorney Edward Foley told the jury that his client, whom he described as a warm and friendly woman, was completely innocent. He stated that the sheriff's department had made numerous errors in their examination of the accident scene and had rushed to judgment in arresting his client. The evidence would show that the fire had started accidently and that his client had tried desperately to pull her husband from the burning car. Mrs. Miller was a decent, law-abiding wife and mother, said Foley. She needed to be sent home to be with her children, including the one she was expecting.

The first witness called by the defence was Priscilla "Sandy" Slagle, a twenty-three-year-old medical student at Loma Linda University who had lived with the Millers since 1959. Despite their money troubles, Dr. Miller was assisting her financially with her medical studies and she would often babysit the children. Sandy described Dr. Miller as a kind and introverted man who suffered from depression. When questioned about his drug use, she stated that he would often take sedatives that would make him groggy. She said Dr. Miller knew he was addicted and had asked her how he could cut down on using the pills. She had suggested he get professional help. When asked if she had ever heard Dr. Miller threaten suicide, Slagle said yes, on multiple occasions. According to her, Dr. Miller would threaten his wife by saying he was going to go to the mountains and drive his car off a cliff. Whenever this happened, she said that she and Mrs. Miller would hide the car keys from him until he calmed down.

The next witness to testify for the defence was fourteen-year-old Debbie Miller, the oldest of the Miller children. When asked about her parents' marriage, the teenager described a volatile home where her parents fought constantly. She told the court that her dad had moved out once, but returned and reconciled with her mother. Debbie admitted that she was aware that her dad was taking pills for his depression and headaches. She said her mother had confided in her that he was also suicidal, something she admitted was hard for her to understand.

Over the next few days, the defence called several more witnesses who spoke positively of Lucille Miller's character. Her lawyer knew that his client's moral character would be front and centre in the jury's minds as they weighed the evidence that would be presented by the prosecution.

The first witness called by the prosecution was William Snare, an automobile arson expert who had been an investigator for over twenty-six years. He testified that from his examination of the vehicle, he believed that the fire had begun inside the Millers' Volkswagen rather than from a gas leak. "It was deliberately set," said Snare. "Gasoline or some highly volatile fluid was poured over the interior of the car and ignited." Continuing to focus on the car, the prosecution then called two Volkswagen experts to the stand. Both mechanics said they found no deficiency in the steering mechanism of the Millers' car that would have caused it to veer off the road as Lucille Miller had indicated, but that a nail had been found in one of the front tires. Then, in a surprise announcement, the prosecutor advised the court that the sheriff's office had conducted a secret experiment on a car that was identical to the Millers' Volkswagen Beetle. Investigators had gone to a local wrecking yard and torched a Beetle from the inside to determine the fire pattern. The results were almost identical to the charred remains of the Millers' car. The prosecution told the court that the experiment had been filmed, but under strenuous objections from the defence attorney, the judge ruled the film inadmissible. The jury would never see it.

The next witness called by the prosecution was a middle-aged woman who had seen the Millers on the night of the car fire. She stated that she had spotted Mrs. Miller inside the all-night Mayfair Market on the night of October 7, just after midnight. Outside, in the parking lot, she noticed that Lucille Miller was driving and there appeared to be something slumped in the front seat. At the time, she said, she thought it was a bundle of clothing.

Later, on the same day in court, a criminologist for the San Bernardino sheriff's department testified that a toxicological examination of Dr. Miller's vital organs showed enough barbiturates to put a normal man into a coma or a deep sleep. Gordon Miller had sustained no other injuries. He had burned to death.

Finally, on February 4, the prosecution called Arthwell Hayton to the stand. The handsome forty-one-year-old San Bernardino lawyer had previously denied having a romantic relationship with Lucille Miller, but in the intervening months, his story had changed. Now, under oath, he admitted that he and the accused had been secret lovers despite his earlier very public denials. Arthwell said that he and Lucille had known each other for several years. The two couples and their children had been friends and attended the same Seventh-day Adventist church. Their affair began in November 1963, a year before Gordon Miller's death. The secret lovers would check into local hotel rooms and had spent a few weekends together in Palm Springs. According to Mr. Hayton, Lucille Miller had even proposed marriage. But Hayton told Lucille that he had no plans to leave his wife. Apparently, Lucille did not take the news well.

Then, five months after their affair began, Arthwell's wife, Elaine, died suddenly. It was Saturday, April 24, 1964. Arthwell had taken his boat over to Catalina Island that weekend with his eldest son. "When I kissed my wife goodbye, she was her happy, vibrant self," said the widower. He said he called home at nine o'clock on the Friday night but did not talk to his wife because Lucille Miller answered the telephone and said that Elaine was showering. He didn't think much of it at the time because the two women were friends. The next morning, the Haytons' fifteen-year-old daughter found her mother face down in her bed. She was dead. Thirty-six-year-old Elaine Hayton, a registered nurse and a healthy mother of four, had apparently choked to death while under the influence of a heavy dose of barbiturates.

At the time, the local coroner ruled the death an accident, and when Arthwell Hayton flew home from Catalina Island that weekend, a comforting Lucille Miller met him at the airport. After his wife's death, Hayton said, he ended the affair, but Lucille continued to harass him. In the summer of 1964, she apparently called him so frequently that he had to change his telephone number. The calls continued, and when he still refused to see her, he said she began threatening him. According to Arthwell, Lucille threatened to expose their affair to his work colleagues and to their minister. "She said she would ruin me," he said. Alarmed by her threats, he told her he would go to the police if she continued.

The prosecutor then reminded the jury that it was around the same time, in July 1964, that Lucille Miller told her attorney to drop her divorce proceedings, which she had filed a few months earlier. It was at this time that the Millers decided to have a fourth child. In late September, just days before his death, Gordon Miller told his mother that he and Lucille were expecting a new baby.

Under cross-examination by the defence, Hayton was asked if he had ever told the defendant he was in love with her. "No," he replied. "I may have whispered sweet nothings into her ear, but the relationship was never about love." At the end of Arthwell Hayton's testimony, the state rested its case, but the defence had one more witness to call.

Dressed in a smart brown maternity dress, Lucille Miller took the stand. With guidance from her lawyer, she retold the series of events leading up to the death of her husband in the early-morning hours of October 7, 1964. Yes, she admitted that they had marital problems, but with a new baby on the way, they were both hopeful that things would improve. And while she admitted to the affair with Arthwell Hayton, she said she no longer loved him. She loved her husband and wanted to keep her family together. "I didn't kill him," she said.

In his closing remarks, prosecutor Don Turner reminded the jury to simply focus on the evidence and the motives. Reviewing all that had been heard during the seven-week trial, Turner said Lucille Miller had two very strong motives in wanting her husband dead: money and lust. "She was sick of her mentally fragile husband, who only earned $30,000 a year as a dentist," said the prosecutor. "She wanted to be the wife of Arthwell Hayden, a successful attorney." Then, the prosecutor outlined a deliberate effort by Lucille Miller to get rid of her husband and collect the $140,000 double indemnity payout by making his death look like an accident. He told the jury that Gordon Miller was drugged and then burned alive to obliterate any traces of the barbiturates he had been given. "The defendant was concerned about an autopsy," said the prosecutor. "So, she cremated him. If you look at the facts and the evidence, I am convinced you will come back with a verdict of first-degree murder," said the prosecutor. "I know justice will prevail," he added.

In his summation, defence attorney Edward Foley began by urging the jurors to have open minds and to cleanse their hearts of any bias or prejudice. He knew his client's moral character was on trial. "Remember what Christ said of the prostitute at the well," said the lawyer. "'Let him among you who is without sin cast the first stone.'" He reminded the jury that his client was on trial for murder, not adultery. "The commandment with which we are concerned here is 'Thou shalt not kill,'" said Foley. The lawyer characterized Lucille as a woman of human frailty, as expressed in her affair with Arthwell Hayton. And while he said that he did not condone adultery, his client should not be judged for her mistake. He ridiculed the prosecution's contention that the alleged murder was motivated by Lucille Miller's love for Hayton. "I say poppycock, pure and simple," he exclaimed. "Where's the proof?"

"Regardless of the affair, her real love was for her husband and her family," said the defence lawyer. This was evident when she cancelled her divorce plans and agreed to have another child. "Would she want another baby by a man she was planning to kill?" asked Edward Foley. While the prosecution painted Lucille Miller as a diabolical killer, her lawyer asked, "If this was a carefully plotted, fiendish scheme, why would she leave the gas can and cap in the car? That would be the stupidest thing she could do," he added. "You must realize that the prosecution's case is weak and is purely based on speculation. My client's life and liberty hang on speculation." Looking over at his pregnant client, who remained unemotional, Foley said, "Lucille Miller should be acquitted and sent home to her family, so that her baby can be born at home and not in a prison."

Superior Court Judge Edward Fogg instructed the jury that they could return with three possible verdicts: they could find Lucille Miller guilty of first-degree murder, guilty of second-degree murder, or innocent of all charges.

The sensational trial had lasted seven weeks. On Friday, March 5, 1965, after four days of deliberations, the jury of eight women and four men returned with their verdict. "Guilty of murder in the first degree," read the jury foreman. The courtroom erupted.

"Oh my God, no!" cried Lucille as Edward Foley tried to comfort her. Sitting behind her mother, Debbie Miller couldn't believe what she had just heard. "No, no," the distraught teenager cried out. "She didn't do it. I'll never see my mother again!" As the jury filed out of the courtroom, Sandy Slagle, the young medical student who had lived with the Millers, charged towards the jury, yelling, "You're murderers! Every last one of you is a murderer. You know she's innocent!"

The jury had ultimately agreed with prosecutor Don Turner's argument that Lucille had deliberately set fire to the Volkswagen with her drugged husband inside it in order to get out of the marriage and collect on the life insurance. A member of the jury later revealed that the lurid details about Lucille's extramarital affair had no bearing on their deliberations, but they kept coming back to the uncapped gas can found in the back seat of the car.

The jury now had to decide whether the raven-haired widow would be executed in a gas chamber or sentenced to life in prison. A pregnant woman had never been sentenced to death in the state.

Three days after Lucille's conviction, Turner waived his original request for the death penalty and settled for life imprisonment with the possibility of parole. Lucille Miller was remanded to the California Institution for Women at Corona, not far from Alta Loma, where she had once lived with her family in a beautiful new home.

Three months later, on June 6, 1965, Lucille Miller gave birth to a healthy seven-pound baby girl at St. Bernardine's Hospital in San Bernardino while a prison guard stood outside her delivery room. She had petitioned Governor Edmund Brown to have her baby away from the prison. Her daughter Debbie took the baby home from the hospital and named her Kimi Kai. The Miller children were now living with family friend and lawyer Harold Lance and his wife.

Lucille Miller was never charged in the murder of Elaine Hayton. The San Bernardino County District Attorney's Office dropped its investigation into her death, even though an exhumation of Elaine Hayton's body revealed a high level of the same barbiturate found in Gordon Miller's body, and despite the fact that Lucille had been the last person to see Elaine before her death. Arthwell Hayton, the man Lucille loved and apparently killed for, went on to marry his children's much younger Norwegian nanny. Life moved on in the golden country.

In 1967, Lucille Miller lost her last appeal in the United States Supreme Court. Even her new, high-profile defence attorney, F. Lee Bailey, was unable to sway the court's decision. She would spend five more years behind bars before being paroled on May 10, 1972. After leaving prison, Lucille Miller changed her name and moved to Los Angeles to be closer to her children. One year later, she was back in the news when she was arrested for shoplifting.

For iconic writer Joan Didion, the Millers' story wasn't just another sensational tale of a love affair and a murder in the suburbs. For her, it represented California and the idea of perfection that so many couples like the Millers had aspired to. Dreamers of the golden dream who looked west for better lives.

In 1991, twenty-five years after "How Can I Tell Them There's Nothing Left?" was published in the *Saturday Evening Post*, the now famous Didion received a letter that read, "It helped to make you famous but it's my life." It was written by the Millers' eldest daughter, Debra (Debbie) Miller. Five years later, the two women met for the first and only time.

In 2006, Debra, now a retired Los Angeles teacher, wrote a personal essay for the *Los Angeles Times* called "A Mother's Crime." She was only fourteen when her father died and the state convicted her mother of his murder. Finally, at age fifty-six, she was ready to relive those harrowing days.

In her intimate essay, Debra wrote about her unhappy home, where her parents constantly fought behind a closed bedroom door and where her dad was always threatening to leave. "Hide the car keys," her mother would yell when things got really bad. Debra knew her dad was sad and took a lot of pills, but still, she said, nothing prepared her for the moment when he was gone. Had he finally done it? Killed himself? No, it was an accident, her mother told her that fateful October morning in 1964. In that moment, Debra Miller remembered feeling an odd sense of relief. With her dad gone, there would be no more fighting. "In my mind I had created a whole new better life for all of us," she wrote. "I loved my daddy. It wasn't like I was glad he was dead but if I'd had to pick, I would have picked her to die."

According to Deborah, her mother died of breast cancer in 1986, broken and estranged from her children. She was fifty-six years old.

# 11 BLACK WIDOW

## THE MANY LIES OF EVELYN DICK

Eight-year-old Faith Reed loved hanging out with her older brother David, who was eleven. They were part of a whole gang of kids from their neighbourhood who often played on the street or went exploring. It was 1946 in Hamilton, Ontario, a blue-collar town supported by steel mills and factories.

On this particular cool spring morning in March, David and Faith were meeting up with the Weaver brothers, Fred, Robert and Jimmie. The five young friends planned a picnic outing to Albion Falls, a well-known spot located a few kilometres east of the city on Hamilton Mountain. The kids took a bus to the top and got off on Mountain Brow Road. They walked along the edge of the road for a while, then two of the Weaver boys headed down a steep hill. Grabbing onto the underbrush to keep from slipping, they made their way down the embankment. Then they spotted something lying under some fallen trees and brush.

"What's that?" said one of the boys.

It looked like a dead pig, but when the boys got closer, they noticed bloodied clothing. The Weaver boys ran back up the hill, screaming that they had found a dead man. The terrified kids formed a human chain in the hope of stopping a passing car. Eventually, a man and his wife pulled over and the kids assured the man it wasn't a prank. The man got out of his car and headed down the hill. He soon discovered the children weren't lying.

When the Ontario Provincial Police arrived on the scene at eleven o'clock that morning, they confirmed the discovery of a human body missing its head, arms and legs. When they turned the torso over, they discovered two bullet holes in the chest, and it also looked like someone had tried to cut the body in half.

Three days later, the torso was identified as John Dick, a thirty-nine-year-old Russian immigrant and Hamilton streetcar conductor who had been reported missing. And it didn't take long for the police to zero in on a prime suspect: John Dick's beautiful new wife, Evelyn.

Evelyn Dick (née MacLean) was born on October 13, 1920, in Beamsville, Ontario, to Scottish immigrants Donald and Alexandra MacLean. A year after Evelyn's birth, the family moved to Hamilton, an industrial city on the western edge of Lake Ontario. The MacLeans moved into a small red-brick house at 214 Rosslyn Avenue in the city's south end.

As an only child, Evelyn was overindulged by her mother and was not allowed to play with neighbourhood kids. Evelyn was sent to an exclusive all-girls private school and was always impeccably dressed in fur coats and expensive jewellery. Many wondered how her parents could shower their only daughter with so many luxuries, given Donald MacLean's workingman's salary with the Hamilton Street Railway. Although other girls envied Evelyn's fashions, they were not inclined to befriend the girl from the wrong side of the tracks. But what Evelyn lacked in female friendships, she made up for with the opposite sex.

By the age of sixteen, men around Hamilton were beginning to take notice of the sultry-eyed beauty, and she became a quick study in how to manipulate her many admirers. As a rebellious teenager, Evelyn began spending time away from school and was often seen in the company of older men from Hamilton and Toronto.

After graduating from high school, Evelyn continued to seek the affections of wealthy, influential men who provided her with a comfortable lifestyle. Rumours began to circulate around town that she was a paid escort. She apparently had a list of her customers—a little black book with a record of her (mostly married) lovers. It was alleged to contain the names of some very prominent Hamiltonians, including lawyers, store owners, financial heavyweights, and even a judge's son. That little black book may have also contained other damning information when, on July 10, 1942, at the age of twenty-two, Evelyn gave birth to a baby girl she named Heather Maria White. A baby born out of wedlock in the 1940s was quite the scandal. But even before the baby was born, Evelyn had devised a ploy to avoid the gossip and stigma attached to being an unwed mother. She simply created a husband for herself. Evelyn's pretend spouse was Norman White, who was proudly serving in the American navy. No one ever recalled meeting the sailor, and Evelyn and her newborn daughter returned to live with her parents at their Rosslyn Avenue home.

After Heather was born, Evelyn continued dating, and one year later she gave birth to another daughter, but the baby was stillborn. And then, eleven months later, Evelyn was pregnant again. She maintained that her fake husband, Norman White, was the father. When Evelyn's father found out about her third pregnancy, he was livid. He didn't want any more children living in his home. Evelyn found a vacancy at the exclusive Henson Park apartments at 316 James Street South in Hamilton. But she had a problem: she had one child, and another one on the way, with no visible husband. So, Evelyn came up with another lie. She told the owner of the building that she was pregnant with her second child but that the baby was stillborn and she would be going to the hospital to have it delivered. The building owner felt sorry for the young mother and rented her the apartment.

On September 5, 1944, Evelyn gave birth to a healthy nine-pound baby boy at Mountain General Hospital. She registered the baby's name as Peter David White. Evelyn's mother, Alexandra, visited her healthy new grandson five days after his birth. She brought a large beige suitcase with some clothing for Evelyn and a beautiful white dress, woollen jacket and booties for the baby. A few days later, a taxi pulled up outside the MacLean house on Rosslyn Avenue. Inside it was Evelyn, carrying the suitcase her mother had brought her in the hospital, but nothing else. She did not have the baby. Evelyn told her mother she'd left him with the Children's Aid Society and had agreed to put him up for adoption. Mrs. MacLean blamed her husband for Evelyn's decision.

A short time later, Evelyn moved into her new apartment and resumed her busy social life. But it wasn't long before her mother moved in with her. Her parents' marriage had finally disintegrated after Alexandra MacLean grew tired of Donald's alcoholic abuse. But it turned out that matrimony was on the horizon for someone else in the family. In the fall of 1945, Evelyn announced she was getting married. Her fiancé's name was John Dick.

John Dick was born on May 25, 1906, in New Halbstadt, Russia. In 1924, at the age of eighteen, he immigrated to Canada with his family and settled in the Beamsville area. The Dick family were part of a large number of German-speaking Mennonites who fled the Russian revolution and came to Canada between 1922 and 1930. John eventually moved to Hamilton, where he worked at various jobs before landing a steady position with the Hamilton Street Railway as a streetcar operator.

As a man in his late thirties, John was living the life of a carefree bachelor. He enjoyed drinking with his friends at the local hotels and definitely had an eye for the ladies. He just hadn't met the right girl to settle down with. But that was about to change. On a hot day in late August of 1945, while driving his regular route, an attractive young woman stepped onto John's streetcar. The dark-haired beauty introduced herself as Evelyn White. She told John she was a widow with one child. After their first meeting, Evelyn became a regular on John's streetcar, and soon the two were dating. Three months later, John announced to his family that he was getting married. But while John Dick was excited about putting his bachelor days behind him, his bride-to-be wasn't quite ready to give up her busy social life, and she already had another man in her sights.

William (Bill) Bohozuk was a tall, handsome athlete. He was an accomplished oarsman with the Leander Boat Club in Hamilton. Bill worked at the Dominion Foundry and lived with his family at 21 Picton Street. Other than rowing, he liked cars, fine clothing, horses and pretty women. And it was at a racetrack in 1944 that Bill met an attractive widow named Helen Kleean Mitchell. They began dating, and one day Helen introduced him to another young widow she had known for several years. Her name was Evelyn White. Bill thought the woman was pretty, but at the time he only had eyes for Helen. A month after their chance meeting with Evelyn, Bill and Helen got married. But just three months after their wedding, Helen suddenly packed up and left. Bill was devastated, but a few months later he happened to run into Evelyn again. After talking for a while, the young widow handed Bill her phone number. "Call me sometime," she said. Bill called many times over the next few weeks, but never got an answer. It would be several months before he ran into Evelyn again, but this time he wasn't going to let her get away without agreeing to go on a date with him. A decision he would end up regretting for the rest of his life.

|||||||||

On the afternoon of October 4, 1945, twenty-four-year-old Evelyn MacLean married John Dick, who was fifteen years her senior. The wedding was a simple affair. Evelyn's parents refused to attend the ceremony, feeling that John was not suitable for their daughter. He was a foreigner and a streetcar operator with a paltry income. He did not have the class or pocketbook of the husband Alexandra MacLean desired for her daughter.

Two weeks after her wedding, Evelyn ran into Bill Bohozuk again and agreed to go for drinks. She told him her (made-up) naval husband had been killed in the war but failed to mention she had just gotten married to another man. Evelyn and Bill agreed to meet again the following Sunday. While Evelyn was planning her next date with Bill, her new husband, John, was desperately trying to find a home for himself and his new bride. But he had one small problem: he had no money. When the rooming house he was living in went up for sale, John approached Evelyn and her mother for a down payment. But both women refused to lend him the money, and for Evelyn's mother, this was further proof that John Dick was a poor choice for a husband.

But John's money woes weren't his only problem. It didn't take him long to figure out that Evelyn was sleeping with another man. She had been seen around town with Bill Bohozuk. John confronted Bohozuk at his workplace and told him to stay away from his wife. "Wife?" said a confused and surprised Bill. He had no idea she was married. Bill promptly cut off all communication with Evelyn. But, unfortunately for the handsome oarsman, he hadn't seen the last of Mrs. Dick.


With her love life temporarily interrupted, Evelyn turned her attention back to her living situation and purchased a house in

Hamilton for $6,300. For a woman who had never held a job, she was always flush with cash. On October 31, 1945, Evelyn, her mother and her daughter moved from the Henson Park apartment into a three-storey brick house at 32 Carrick Avenue. John Dick was there to meet them and, much to her mother's displeasure, Evelyn allowed her husband to move in with them. But a happy home life was not in the cards for the newlyweds. While John initially helped with cleaning and repairs around the house, when he found out his name had been excluded from the mortgage and title to the home, he refused to do any further work in the house or contribute financially. A few weeks after moving into the Carrick Avenue house, Evelyn went to a lawyer to get a separation agreement. But when she presented it to John, he refused to sign. He was determined to make his marriage work. John and Evelyn spent Christmas of 1945 together, but as far as Evelyn was concerned, their marriage was over.

In the new year, John moved in with his cousin Alex Kammerer. But every day before work, he would stake out Evelyn's house. He wanted to know if she was still seeing Bill Bohozuk. Or if there was someone else. John's obsession with getting his wife back eventually caused problems at work. He had four traffic accidents while driving his streetcar route, and his boss threatened to fire him if his performance didn't improve. And making his work life even worse was having to deal with Evelyn's father, Donald MacLean, who also worked at the Hamilton Street Railway. MacLean hated John Dick and was happy to tell anyone who would listen. According to Evelyn's father, his daughter had married a scrounger and a scoundrel.

Eventually the arguing and tension between Donald MacLean and John Dick became unbearable for their work colleagues. Their supervisor, Raymond Castle, threatened them both with dismissal if they couldn't keep their domestic issues out of the office. Relations between the two men seemed to quiet down, but a few weeks later, Castle received a call from the Hamilton police. Apparently, Donald had threatened to shoot John. Castle called MacLean into his office to ask him about the threat, but he denied it, saying he didn't even own a gun.

What neither the police nor Castle knew at the time was that John Dick had confronted his father-in-law and threatened to expose him unless MacLean convinced Evelyn to stay with him. John knew that MacLean was stealing cash and used bus tickets from the company, and had been for years. This was how the MacLeans had afforded so many luxuries for their daughter while she was growing up. And, in fact, it was Evelyn who told John all about her father's scheme. Maclean had stolen the combination to the cashier's vault and would pilfer the cash boxes before his boss arrived each morning. Then he would resell the used bus tickets. Donald MacLean was furious and threatened to kill Dick if he ever said anything.

At the end of January 1946, John Dick contacted the Hamilton police to report his father-in-law's threat. Just five weeks later, on Wednesday, March 6, 1946, he failed to show up for work.

Ten days after John Dick was a no-show at his work, five young kids out for a hike to Albion Falls stumbled upon a human torso on Hamilton Mountain. The torso was clothed in a one-piece underwear garment—size 44, according to the label—with the legs and arms cut off where the limbs of the body had been severed. Sergeant Carl Farrow of the OPP noted that the torso was frozen with no decomposition, and it appeared that all the blood had been drained from the remains. The torso was photographed at the hillside site, then was hauled up the escarpment using a rope and a basket. None of the missing body parts were found in the area, leading the police to assume that the murder had taken place somewhere else. Hamilton Mountain was just the dumping ground.

Later that Saturday, Inspector Charles Wood of the OPP's Criminal Investigation Branch arrived from Toronto to take charge of the investigation. An official autopsy was scheduled for Monday, March 18, but until then, Inspector Wood needed to try to figure out whose torso was lying in the city morgue.

News of the gruesome discovery travelled fast throughout the working-class city, and this wasn't the first time some residents had heard about a body dumped on Hamilton Mountain. Hamilton was a rough, blue-collar town with big-city problems like prostitution, illegal gambling, drug trafficking and a strong Mafia presence. So, the discovery of a decapitated body led to all sorts of speculation. Was it a mob hit? Maybe it was the remains of reputed mobster Rocco Perri, known as "king of the bootleggers," who had disappeared two years earlier. His wife, Bessie, had been shot to death in 1930, and local journalists speculated that maybe Rocco had finally met his end, too.

The day after the story of the torso hit the newspapers, an employee of the Hamilton Works Department contacted the police to tell them that he and his co-worker had come across a man's blood-soaked dress shirt near Mountain Brow Road on March 7. He told the police the arms of the shirt appeared to have been cut off, and there was a lot of dried blood around the collar. Not sure what to make of it at the time, the workmen kicked it into the ditch and drove away. Later that day, the police retrieved the blue pinstriped shirt from where it had been left by the workmen. The garment offered a clue as to when the murder had taken place—sometime before March 7—but didn't give them any further information as to who it belonged to. They had a bloody shirt and a man's dismembered remains, but what they really needed was an identity.

The day before the body was found, Raymond Castle had called the police to report one of his streetcar operators missing. John

Dick hadn't been to work since March 6. Castle gave the police an address on Carrick Avenue—he said it was the home Dick had shared with his wife, Evelyn, until their separation two months earlier.

John Dick's supervisor wasn't the only person looking for him. John's cousin, Alex Kammerer, was also concerned about his whereabouts. Initially, he thought John might be visiting his mother and sisters in Vineland. But no one in the family had seen or heard from John in a few weeks, and they feared the worst.

On the morning of March 18, Dr. William J. Deadman performed a post-mortem examination on the torso that had been discovered two days earlier. The doctor, aptly named for his position, was one of Canada's first forensic pathologists. Also in attendance at the autopsy were Inspector Charles Wood of the provincial police and Detective Sergeant-Clarence Preston of the Hamilton police—this would be a joint investigation between the two forces.

Deadman estimated that the victim had died ten to fourteen days earlier, and that the torso belonged to a fair-skinned male, weighing approximately 185 pounds, standing between five foot ten and five foot eleven, and forty to forty-five years old.

The victim's genitals were intact, but the body had one undescended testicle. Dr. Deadman concluded that the head, arms and legs had been crudely hacked off in an amateur way with a saw rather than with a sharp cutting instrument. And there was a ragged cut, about thirty centimetres long, just above the belly button, indicating that someone tried to cut the body in half but had abandoned the grisly task before it was completed. There were two gunshot wounds—one entry, and one exit wound above the right nipple caused by a .32-calibre bullet—but they appeared to be superficial and non-fatal. In his summary, Dr. Deadman wrote, "The cause of death cannot be determined by the post-mortem examination, but death may have been caused by injury to the missing head."

On Tuesday, March 19, John and Jake Wall, two brothers married to John Dick's sisters, arrived in Hamilton to help search for their missing brother-in-law. But his whereabouts would not remain a mystery for long. The night before, Alex Kammerer had contacted the police when he heard a body had been found on Hamilton Mountain. When he described John Dick, the police suggested the remains were likely those of his cousin. The next morning, the Wall brothers and Kammerer arrived at the city morgue. They were ill prepared for what they were about to see. Lying on a metal table was the bloodless midsection of a human body with jagged, fleshy stumps where the head and limbs had once been. Jacob Wall took one look and ran out of the room. John Wall immediately recognized the torso.

Three days after the gruesome discovery, the police were able to confirm the identity of the headless torso. It was the missing thirty-nine-year-old streetcar operator, John Dick. Now they needed to find out who had murdered him. The Wall brothers and Alex Kammerer did not hesitate to point the finger directly at one person: Evelyn Dick, the murdered man's estranged wife.

That same day, Evelyn Dick and her parents were sitting down for a leisurely lunch when there was a knock at the door. It was four police officers with a search warrant. Evelyn did not appear concerned by their arrival. Asked when she had last seen her husband, she replied, "March 4." Inspector Wood then advised her that the torso discovered on Hamilton Mountain had been identified as John Dick. "Don't look at me, I don't know anything about it," she exclaimed. The seasoned detective was shocked by her reaction. "Get your coat on," Wood said to Evelyn. They were taking her in for questioning. Donald MacLean asked if he could accompany his daughter. The police agreed. They had some questions for him as well.

When they arrived at the police station, Evelyn and her father were separated. Inspector Wood began the interview with Evelyn. After considerable back and forth, she admitted that she had borrowed a car from a friend on Wednesday, March 6, the last day John Dick was seen alive. She said she did some shopping and returned the car later that day.

Bill Landeg owned the Grafton Street Garage, and he would often lend Evelyn his car. It was a black 1938 eight-cylinder Packard sedan. When questioned by the police, Landeg had no trouble remembering the last day Evelyn had the car, because she had returned it damaged. The front running board was bent, the car was covered in mud, and when he got into the car, he noticed a dark, wet spot on the front seat. Touching it, he realized it was blood. But Evelyn had left him a note, explaining that the blood was from her daughter, who had cut her face. She promised to replace the seat cover and a missing blanket.

As the interview at the police station continued, Evelyn said she knew nothing about her husband's demise but suggested she could provide a motive for his murder. She told the detectives that her husband had been seeing other women—married women. And in fact, an angry husband had come to her house, looking for John. The man told Evelyn that John was seeing his wife, and if he didn't stop, he was going to "fix him." Evelyn said the man was Italian, so she understood what "fix him" meant.

Evelyn reiterated that she had gone shopping on March 6 and had dropped the Packard off at the garage at approximately 5 p.m. before returning home. But then, a few hours into the interview, there was more to her story. Shortly after getting home that evening, Evelyn said she received a call from someone she described as "a gangster from Windsor." The man told her John Dick had gotten a friend's wife pregnant, so he had been hired to "put John out of business." According to Evelyn, the gangster on the phone demanded that she drive to a rendezvous point to meet him. Naturally, Evelyn did as she was told and went to meet the stranger. But when she arrived at the designated spot, there were two men. One stayed in his car while the other approached her, dragging a large, heavy sack. The man told her he needed to get rid of the sack and threw it in the front seat of the Packard she had borrowed from Bill Landeg.

"Did he tell you what was in the sack?" asked Detective Wood.

"Yes," said Evelyn matter-of-factly. He said it was John.

The gangster then instructed her to drive towards Albion Falls on Hamilton Mountain. When they reached Mountain Brow Road, he told her to pull over. Then he pulled the sack out of the car, removed John's body (or what was left of it) and threw it over the embankment. The gangster threw the front seat covers out of the car, along with John's shirt, as they drove back down the mountain. Then he instructed Evelyn to drop him off at the Royal Connaught Hotel.

The two seasoned detectives weren't quite sure what to make of Mrs. Dick's bizarre story. Wood asked Evelyn why gangsters would have involved her if they had already killed her husband and cut up his body. Evelyn had no plausible answer, but she stuck to her story. She described the man who had dumped John Dick's torso as a short, stocky Italian with a slight foreign accent. Inspector Wood had finally heard enough.

"Mrs. Dick, did you take any part in the murder of your husband?"

"No, no," replied Evelyn. "I don't know nothing about where his legs, arms or hands are."

Finally, Evelyn decided she had said enough and told the detectives she was afraid that the Italians might come after her if she talked too much. They might put a bomb under her house. But the detectives wanted to keep Evelyn talking and they needed more time. While she was sitting in the interview room, chain-smoking and eating chocolate, the police were gathering crucial evidence. Bill Landeg's Packard was impounded and brought to the police garage. And other officers were searching Evelyn's Carrick Avenue house and Donald MacLean's home on Rosslyn Avenue.

At Evelyn's home, they found the blanket that was missing from the Packard, a gold watch chain belonging to John Dick, and the dress Evelyn said she was wearing the night John was killed by the Italians. At Donald MacLean's house, the police found a .32-calibre Harrington & Richardson revolver hidden in a drawer.

Later that afternoon, Inspector Wood asked Evelyn if she would take a drive up the mountain to point out where John Dick's torso had been discarded and where the other items had been thrown out of the car. Evelyn was happy to help. When they got to the intersection of Mountain Brow Road and Flock Road, Evelyn told the detectives that that was where the gangster had dumped John's remains. But suddenly she had a new detail: the gangster's name was Tony Romanelli.

The detectives still couldn't believe what they were hearing. Did Evelyn really think she could charm her way out of a murder charge with such a ridiculous story? Did she think the cops were that dumb? When they returned to the station, the investigators noted that Evelyn was in good spirits. But when she was told she would be spending the night in jail, her mood quickly soured. The following day, Evelyn was remanded into custody for one week.

While Evelyn sat behind bars at the Barton Street jail, the police continued their investigation. Dr. Deadman examined the Packard sedan and immediately noticed several stains in the car that "appeared to be blood." When the doctor looked in the back of the car, he noticed something jammed in the corner between the seat and the door frame. It was a man's necktie that was still tied and bloodstained. When shown the tie, Bill Landeg suddenly remembered something he hadn't told the police. On the day after

Evelyn returned the car, he found a man's sweater in the back seat. It was a blue, sleeveless pullover with a couple of holes in the front and a tear in the back. Landeg assumed the dark reddish stains on the sweater were car oil. Not knowing whose it was, he tossed it onto the floor of the garage and forgot about it. But luckily, it was still there. When the police examined the sweater, the stains were confirmed to be blood type O, the same type as John Dick's. The evidence against the young widow was starting to pile up.

During the search of Evelyn's home, the police had also found a purse belonging to her. Inside, there was a small snapshot of a handsome, husky, well-built man. In the attic, they found two more photographs of the same man. But who was he? They soon learned that he was Bill Bohozuk, a well-known Hamilton oarsman and bachelor about town. His name was also found on a scrap of paper amongst John Dick's possessions. What was his connection to Mr. and Mrs. Dick?

The police decided to pay Bohozuk a friendly visit, but when a search of his home turned up a .32-calibre revolver—the same calibre that John Dick had been shot with—they suddenly had more questions for the Hamilton athlete. Little did the police know that, by bringing Bill Bohozuk into the police station, they were handing Evelyn Dick the basis for her next story.

While Evelyn sat at the police station, waiting to sign her statement from the previous day, the one about the hired hit man named Tony Romanelli, she learned that her ex-lover Bill Bohozuk had been brought in for questioning. She soon wanted to amend her statement. Evelyn proceeded to tell Inspector Wood and Sergeant Preston that Bill had borrowed $200 from her for a job he was arranging.

"What kind of job?" asked Inspector Wood.

"For John to be fixed," replied Evelyn.

According to Evelyn, Bill wanted John dead because John had embarrassed him by confronting him at work about sleeping with his wife. The $200 was a down payment for the mobsters in Windsor who were going to do the job. But Bill eventually returned the money, saying the Italians had upped their price and the hit was just too expensive.

But no sooner had Evelyn implicated her ex-boyfriend in the murder of her husband than she reverted to her previous story—this time, with more details. According to her, the Windsor gangsters met John Dick for a drink at the King George Hotel on the afternoon of March 6. Then they invited him to go for a drive up Hamilton Mountain, where they pulled over in a secluded area and consumed more alcohol. An argument ensued and, according to Evelyn, Romanelli let him have it.

"What do you mean?" asked Inspector Wood.

"One shot in the back of the neck and one through the right eyeball," said Evelyn.

Then, according to Mrs. Dick, the two gangsters took John's body to a house in the north end of the city, cut it up and burned the head, arms and legs in a furnace. But if Evelyn wasn't there when John Dick was killed, how did she know all these details? According to the talkative widow, Tony Romanelli told her the whole sordid story when she met him later that day to dispose of John's remains back up on Hamilton Mountain. And, just to conclude, in case the police weren't sure where this new narrative was going, Romanelli told Evelyn it was Bill Bohozuk who paid him to get rid of John Dick.

The police were starting to put a timeline together of the day John Dick disappeared, and Evelyn's various stories just weren't matching up. Witnesses saw Evelyn trying to back the Packard into her garage the afternoon John Dick disappeared. Were parts of John's body in that car when Evelyn was seen behind the wheel? The police needed to pay another visit to the house on Carrick Avenue.

On the morning of Thursday, March 21, Wood and Preston arrived at Evelyn Dick's house. Evelyn's mother spoke with Wood in the living room while Preston looked around. In the attic, Preston noticed a large trunk that had been locked the last time he searched the house. But now, it looked as though someone had broken open the lock. He looked inside and saw some bath towels, old clothing and a few books. When questioned about the trunk in the attic, Alexandra MacLean told the sergeant that her husband, Donald, had broken into it the night before. According to Mrs. MacLean, her estranged husband had shown up drunk, and when he found out the police had searched the attic, he rushed up there. He then asked her for a hammer and screwdriver to pry open the lock on the trunk, but she didn't see if he had removed anything from it.

Preston made note of the trunk and continued to search the rest of the house. Taking the stairs down to the basement, Preston noticed a bushel basket containing ashes as well as a small pile of ashes on the floor. Dark stains on the basket looked like blood. Preston carried the basket out to the garage, where he dumped the ashes on the cement floor and grabbed a nearby rake to spread them out. Mixed in with the dusty grey particles, the sergeant spotted small white fragments. He opened the garage doors to allow light in and saw more white bits catching the light. Then, walking towards the driveway, he could see more ashes and more white fragments. Bending down, he picked something up. It was a human tooth. Preston quickly realized he was standing right in the middle of a crime scene.

Later that same afternoon, Dr. Deadman and his assistant arrived at the Carrick Avenue address to assist the police in gathering the disturbing evidence. They found several more pieces of what appeared to be bone material and teeth fragments. All of the ashes from the basement, garage and driveway were collected and sent to the city morgue, where they would be sifted and sorted.

After returning to the police station that evening, Wood and Preston reviewed their notes. They were sure they had found some of John Dick's burned remains, thereby further implicating Evelyn in her husband's murder, but something was still bothering Sergeant Preston: that trunk in the attic. Why did Donald MacLean break it open, and what did he remove? The two detectives decided that a further search of the Carrick Avenue house would be conducted the following day.

On Friday, March 22, Detective John Freeborn, a twenty-six-year veteran of the Hamilton police force, was assigned to accompany two OPP officers to conduct another search of Evelyn Dick's house. It was a routine search, the kind the detective had conducted many times in his career, but this was a day that he and the other two officers would never forget.

When they searched the tidy house, they found several items of interest. In Evelyn's bedroom they found a human tooth in a purse and man's gold watch chain. The watch appeared to have bloodstains on it. Heading up to the attic, they noticed several unlocked trunks and old suitcases. But then Freeborn noticed a beige suitcase in the corner of the attic. It was locked. Freeborn didn't know it at the time, but it was the suitcase Evelyn's mother had brought to the hospital when Evelyn gave birth to her son.

Detective Freeborn brought the suitcase down from the attic. It was very heavy. He pried open the lock with a screwdriver and was immediately taken aback by a strong, foul odour. Inside the suitcase was a burlap bag covering a wicker basket, and inside the basket was a cement-filled cardboard box with pieces of clothing protruding through the cement. Freeborn had no idea what he had just discovered, but he knew he needed to get it to the police station right away. On his way out of the house, Freeborn asked

Alexandra MacLean who the suitcase belonged to. "Evelyn," she replied.

After the discovery of the suitcase at Evelyn's home, the police decided to search Donald MacLean's house again. They had already found a .32-calibre handgun there, and this time they discovered a gun locker in the attic. An interesting find, since MacLean claimed he didn't own any guns. In the locker, they found two shotguns and two rifles. But even more interesting than the guns was an envelope full of cash—over $4,000. They also discovered bags full of used streetcar and bus tickets—26,000 of them, to be precise.

The police made some other disturbing discoveries. Beneath a workbench in the basement, they found a pair of muddy black oxford shoes with what appeared to be bloodstains on them. There was also a butcher's knife with a thirty-eight-centimetre blade and a small carpenter's strip saw. The shoes were later identified as belonging to John Dick.

Later that day, the suitcase found in Evelyn's attic was photographed and reopened by the pathologist, Dr. Deadman. When he chiselled away the cement, it revealed a shopping bag. Beneath the shopping bag, stuck to the cement, was a khaki-coloured skirt with a waistband that bore a name tag: E. MacLean, 1941. This was later identified as part of the Red Cross uniform Evelyn had purchased to impress the local military men. And inside the shopping bag? The partially mummified remains of a newborn baby boy. The baby was fully clothed in a diaper, a cotton shirt, an infant's dress and a knitted wool sweater. Decomposition was so advanced that the left foot and ankle were missing. The pathologist initially wondered if the baby had died a natural death shortly after birth, but that possibility was quickly excluded when he saw the heavy string looped around the baby's neck. The newborn infant had been strangled. Now the police had two murders on their hands.

||||||||||

The dead infant in the suitcase was quickly identified as Peter David White, the healthy son Evelyn had given birth to eighteen months prior, in September 1944. Evelyn left the hospital with the baby and he was never seen again. But before confronting Evelyn about the horrific discovery, Inspector Wood and Sergeant Preston wanted to question her about the human bone fragments found in the ashes in her basement and driveway. Evelyn was brought to the police station from the Barton Street jail and told what the police had uncovered at her home. Without seeming surprised or concerned, she informed the police she would now finally tell them the whole story—and it was a continuation of the previous one, in which she blamed her ex-lover Bill Bohozuk for the murder of John Dick.

Wood then informed Evelyn that the body of a baby boy encased in cement had been found in a suitcase in her attic. Without batting an eyelash, she told the inspector her lawyer told her not to say anything. Later, after Wood left the room, Evelyn informed Preston that she did indeed have something to say about the baby in the attic. She knew who killed him. It was Bill Bohozuk.

Preston wasn't surprised that Evelyn was immediately pointing the finger at someone else. But before he could question her any further, their interview was interrupted by her lawyer, who instructed Evelyn to say nothing further. The police had heard more than enough from Evelyn Dick, and they could see how she was changing her story each time new evidence was uncovered. But regardless of her many contradictory statements, the police had collected valuable physical evidence, and this evidence was going to tell them the truth about what had happened to John Dick. It was obvious to the police that he had been murdered in the Packard sedan that Evelyn borrowed, and the body parts removed from John's torso had been burned at Evelyn's house, with the ashes then spread out in the garage and driveway. The physical evidence was clear, but it still didn't tell the police who killed John Dick and then dismembered him. His estranged wife was certainly involved, but how?

On Tuesday, March 26, ten days after John Dick's torso was discovered on Hamilton Mountain, his attractive widow, Evelyn, was charged with his murder. Asked if she had anything to say, she admitted that the first two statements she had given the police were false, but her third one had been the truth. She wanted to finish her last statement, but her lawyer was very direct with her and warned her to stop talking. That seemed difficult for Evelyn, and before she was escorted back to the Barton Street jail, she asked Inspector Wood one final question: When would they be charging Bill Bohozuk with murder?

Three days later, Bohozuk was also charged with the murder of John Dick. And as he and Evelyn stood in front of the same magistrate at the Hamilton Courthouse, they were also jointly charged with the murder of Peter David White, Evelyn's newborn son.


While Evelyn Dick and Bill Bohozuk sat in jail, awaiting their preliminary hearings, the police continued their investigation. Having confirmed that the bloodied shoes they discovered at Donald MacLean's house were indeed John Dick's, they returned once again to the cellar of the house at 214 Rosslyn Avenue. Using a powerful searchlight, they discovered a bullet-sized hole in a furnace pipe and another in a large wooden box. Moving the box, they found a spent .32-calibre bullet on the floor. Donald MacLean had already been charged with stealing from his employer and was out on bail, but Evelyn would soon change that.

From her jail cell, Evelyn asked to speak with Sergeant Preston. She had another question. This time, she wanted to know when the police were going to arrest her father.

The detective asked why.

"Because he loaned Bohozuk the gun," said Evelyn. She went on to further implicate her father by saying he was the one who paid Bohozuk to get rid of John. "My father hated John's guts," she added.

On Monday, April 15, Donald MacLean was charged with John Dick's murder. But as he stood in the prisoner's dock, waiting to hear the charges against him, the stocky Scotsman was not alone. Evelyn's mother, Alexandra MacLean, stood beside her estranged husband—and was also charged with murder.

On the morning of April 24, 1946, a large group of spectators gathered at the Barton Street jail to catch a glimpse of the four co-accused. Hundreds more waited at the courthouse, hoping to get a seat inside the small courtroom for the preliminary hearing. Dozens of newsmen and photographers had also descended upon the city to report on what was shaping up to be a sensational murder trial. For the next six months, every aspect of the case, including Evelyn Dick's courtroom fashions, would be splashed across the front page of every major newspaper in Canada and even south of the border.

On the first day of the preliminary hearing, Crown Attorney Harvey McCulloch proceeded with the charges against Bill Bohozuk and Evelyn Dick on the murder of her newborn baby. At first, Evelyn refused to testify against Bohozuk, but when the judge threatened to find her in contempt of court, she said that Bill was the father of the dead baby and that he had strangled it. Bohozuk's lawyer knew there was no other evidence against his client other than Evelyn's wild accusations. He knew she was lying. He then proceeded to ask her about other men she had slept with. Wasn't it a fact that she'd had intercourse with multiple men? "Only a few," stated Evelyn. But the lawyer pressed on. He wanted names. "Bill Bohozuk," replied Evelyn. And who else? the lawyer demanded.

"The judge's son," said Evelyn calmly.

There was a stunned silence in the courtroom. Evelyn Dick had just admitted to sleeping with the presiding judge's son. But even that startling admission wasn't enough for Bohozuk's lawyer. He then proceeded to list the names of other prominent Hamilton men. Had Evelyn's little black book of secrets been exposed? To say the least, the judge was not amused.

Bohozuk's lawyer then accused Evelyn of lying about the father of her children by inventing a military husband, Norman White. She didn't want people knowing her children were born out of wedlock—or, was she covering up something even more sinister? Bohozuk's lawyer suggested that Evelyn was having an incestuous relationship with her father, resulting in the pregnancy. Evelyn emphatically denied the accusation.

Despite other theories and no real evidence tying Bill Bohozuk to the murder of Evelyn's infant son, the judge decided that the twenty-seven-year-old oarsman would stand trial for the murder of the baby. Bohozuk and his lawyer were stunned. How could this be possible? they wondered. He'd had nothing to do with the creation or the demise of Evelyn Dick's baby. He'd been railroaded! But for the normally confident and carefree athlete, his nightmare was just beginning.

The following day, Evelyn was back in the witness box. Sticking to the last story she gave the police, she testified that Bill Bohozuk killed her husband with her father's gun, and together, the two men had disposed of the body. After three hours of testimony, the judge ordered Bill Bohozuk, Donald MacLean and Evelyn Dick to stand trial for the murder of John Dick. The judge declared there wasn't enough evidence to proceed against Evelyn's mother, Alexandra.

||||||||

The day after the preliminary hearings, every major newspaper across Canada was covering the story. *Time* magazine and *Newsweek* ran features on the case. It was the first big news story after the war, and the public were riveted by every gruesome detail. Television broadcasting was still several years away, so people turned to newspapers and the radio to get the latest gossip on the now famous femme fatale.

In Hamilton, it seemed everyone had a story about Evelyn Dick. Rumours of her sexual exploits were a hot topic in every social circle. Was she a paid escort, or simply a party girl with a less than stellar reputation? Who were the powerful and mostly married men supposedly listed in her little black book? And did any of them father her three children? But the residents of Steeltown and the rest of the country would have to wait until the murder trial to find out if Evelyn would reveal any of her salacious secrets.

The first day of the trial was October 7, 1946, a week before Thanksgiving, and hundreds of spectators carrying their lunches lined up for hours, hoping to get a seat inside the courtroom or at least catch a glimpse of the famous accused as she was led into the seventy-year-old courthouse on Main Street.

Wearing a fashionable black dress, a sequin-studded skullcap and bright red lipstick, Evelyn Dick looked more like a movie star than an accused murderer as she stood to answer to the charges against her. Her twenty-sixth birthday was just six days away, and she was now on trial for her life. Only nine women had been hanged in Canada during the past century, but if she was found guilty of murder, Evelyn would likely become the tenth.

Accompanying her on the first day of her trial was her new Hamilton lawyer, John Sullivan, a tall, good-looking man in his early forties. Representing the Crown was Timothy Rigney, from Kingston, Ontario, who was often called in on high-profile cases. He was considered the best prosecutor in Ontario at the time. As the trial got underway, Crown Attorney Rigney announced he would try Evelyn first. Once her trial was concluded, he would try the other two accused—Donald MacLean and Bill Bohozuk—together.

Evelyn faced an all-male jury, since most Canadian provinces still did not accept female jurors. With the jury in place, Rigney called a string of witnesses—the police who recovered the torso, and the detectives who had searched Evelyn's Carrick Avenue house and Donald MacLean's home on Rosslyn Avenue.

The first witness was Mrs. Anna Kammerer, the wife of John Dick's cousin Alex. John had been living with the Kammerers before his disappearance, and Anna was able to identify the bloody clothing as the items John was wearing when she last saw him on the morning of March 6. She also identified his bloodstained black oxford shoes, which had been found in Donald MacLean's basement.

The Crown also called William Landeg, who repeated what he had told the police about lending Evelyn Dick the Packard sedan on March 6, and the condition of the car when it was returned. With respect to Evelyn's movements with the car, a young man who had been renting a room at the Carrick Avenue address said he had watched Evelyn from an upstairs window as she tried to back the Packard into her garage that evening. But she kept hitting the running board against the side of the garage. Several of Evelyn's neighbours also testified that they had seen her trying to manoeuvre the car into the garage that same night.

Dr. Deadman described the dismemberment and decapitation of the torso. The head had been severed just above the fifth neck vertebra. And the lacerations to the flesh on the torso indicated that the limbs had been severed with a saw instead of a knife. "Rough dismemberment such as this," he said, "did not require experience or knowledge." The pathologist also gave evidence concerning the ashes collected from Evelyn's home. He confirmed that human teeth and bone fragments, now contained in over sixty small boxes, had been discovered amongst the ashes and that the bone fragments coincided with the missing body parts. Dr. Deadman also confirmed that bloodstains discovered in the Packard sedan and on all of the other evidence gathered from Evelyn's home and Donald MacLean's house was human blood type O, the same as John Dick's.

For Hamiltonians, every day of the trial brought more intrigue and excitement. Witnesses' testimony was deciphered and debated in the local bars and coffee shops. Public opinion was divided—did she or didn't she do it? By the third day of the trial, the crowds outside the courthouse were reported to be in the thousands when word spread across the city that Alexandra MacLean, Evelyn's mother, would be in the witness box that afternoon.

The plain, grey-haired grandmother began her testimony by reiterating her strong disapproval of Evelyn's marriage to John Dick because he had no money. She then described the couple's brief marriage and constant quarrelling until John left for good in February, a month before he disappeared. Asked to recall Evelyn's movements on March 6, Mrs. MacLean testified that her daughter left the house around 1:30 p.m. and returned at 6 p.m., driving the black Packard. Mrs. MacLean said she watched as her daughter tried to back the car into the garage, which she found strange since Evelyn never used the garage. Two days later, Mrs. MacLean said she took her granddaughter, Heather, to watch John Dick's streetcar pass by on his regular route. The little girl liked to wave at him. But John was not driving that day. When Mrs. MacLean told Evelyn that John was not on his streetcar route, Evelyn snapped at her mother and told her she would never see John Dick again.

"Why?" asked Mrs. MacLean. "Has something happened to him, has he been killed?"

"Yes," said Evelyn. "John Dick is dead, and you better keep your mouth shut!"

A collective gasp could be heard in the courtroom, and then all eyes turned to the woman sitting in the prisoner's box. Evelyn showed no reaction to the damning testimony her mother had just given.

For the next few days, the Crown called more witnesses. The jury heard a lot about the physical evidence collected by the police, and most of it pointed directly at the accused, but they still hadn't heard from Evelyn directly. Her lawyer, John Sullivan, wanted Evelyn's multiple statements to the police excluded from testimony. He knew they would be extremely damaging for his client. He argued that they had been obtained improperly, but the judge disagreed.

Over the next two days, any spectators lucky enough to get a seat in the courtroom heard all four of the contradictory and confusing statements Evelyn had given to the police. But the question on everyone's mind was whether she would testify in her own defence. And if she did, which story would she stick with? Was John Dick murdered by an Italian mobster out for revenge, or was it her former lover Bill Bohozuk? And how was her father involved? Or, would she finally come clean and tell the truth about her involvement in her husband's grisly demise?

But Evelyn's lawyer advised the court his client would not be giving testimony.

On the ninth and final day of the trial, and after forty-two witnesses, John Sullivan addressed the jurors. Portraying his client as childlike and naive, he claimed that she lived in a fantasy world in which she dreamed of elevating her station in life. She was a pretty, photogenic woman who had never worked a day in her life. And, according to him, her contradictory statements to the police did not show an intention to deceive, but rather a young woman of questionable mental capacity who had suffered from a very unhappy home life.

Sullivan then questioned the testimony of Mrs. MacLean and asked the jury to contemplate why a mother would testify against her own daughter. With respect to most of the physical evidence, Sullivan said it was suspicious that there was so much evidence lying around the Carrick Avenue house that connected Evelyn to the murder of her husband. Why would a guilty person be so careless? And he pointed out that it would have been impossible for his petite client—"this little girl," as he referred to her—to have either carried John Dick's body or cut it up. In his final remarks, Sullivan concluded that Evelyn Dick had no reason to kill her husband; the usual motives of money, love or passion just didn't exist in this case. Therefore, in his opinion, the jury should return with a verdict of not guilty.

Up next was Crown prosecutor Timothy Rigney. His comments were brief, and he intended to use Evelyn's own words against her. As expected, he reiterated Alexandra MacLean's testimony about Evelyn telling her that John Dick was dead. "Her own mother thinks she did it," said the prosecutor. And in one of her statements to the police, Evelyn said she wasn't going to take the rap for John Dick's murder alone. "Are those the words of an innocent person?" Rigney asked. In closing, Rigney urged the jury to consider the evidence and return a verdict of guilty.

After reading from the Criminal Code and defining murder for the jury, the judge said: "If you conclude that the accused, Evelyn Dick, killed her husband intentionally then she is guilty of murder. Or if you conclude beyond a reasonable doubt that she did not actually shoot John Dick, but aided and abetted in the murder, then she is just as guilty as the person who fired the shot."

With those final words, the jury filed out of the courtroom to begin their deliberations. Evelyn was escorted to a dingy room down the hall where she would await her fate. But she didn't have to wait long. The jury returned in less than two hours. "Guilty," announced the jury foreman. The now convicted killer showed no reaction. "Evelyn Dick, stand up," ordered the judge. Then he addressed her directly and said, "Evelyn Dick, the sentence of this court is that you be taken from here to the place whence you came, and there be kept in close confinement until the seventh day of January in the year 1947 and upon that date that you be taken to the place of execution and that you be hanged by the neck until you are dead. And may the Lord have mercy on your soul."

In short order, twenty-six-year-old Evelyn Dick had been found guilty and sentenced to hang for the murder of her husband. While news of her date with the hangman travelled fast, the condemned woman sat alone in a small, windowless cell on the third floor of the Barton Street jail. She was now on death watch, which meant she would be guarded twenty-four hours a day until the date of her execution. Her only hope now was an appeal.

The day after Evelyn was sentenced to hang, Bill Bohozuk and Donald MacLean were ushered into the same courthouse to answer to the charge of murdering John Dick. Timothy Rigney again represented the Crown.

After a brief outline of the Crown's case against the two, Rigney called many of the same witnesses who had appeared during Evelyn Dick's trial. The jury and courtroom spectators listened intently to the police evidence and medical testimony, but many were really hoping to hear what the Crown's star witness had to say.

Finally, on the second day of the trial, Evelyn Dick was escorted into the courtroom and presented as a Crown witness. But her appearance in the witness box didn't last long; she refused to be sworn in and refused to give testimony against either of the accused. Not sure how to proceed, the judge excused her. The following day, Evelyn once again refused to take the oath or give testimony. This put the Crown in a difficult predicament. She was their key witness against Bohozuk and MacLean, but the judge had no judicial tools to compel her to testify. After all, how could you threaten a woman with contempt of court when she had just been sentenced to hang? Rigney requested that the judge discharge the jury and delay the trial to the next session of the court, which was the following January. The judge agreed, and the jury was dismissed. A new trial for Bill Bohozuk and Donald MacLean would have to wait.

But the clock was ticking for Evelyn. Her execution date was looming. On November 14, Evelyn's lawyer, John Sullivan, sought leave to appeal her murder conviction. This was her only hope. The Ontario Court of Appeal granted Evelyn's request. If her appeal failed, she would go to the gallows. She was in a fight for her life, and she needed the best lawyer money could buy.

Evelyn's new lawyer was forty-one-year-old J.J. Robinette, a prominent and well-respected academic lawyer from Toronto. On January 9, 1947, the hearing began at Osgoode Hall in Toronto. Evelyn was given a one-month stay of execution. If the appeal was unsuccessful, she would hang on February 7.

After two and a half days of arguing the case before the Court of Appeals, Robinette won the appeal on the grounds that evidence had been improperly obtained by the police and the judge's instructions to the jury were deficient. The judgment of the court was unanimous, and a new trial was granted for Evelyn Dick.

On February 24, 1947, the new trial of Evelyn Dick, William Bohozuk and Donald MacLean, under a joint indictment for the murder of John Dick, opened in Hamilton before the Honourable James McRuer. Timothy Rigney, representing the Crown, requested that Evelyn Dick again be tried first and separately from the other two accused. Addressing the jurors, Chief Justice McRuer, one of the most respected judges on the bench, warned the twelve men that they must ignore anything they might have heard about the case up to this point. Crown Counsel Rigney also addressed the high degree of media attention the murder

trial had received and asked the jurors to dismiss any precon-
ceived ideas or theories they might have about the guilt or innocence of the accused. He then introduced the characters in the
case and outlined the series of events related to the murder and
dismemberment of John Dick.

After a week of witness testimony, the judge held a second
in-trial hearing without the jury to determine the admissibility of
the statements that Evelyn had given to the police. Would the jury
get to hear Evelyn's wild and contradictory stories? This time, the
answer was no. McRuer ruled that Evelyn's statements were inadmissible and would not be admitted into evidence. This was a huge
victory for the defence, but Robinette still needed to convince the
jury that his client was not guilty of murder.

On March 5, Evelyn's lawyer began his closing address to the
jury. This was only his second murder trial, but he was determined
to win. His argument was clear and concise: even if the Crown's
evidence was fully accepted, it pointed only to Evelyn being an
accessory after the fact in the death of John Dick. "And that, gen-
tlemen, does not constitute murder," said a confident Robinette.
Robinette then went on to suggest that Donald MacLean was the
murderer. Most of the police evidence pointed to him, and it was
well known that he hated John Dick. And it was MacLean who
had a motive to kill. He needed to make sure John didn't tell their
employer that he was stealing from them. Evelyn, on the other
hand, had no reason to kill John. She could have just divorced him.

Robinette concluded by telling the jury that the case had many
mysterious elements and questions that still could not be answered.
But they must base their verdict only on the evidence as they had
heard it, and the verdict must be not guilty.

While the jury deliberated, Evelyn Dick found herself sitting
in the same dingy prisoner's room down the hall, where she had
waited during her first trial. But this time was different. There
would be no more appeals if the verdict came back as guilty. This

was the end of the line for her. Five hours later, the jury announced they had reached a verdict. A visibly pale Evelyn was escorted back into a silent courtroom. "They'll hang her," a spectator was overheard whispering. It was one year to the day that John Dick had been murdered. Outside the courthouse, a crowd estimated at over six thousand had gathered to await the fate of Evelyn Dick.

"Not guilty," announced the jury foreman. A collective gasp resonated in the courtroom as all eyes turned to the woman standing in the prisoner's box. According to witnesses, Evelyn Dick appeared almost stunned by the words she had just heard. But then a broad smile appeared on her face and she raised her clasped hands in a thank you gesture towards the jury. Evelyn had escaped her date with the hangman, but she wasn't going home any time soon. She still had to answer for another murder.

Three weeks after her acquittal in the murder of John Dick, Evelyn was back in court on the charges of murdering her infant son. Once again, the Crown was represented by Timothy Rigney, while J.J. Robinette continued to act on Mrs. Dick's behalf. Rigney's first witness was Evelyn's mother, Alexandra MacLean, who told the court how she had seen her daughter and newborn grandson in the hospital five days after his birth. She had brought clothing for Evelyn and the infant in a beige suitcase. Then Mrs. MacLean was asked to identify the exhibits sitting on a table in front of the jury. As spectators stood up to try to catch a glimpse of the morbid items, Mrs. MacLean confirmed that the torn and mouldy garments were the baby's clothing and the suitcase was the same one that belonged to her daughter.

Next in the witness box was Dr. Deadman, who described the autopsy he performed on the mummified remains of the infant. When Robinette tried to suggest that the baby found in the suitcase might have been from another pregnancy that had been aborted, Dr. Deadman quickly confirmed that the dead infant was a full-term pregnancy.

Following the pathologist's testimony, the Crown called on Samuel Henson. He repeated what Evelyn said when she was trying to rent an apartment in the upscale building he owned. She had told him that she was a widow with one child, and the baby she was carrying was stillborn. Did Evelyn's words foretell the fate of her son, as the Crown was contending? Or was she just a desperate single mother trying to secure a home for herself and her child, as Robinette suggested?

Robinette called no witnesses, and in his summation to the jury he described his client as a loving mother to her daughter, Heather. But what about the father of this baby? Who was he? asked the defence lawyer. Was he a prominent Hamiltonian, perhaps a married man? If so, he would have had a motive for wanting the infant dead.

In his charge to the jury, the judge reminded them that the Crown must prove beyond a reasonable doubt that the baby died as a result of a criminal act and not from natural causes. But he then speculated, "Are children who die from natural causes encased in cement and kept in a locked suitcase? Is an eighteen-inch-long baby stuffed into a thirteen-inch zippered bag? And what about the cord around the infant's neck?" He went on to remind the jury that the accused left the hospital with a healthy newborn and it was never seen alive again.

The jury deliberated for less than five hours before finding Evelyn Dick guilty of manslaughter. Evelyn's star lawyer had saved her from another possible death sentence, but he had not saved her from prison. Robinette made a strong plea for mercy in his client's sentencing. In his view, Evelyn Dick could be reformed. But the judge was not of the same mind and imposed the maximum sentence: Evelyn Dick would spend the rest of her natural life in prison.

Or would she?

|||||||||

On July 16, 1947, Evelyn was transferred to the Kingston Prison for Women to begin serving her life sentence for the murder of her baby boy. After seventeen months in the decrepit Barton Street jail, the federal prison would be her new home.

With Evelyn securely ensconced in the penitentiary, the Crown still had three more trials to attend to. Bill Bohozuk and Donald MacLean were waiting for their day in court and had already spent over a year in jail. First to stand trial was Bohozuk, who was defending himself against the charge of murdering Evelyn's baby. The Crown's witness list included many of the same people who had given evidence at Evelyn's trials. Evelyn's mother testified she had never met Bohozuk and that her daughter had told her another man was the baby's father. Detective Preston then testified that Evelyn had told him Bohozuk was the father of the infant and he strangled the baby in the car the day she left the hospital. But when asked about her relationship with Bohozuk, Evelyn admitted she had only been intimate with him on one occasion, which happened to be thirteen months after the baby was born. Clearly, the dates didn't add up, but maybe the Crown's next witness could clarify.

Evelyn Dick was called to the witness box, but once again she refused to be sworn or to testify against her former lover. But, unlike Evelyn, Bohozuk was more than ready to talk and to take the stand in his own defence. Bohozuk said that he first met Evelyn in the summer of 1944, before he was married. After his wife left him, he went out on a few dates with her in October 1945. She told him she was a widow. They were intimate once, but after he discovered she was married, he stopped seeing her. Bohozuk swore he was not the father of the infant boy, nor had he murdered him.

It took the jury only twenty-three minutes to acquit Bill Bohozuk of murdering Evelyn Dick's baby. The husky labourer was visibly relieved. But Bohozuk still wasn't in the clear. Two days later, he was in the same courtroom to answer to the charges of murdering John Dick. Prosecutor Timothy Rigney outlined the Crown's case against Bohozuk and called his first witness: Mrs. Evelyn Dick. As she had done on every other occasion, Evelyn refused to take the Bible in her hand to be sworn in before the court. Rigney was beaten. Without Evelyn's testimony, he could not proceed with the trial against Bohozuk. There were no other witnesses or evidence that tied him to the crime. The judge turned to the jury and instructed them to acquit the defendant immediately. Bohozuk was ecstatic. After more than a year in prison on two charges of murder, he was finally going home.

The Crown had one last opportunity to convict someone for the murder of John Dick. Donald MacLean's trial began soon after Bohozuk left the courtroom. Sitting alone in the prisoner's box, Evelyn's father listened as Rigney introduced evidence found at his Rosslyn Avenue home, including John Dick's bloodied shoes, a butcher knife, several guns and a box with a bullet hole in it. While the evidence was incriminating, it still didn't prove that MacLean had been directly involved in John Dick's murder. The following day, a deal was struck and MacLean pleaded guilty to a lesser charge of being an accessory after the fact. The judge sentenced him to five years in federal prison to run concurrently with a five-year term he was given for the theft from his employer. The seventy-year-old Scotsman was sent to Kingston Penitentiary to serve out his time, but at least he would be closer to his daughter.

Across the street, at the women's penitentiary, Evelyn was adjusting to prison life, and according to reports from the day, she was a model prisoner. She was polite and followed all the rules. She was a natural leader and she helped other inmates with their reading and writing skills. Eventually, Evelyn's good behaviour and leadership skills caught the attention of a prominent lawyer and supporter of penal reform, who took a personal interest in her future.

Alex Edmison, who would serve on the National Parole Board from its founding in 1959 until his retirement in 1971, was particularly impressed with Evelyn Dick when he met her in Kingston. He felt the now thirty-eight-year-old inmate had been reformed and could go on to lead a productive life if she were released from prison. But, given the notoriety of her case, he decided she was going to need special help if she was going to succeed. In short, Evelyn Dick had to disappear.

After serving eleven years of a life sentence for the murder of her infant son, Evelyn Dick was secretly taken from the Kingston Prison for Women in the dead of night and transported to an undisclosed location. Given a new name, new home and new job, the woman formerly known as Evelyn Dick, Evelyn White and Evelyn MacLean was gone forever.

But while Evelyn was enjoying a secret new life, none of the other characters in her story fared quite as well. Donald MacLean, Evelyn's father, was released from Kingston Penitentiary in 1951 after serving four years of his two concurrent five-year sentences. The man who stole thousands from his former employer returned to Hamilton penniless and alone. He and his wife, Alexandra, never reconciled, and he never saw his daughter again. If he was involved in the murder and dismemberment of his son-in-law, John Dick, he took those secrets to his grave in 1955.

Bill Bohozuk, Evelyn's former one-time lover, returned to his former job at the steel mill in Hamilton and resumed his rowing hobby. But life was never the same. Even though he had been found innocent of all charges, rumours and hearsay continued about his involvement in the murder of John Dick and Evelyn's infant son. Bohozuk never spoke to the press about his ordeal and ended up changing his name. "He was persecuted all his life," said his wife after his death in 1996.

As for the women in Evelyn's life, their lives were impacted forever, too. When Evelyn was given a new identity, it meant she had to leave her entire past behind her, including her mother and her own daughter, Heather. After Evelyn went to prison, Mrs. MacLean continued to care for her granddaughter. Although she testified against Evelyn in all three of her trials, Alexandra MacLean otherwise remained faithful to her only daughter until her death in 1964.

Evelyn's daughter, Heather, who went by the name Maria MacLean to avoid any negative association with her notorious mother, was never told anything about Evelyn's new identity or whereabouts while she was growing up. In 1965, she was finally reunited with Evelyn at a hotel in Ottawa with the assistance of Alex Edmison from the Canadian Parole Board. Twenty-three-year-old Heather, who by then was a mother herself, introduced Evelyn to her five-year-old granddaughter Cindy. Heather has never spoken about her mother.

In his 2001 book *Torso Murder: The Untold Story of Evelyn Dick*, author Brian Vallée speculated that Evelyn remarried and started a new life somewhere out west. For years, the press continued to hunt for any small clue about her whereabouts. And Evelyn's secret identity was further protected when, in 1985, at age sixty-five, she was granted a federal pardon under the Royal Prerogative of Mercy. The pardon meant she no longer had to report to the police or the parole board, and her file was forever sealed. Evelyn Dick, the number one suspect in her husband's gruesome murder and a convicted baby killer, was given complete clemency by the Canadian government, and today her criminal file no longer exists.

Almost eighty years after a headless human torso was found on Hamilton Mountain and a dead baby was discovered in an attic, the woman at the centre of both crimes remains an enigma, and there are still so many questions left unanswered. To this day, the Evelyn Dick story remains part of the lore and history of Hamilton, the working-class city where she grew up and tried so desperately to improve her social standing. The infamous femme fatale will always be connected to Steeltown. But it's doubtful she ever returned to the place that held her secrets and to this day continues to whisper about her murderous deeds.

# NO WAY OUT

## THE JANE STAFFORD STORY

On the morning of Friday, March 12, 1982, sixty-three-year-old Carl Croft got up at his usual time, four o'clock, to do his chores before he went off to work. Carl had lived on the small rural Nova Scotia property all his life, and his daily routine rarely deviated. He would feed his animals and then eat breakfast before catching a ride to his job in Liverpool at Steel and Engine Ltd., which specialized in repairing fishing boat engines and repairing hulls.

As usual, on that cold and misty spring morning, Carl left his house at 7:15 and walked down River Road to meet his ride. River Road was an isolated dirt road that saw little traffic, so Carl was surprised when he spotted a truck pulled off to the side in the ditch. Everyone in the area drove a truck of some sort, but he didn't recognize the half-ton grey Jeep. Moving closer to the driver's side, he noticed something on the door. It looked like blood. Maybe someone had an accident, he thought as he looked around. Then, peering into the window, he saw a man lying against the driver's side of the door. There was blood everywhere. Carl knew right away that the person inside the truck was already dead because, whoever he was, his head was gone.

By 8:00 a.m., officers from the local RCMP detachment in Liverpool had arrived at the isolated spot on River Road. At the scene, they found a truck with Nova Scotia licence plates. Inside the vehicle was an unknown male who had been decapitated. The cab was splattered with blood and brains. The keys were still in the ignition, and outside on the ground, near the driver's-side door, was more blood, brain matter and a set of false teeth.

When the local coroner arrived at the location, he determined that the victim had likely been killed by a gunshot blast to the face. Sadly, there had been several suicides in the area in the previous year, and at first, this looked like another one, except for one small problem: there was no gun. An hour after the body was discovered, Corporal Howard "Howie" Pike arrived at the crime scene. The thirty-five-year-old officer had been with the RCMP for fifteen years and had worked at the local Liverpool detachment for the past four. He knew most of the locals and recognized the truck right away. It was Billy Stafford's. Stafford lived about ten kilometres up River Road in the tiny hamlet of Bangs Falls. Looking into the truck, there was no face to see, but judging by the clothing and the size of the body, Pike was sure it was Billy Stafford, and he was certain he had been murdered. "Couldn't have happened to a better guy," said Pike. No one was going to be upset that Billy Stafford was dead.

Queens County, Nova Scotia, lies midway between Halifax and Yarmouth on the southwest shore of the Atlantic province. With its beautiful sandy beaches, unspoiled rivers and lush Acadian forests, the area is a well-known summer destination for Canadians and Americans. Liverpool, the county's largest city, was founded in 1759 and was the only place in British North America to be settled by the descendants of the *Mayflower*. It eventually became the fourth-largest shipping and shipbuilding port in Canada. But after World War II, the economic prosperity of the area declined, and most families relied on the fishing and logging industries.

Jane Marie Hurshman was born on January 25, 1949, in postwar Queen's County. She was the second born in the Hurshman household, and two more daughters would eventually follow. Her father, Maurice, worked in the local sawmill and carried wood home every night to heat their house, which had no indoor toilet or running water. A year after Jane's birth, her father joined the Canadian army and was shipped to Korea. When Maurice returned to Canada in 1952, he stayed in the military as an army chef. But military life meant constant upheaval, and the family moved every few years—first to Truro, Nova Scotia, then to New Brunswick and eventually to Germany for three years.

With four children on a military salary, money was tight and Jane's dad began drinking heavily, which seemed to be the norm among the other families Jane knew on the army base. But when Maurice drank too much, he would get physically abusive towards Jane's mother, screaming at her and hitting her. Jane and her two younger sisters would hide, hoping her father's wrath didn't turn on them.

In 1964, when Jane was fifteen, the Hurshmans returned to Canada from Germany and settled in Winnipeg, Manitoba. Jane hated the harsh winter, so the following summer she moved back to sleepy Liverpool, Nova Scotia, to live with her grandparents. After years of moving and dealing with her father's alcoholism and abuse, Jane finally felt safe and knew she would never return to live with her parents, who had never expressed any love towards her. She enrolled at Liverpool Regional High School and started dating a local guy named Marty who was nine years older than her. Then, two months after turning sixteen, Jane discovered she was pregnant.

Jane and Marty got married and moved in with his grandparents. On October 9, 1965, Jane gave birth to a baby boy they named Allen. Jane was thrilled to be a new mother, but her husband no longer seemed interested in her or the baby. He began spending more time at the local tavern than at home with them. Jane quit school and took a job at a local grocery store, while Marty's grandparents cared for the baby.

In 1972, Jane gave birth to another baby boy they named Jamie. She was happy that seven-year-old Allen now had a baby brother, but by that time her marriage was on the rocks. Marty had lost his job because of his heavy drinking, and he was having an affair. Jane stuck it out for a few more years, but by the beginning of 1976, she had finally had enough. She wanted a divorce.

By this time, Jane was also having an affair, although it was complicated, since he was a good friend of her husband's. But he was kind, gentle and listened to Jane talk about her marital troubles. Within a few months, Jane finally left Marty and moved in with her new lover. His name was Billy Stafford.


Lamont William "Billy" Stafford was born on February 13, 1941. He was the second of six children. The Staffords lived in a modest home in Liverpool. Billy's dad ran a successful junkyard business, and his mother ran a strict household. Friends who grew up with Billy remembered a kid who always had a nasty streak and wasn't afraid to use his fists. As a teenager, Billy dropped out of high school and went to work on the boats as a merchant seaman.

In 1962, at the age of twenty-one, Billy married his pregnant girlfriend, Pauline Oickle. The couple had five children in six years before Pauline was granted a divorce on the grounds of cruelty. Billy would beat Pauline and the children on a regular basis. After he tried to drown her by submerging her head in a bucket of water,

Pauline realized her life was in danger. She took their children and fled to Ontario. When Billy discovered she had left, he reportedly beat her mother to find out where she had gone. And while he begged her to come back, she never did.

Two years after his first wife left him, Stafford began living with a woman named Faith Hatt. While Billy could be very charming at the beginning of his relationships, it didn't take long for his dark side to emerge. Within a few months of moving in together, Billy was beating Faith on a regular basis. After discovering she was pregnant, Faith knew she had to escape for her own safety and that of her unborn child. She fled to Calgary and prayed Billy Stafford would never find her.

Stafford treated the women in his life as if they were his property that he could abuse at will. But his violent tendencies weren't just restricted to behind closed doors. Stafford was the well-known bully of Queens County, and people in the area knew not to cross him. At over six feet tall and over 250 pounds, he was an intimidating presence. The local police knew him well, too, since he seemed to think most laws didn't apply to him. He had been arrested numerous times for drunk driving and driving without a licence. Billy hated the local RCMP and often bragged to friends that he wouldn't hesitate to shoot a cop if they ever came near his home. And anyone who knew Billy also knew he had a lot of guns and wasn't afraid to use them. The man was a tyrant, and there were even rumours around town that he had murdered another fisherman by throwing him overboard during a heated argument. In fact, Billy bragged about the deed, but the police could never prove he had been involved.

But they say love is blind, and despite his less than stellar reputation, Jane Hurshman had fallen for the big, burly guy who made her feel safe. Life with Billy in the beginning was good. By May of 1976, Jane's divorce from Marty was finalized, and she and Billy moved into a big, rundown rented house that she cheerfully fixed up. Billy was attentive and generous, but Jane missed her children. Marty had taken the boys and refused to let her see them. He was going to make her pay for leaving him and moving in with his friend. And the family court system appeared to back him up. After all, it was Jane who had left the marriage and had admitted to infidelity. In rural Nova Scotia circa 1976, that meant Jane was considered an unfit parent. Billy encouraged her not to be upset about the children and even suggested they have one of their own. He flushed her birth control pills down the toilet, and by August, eight months into their relationship, Jane was pregnant. Billy seemed happy with the news, and while they decided not to get legally married, Jane began using Billy's surname. It was a whole new beginning for Jane Stafford.

Jane was thrilled about the new baby, but as her pregnancy progressed, something seemed to shift in Billy. The more she began to show, the less he took her out. Soon, he was spending more time away from home drinking, and when he was home, he would criticize her for gaining weight, calling her a cow and then laughing it off. On May 24, 1977, Jane gave birth to a healthy baby boy she named Darren. Billy was out on the boats when the baby was born and didn't come to see her in the hospital until a few days after he had returned. He was unhappy that the baby was a boy and told Jane he didn't want anything to do with him. She was hopeful he would change his mind once they took the baby home. But Jane's dreams of a happy family were soon dashed when she and the baby left the hospital. Things went from bad to worse.

Billy was not interested in their son and continued to criticize Jane. Then, a month after Darren was born, Billy and Jane had to leave the house that Jane had spent so much time fixing up. Fortunately, some friends offered them a plot of land near Bangs Falls, so

Billy purchased a cabin for $1,000 and had it shipped to the lot. It wasn't much, but Jane worked hard to make it a nice home. Billy's moods continued to fluctuate, especially when he was drinking, but Jane learned to stay out of his way and enjoyed the times when he was away at sea.

When Darren was six months old, Billy's verbal abuse finally turned physical. Accusing Jane of flirting with one of his friends, he began slapping, punching and kicking her while calling her every foul name he could come up with. Jane didn't understand what she had done wrong, but believed she must have done something to provoke such an attack. Naturally, the following morning, Billy apologized and promised it would never happen again. But it did happen over and over again, and, according to Billy, it was always Jane's fault.

Over the next few years, Jane endured regular beatings, and by the time Darren was three years old he had also become a victim of his father's violent temper. Billy would slap him, pick him up by the hair and beat him with a mop handle, and if the child dared to cry, he would get hit again until he stopped. Mealtimes were the worst if Billy was in a foul mood. Darren would be so nervous around his father, he couldn't hold a cup steady without spilling it, and if he didn't finish all his food, Billy would force-feed him until he vomited. Then Darren would be forced to eat his own vomit. The only peaceful, happy times for Jane and Darren were when Billy was away on the boats.

But in 1980, Billy was fired and blacklisted from the fishing boats for threatening a ship's captain. He began working on oil tankers, but that job soon evaporated when his temper got him into trouble with co-workers. By 1981, he declared he wasn't working anymore, and Jane, whom he always called "old woman," would have to support them. Jane did as she was told. She had learned not to argue with Billy. She hoped that if she went along with everything he wanted, their lives would get better. But things would only improve for a few days before Billy would fly into a rage again, and Jane would always be the one to bear the brunt of his anger.

Fortunately, Jane had one enjoyable outlet in her life, and that was her job at Hillsview Acres Retirement Home, where she cooked for the elderly residents. Everyone at the home loved Jane. She was very caring and always willing to sit and talk with the lonely residents. But Jane didn't tell anyone what her home life was like, and she always made sure to cover her bruises with makeup. At least her work gave her valuable time away from Billy and their rural home, which she had come to view as her own personal prison.

Jane and Darren had endured years of abuse at the hands of Billy Stafford, and things weren't getting any better. In fact, they were getting worse, because not only was Billy drinking, but he also began using drugs. Billy had beaten Jane unconscious numerous times, but one day he fired a gun at her, narrowly missing her head, and Jane knew then that if she didn't leave, he would eventually kill her.

Gathering all her strength, Jane informed Billy she was leaving him. But, of course, Billy had no intention of letting her go. "You can leave me any time you want, old woman," said Billy. "But if you go, you'll be coming back and you'll bring that little bastard with you. Or I'll start shooting that precious family of yours one by one." Billy's two previous wives had fled the province in order to get away from him, and he wasn't going to let Jane do the same.

Jane knew Billy wasn't bluffing. He would follow through on his threat and kill her family if she left. Jane was trapped. What could she do? She couldn't go to the police because she knew that they seldom got involved in domestic disputes, and husbands rarely went to prison for assaulting their wives. In that moment, Jane felt completely defeated. Any scrap of hope she had was gone. Billy Stafford had finally beaten her down emotionally and physically. She would stay and he would kill her. It was just a matter of time. Her only escape was suicide, but she couldn't leave Darren behind to be raised by Billy. And Darren was the only person who gave her the strength to keep going. She had to survive for him, and there was only one way that was going to happen. Billy Stafford had to die.

Every morning Jane woke up in the bed next to Billy Stafford, she prayed that she would get through the day alive. March 11, 1982, was just another one of those days. Jane had the day off from her job, which meant she could catch up on the laundry and cleaning. If she was busy with household chores, Billy would usually leave her alone. And fortunately for her, Billy was preoccupied with a project that day. He had decided he was going to raise some pigs for slaughter and was building a pigpen behind the barn. But their next-door neighbour, an older woman named Margaret Joudrey, was not happy with Billy's latest money-making venture. The stench from the pigs would be horrible and would devalue her property.

That afternoon, an angry Margaret confronted Billy and told him she had contacted a lawyer to help her put a stop to his pig-pen plan, and she had also contacted the police to report an earlier incident when Billy shot at her trailer. After five years of living next door to Billy Stafford, Margaret said she was fed up. He was a bully and he terrorized everyone, including her and her husband, who had given him the lot to put up his house in the first place. But Billy Stafford wasn't used to being told what he could and couldn't do, and he certainly wasn't going to listen to an old lady. Billy turned on the woman and told her to get out of his house. "You better have a good day, you old bitch," he yelled after her. "Because you'll never live to see another one."

Watching the confrontation, Jane could see that Billy was furi-ous. His face was red, his eyes were bulging and he was foaming at the mouth—all telltale signs of his uncontrollable rage. "Give me some money, old woman. I'm going to town," he yelled at Jane after he had chased Margaret Joudrey away. Jane tried to reason with him. The only money she had was for the truck insurance, which was due the following week. But that wasn't the right answer. Billy slapped her across the face, spat at her and took the money out of her purse. And before he left, he threw the clean laundry Jane had just finished outside into the mud. "That should give you something to do until I get back," he said as he slammed the door behind him. Jane looked over at five-year-old Darren and sixteen-year-old Allen, who was staying with them. The boys had witnessed the violent exchange and could do nothing to protect their mother. The three of them didn't speak a word. Jane picked up the dirty laundry and started washing it again.

Later that afternoon, Billy returned. He was drunk and said he wanted to go visit some friends, which usually meant he wanted to buy drugs. He insisted that Jane come with him. By 8:30 that night, they were driving back home and Billy was complaining about Margaret and their earlier exchange. He was furious that she had spoken to the police. Then he announced he had a plan. He told Jane he was going to burn down Margaret Joudrey's trailer. "When Margaret turns her lights off tonight, it will be lights out for good for her," he laughed. "I'm going to pour gas all around her trailer and watch them burn. They'll never get out!"

Billy kept laughing as Jane kept driving. She knew he was serious about his threat against Margaret and her husband. "And I'll deal with that son of yours at the same time," he added. "I've waited a long time to sort him out, so I might as well clean them all up at once." Billy was referring to Allen, whom he also hated.

By the time they pulled down their dirt driveway, Billy had passed out. Jane sat quietly in the truck, waiting to see if he would wake up. It was one of his rules: Jane wasn't allowed to get out of the truck until he gave her permission to go into the house. Sitting there in the dark, Jane thought about what Billy had threatened to do. Margaret Joudrey had been a good friend to her, almost like a mother, and she didn't want to see her get hurt. And Allen was no match for Billy. Maybe she could warn them. But if Billy found out, they would all be dead.

Rain began pelting the hood of the truck. Jane looked over at the 250-pound hulk of a man next to her. He was a monster who had terrorized her for the past six years. He had beaten her unconscious, knocked her teeth out, shot at her, degraded her sexually, abused their young son and threatened to kill her family if she ever left. And now he was threatening to burn their neighbours alive and harm her eldest son. Maybe she wasn't worth anything—at least, that's what he had instilled in her with every beating—but she was not going to let him hurt other people. Fuck it, thought Jane. She wasn't going to live in terror anymore.

As the rain continued, Jane gently leaned on the truck horn to wake up Allen. A few minutes later, he appeared in the doorway. Jane rolled down the window. "Get the gun and load it," she said. Allen ran back inside the house and loaded a 12-gauge single shotgun, one of the many guns Billy owned. He handed it to his mother. "Go back inside," she told him. Moments later, a single gunshot broke the eerie silence of the dark, rainy night. Allen ran back outside to see his mother standing by the open window of the truck. Jane handed him the gun. She asked him to get her some clean clothes and to call her parents. She needed them to meet her at a remote location about ten kilometres away. Then Jane got back in the truck. "Get rid of the gun," she yelled before driving away.

At the end of the driveway, Jane drove by Margaret Joudrey's trailer and noticed a light on. Margaret and her husband were probably still up, playing cards. Gripping the steering wheel tighter and trying not to focus on what lay beside her on the seat of the pickup truck, she suddenly felt a strange sense of relief. Margaret and her husband were safe. Her sons were safe and she was free. Nobody knew it yet, but Billy Stafford's reign of terror was finally over.

On the morning of March 12, 1982, Jane Stafford woke up in a daze. The clothes she had passed out in were soaked in sweat. She looked over at the empty space in the bed. Was it a dream? The house was quiet. The boys must be still sleeping, thought Jane. Her sons would wake up soon, and today would be the first day they wouldn't have to be afraid. No one was ever going to hurt them again. But was it real? Was the monster dead? Jane didn't have to wait long for an answer. The police were standing at her door by nine o'clock that morning. They informed her that Billy Stafford had been discovered a few hours earlier and he was deceased. Jane fainted at the news. Her nightmare was truly over. But another one was soon to begin.

Just two days after Billy Stafford was found murdered, the police asked Jane to come to the police station in Liverpool to answer some questions. It hadn't taken them long to home in on Jane as their number one suspect. Everyone in town knew the way that Billy treated her, and the police had also heard rumours of Jane trying to hire a hit man.

Jane initially told the police that Billy was probably killed because of a drug deal gone wrong, but finally, after ten hours of interrogation, she admitted she had shot him because she feared he would kill her neighbours and her son. In her statement to the police, Jane took sole responsibility for his death and said she was glad it was all over. "It was either him or me," she told the officers. Jane also admitted to the police that, earlier that same year, she had asked a friend to murder Billy for $20,000, the amount of his life insurance policy. But the friend had turned her down.

Jane Marie Stafford was formally charged with first-degree murder in the shooting death of her common-law husband, forty-one-year-old Lamont William Stafford. If convicted, Jane faced the possibility of twenty-five years in prison before any chance of parole. "That woman deserves a medal," said a senior police sergeant when he walked out of the interrogation room. The police had a lot of sympathy for what Jane had endured, and no one was going to miss Billy Stafford.

Jane Stafford's trial began on November 2, 1982, in the historic 1854 courthouse in Liverpool, Nova Scotia. Jane was thirty-three but looked ten years older. She had spent four months in prison and was taking medication for depression. Standing beside her in court was Alan Ferrier, a young legal aid lawyer. This was only his second murder trial, and this one was unique. The case had attracted nationwide attention and the courtroom was packed every day with people who mostly supported Jane and what she had done. A battered woman had finally fought back against her abuser, and hopefully a jury would see that she had acted in self-defence. Or, would she be convicted of murder despite the horrific abuse she had endured for years? Either way, the outcome of Jane's trial was critical in that it would have a significant impact on how domestic violence was dealt with in Canada.

A famous American case of "battered woman's defence" had garnered worldwide attention just five years before. On March 9, 1977, Michigan housewife Francine Hughes poured gasoline around her husband's bed as he slept and set it on fire, killing him. Hughes, who had suffered from years of abuse, was found not guilty by reason of insanity. The case was chronicled in a book titled *The Burning Bed* and later made into a TV movie starring Farrah Fawcett.

Now, in a Nova Scotia courtroom, Ferrier would argue that at the time of the crime, Jane was living as a battered woman and suffered from extreme fear from which she saw no escape. When Jane killed her abuser, she was acting in self-defence, as she feared for her own life and those of others Billy Stafford had threatened to harm that evening. The Crown's job would be to convince the jury that Jane Stafford was in no immediate harm when she killed Billy because he was asleep, passed out in his truck. The Crown would contend that the murder was planned and deliberate.

In their opening statements, there was little disagreement between the defence and the Crown as to the facts of Billy Stafford's death. On the night of March 11, 1982, Jane took one of Billy's shotguns, put it through the window of the truck while he was passed out and pulled the trigger. She then drove the truck, with Billy's body inside, to a deserted road where she abandoned it. Her parents, not knowing what she had done, met her that night and drove her home. Then her son Allen burned her bloodstained clothes, broke down the shotgun and threw it into the river from the Bangs Falls Bridge.

During the first week of the trial, the defence called sixteen witnesses, all of whom had similar stories to tell. Family, friends and neighbours all testified that Billy Stafford was a tyrant, and many had witnessed the abuse he inflicted on Jane and their son, Darren. A few of the witnesses themselves had gotten on the wrong side of Billy Stafford and had seen first-hand how he would react. So-called friends had been punched, shot at and intimidated by him.

Billy Stafford's ex-wife Pauline testified that he had beaten her and their children regularly. He forced the children to eat cigarette butts and abused the family pets. "He was a very cruel man in the six years I was married to him," said his former wife. His former common-law partner Faith Hatt told the court that she had escaped to Calgary when she was three months pregnant. "He was like a mad dog," she said. "He would actually froth at the mouth when he came after me."

Ferrier then called on Jane's mother. Gladys Hurshman testi-fied that she had also suffered physical abuse for years from her alcoholic husband when Jane was a child. "Maybe she thought that was just the way it had to be," said her mother, choking back tears. But Mrs. Hurshman admitted that Jane had told her very little about what she was going through with Billy. Jane's father, who no longer drank or abused his wife, testified that Billy had physically attacked him once. "After that, we didn't go around to visit often," he added.

Dr. Rosemarie Sampson, a psychologist hired by the defence, testified that Jane Stafford was a woman involved in a seriously sadistic relationship who shot her husband when her anxiety and fears had reached an extreme level. She was in a situation of over-whelming stress, both physical and mental. Her way of coping was to be passive and compliant. Dr. Sampson told the court that Jane had the strength to endure the abuse, but could not see a way out. She believed there was no escape and it was a life-or-death situation.

Dr. Carol Abbott, a psychiatrist who interviewed Jane, talked about the shame associated with domestic violence. She said a lot of women in Jane's circumstances will not tell others about the abuse. Many will isolate themselves from family and friends out of fear of being judged and fear of reprisals if they speak out. Jane had stayed silent for many years, keeping the abuse secret and hiding her bruises.

Now, two weeks into her murder trial, she was finally ready to talk. The courtroom fell silent when Ferrier called his next witness. Looking frail, with dark circles under her eyes, Jane Stafford was clearly nervous as she testified in her own defence. She had lost almost forty pounds on her already petite frame, and the judge had to ask her several times to speak up as her lawyer guided her through her difficult testimony. For more than three hours, Jane recited a litany of physical, sexual and mental abuse that Billy had inflicted on her and other members of her family. He would often beat her into unconsciousness, and he had pointed a shotgun at her head and threatened to pull the trigger. The week before his death, he had beaten her with a metal vacuum cleaner hose, and she was still covered in bruises when she was arrested.

The jury also heard how Jane had been sexually tortured, raped and forced into degrading sexual acts, including bestiality with the family dog. When asked what she did about the assaults, Jane said that she didn't do anything. "Billy would tell me it was always my fault," she said. "And when you hear that so often, you begin to believe it." Questioned why she hadn't left the relationship, Jane told the court that Billy had threatened to kill her if she did. And he had also threatened to kill her parents and her sisters. "And did you take those threats seriously?" asked her lawyer. "Yes," replied Jane. "I knew he would do it. There was no way out."

Under cross-examination, Jane admitted that she wanted Billy dead and had tried to hire someone to kill him. Crown Attorney Blaine Allaby asked her if she was aware of a shelter for battered women in Halifax. Wasn't there indeed another way out? asked the attorney. "If I had tried to leave, there would have been more people dead besides Billy," said Jane. She told the court how Billy had bragged that he had killed before. He told her that he had thrown a man overboard on a fishing boat, so she had no doubts he would follow through on his threats. "His two previous wives had left him," said Jane. "And he always said he wouldn't be a three-time loser."

In his closing arguments, Alan Ferrier told the jury that Jane shot Billy as an impulsive reaction to what he said to her that evening. He intended to burn down their neighbour's trailer with them in it and to harm Jane's son. And, given her violent history with Billy Stafford, she had every reason to believe him. Jane reacted out of a protective nature and her actions were neither deliberate nor planned.

Ferrier then addressed the issue of battered wife syndrome. "Jane

Stafford was a prisoner in her own home," said Ferrier. He went on to say that the expert testimony from psychologists and psychiatrists who had examined Jane spoke of her victimization and how it had amounted to a psychological paralysis. "A woman suffering from battered wife syndrome develops a feeling of powerlessness, becomes passive, and is blind to other options," said the defence lawyer. It is a learned helplessness, which explains why the battered woman does not leave her abuser, continued Ferrier. "In short, Jane Stafford was trapped in the relationship and reacted in self-defence."

In his closing arguments, Crown Attorney Allaby stated that the Stafford murder trial was indeed an important case for battered women in Canada. And while he believed that Billy Stafford was a batterer and a bully, he was not the person on trial. Jane Stafford was—for first-degree murder.

It was the Crown's contention that Jane had planned Billy's murder. She had been unsuccessful in trying to hire someone to kill him, so she waited. Then, on the night of March 11, 1982, she finally saw her opportunity when he was passed-out drunk in his truck. "We may sympathize with Jane Stafford and her situation," said Allaby. "But the law is the law and what Jane Stafford did was planned and deliberate. And, therefore, as to the charge of first-degree murder you must return with a verdict of guilty."

In his remarks to the jury, Justice Charles Burchell advised them that they could return with one of four verdicts: guilty of first-degree murder, guilty of second-degree murder, guilty of manslaughter, or not guilty. He then explained how each verdict could be reached. The jurors had heard from forty-six witnesses in total and the trial had lasted two and a half weeks.

On the morning of Saturday November 20, 1982, seventeen hours after they had begun their deliberations, the jury announced that they had reached a verdict. Jane sat motionless beside her lawyer.

If found guilty of first-degree murder, she would be going to prison for a very long time. She had already said emotional goodbyes to her three sons the night before. "Hang in there, Jane," whispered Alan Ferrier. "It's almost over." Jane could barely hear him over the sound of her own heart pounding in her chest as she stood waiting for the verdict. "Not guilty," said the jury foreman. "Praise the Lord," someone shouted before applause and cheers rang out in the courtroom. Jane couldn't believe what she had just heard. She felt faint. Ferrier grabbed Jane's arm and hung on to her.

With the verdict, the jury of ten men and one woman seemed to be expressing a sentiment shared across rural Queens County and the rest of the country: Jane Stafford was justified in shooting her violent, abusive husband, Billy. Moments after the verdict was read, Jane and her lawyer walked out of the Liverpool courthouse to a cheering crowd and dozens of reporters. "How do you feel?" asked the waiting press. "Super," Jane replied, but in the back of her mind, she later admitted to feeling uneasy. She had prepared herself for the worst, and she did not know how to accept the best. She had killed a man, and now she was free to go. Free to move on with her life. But in her gut, she knew it couldn't be that easy, and sadly, she was right.

News of Jane Stafford's acquittal travelled quickly, and women's organizations across Canada saw it as a possible legal breakthrough for battered women. It was a precedent-setting victory in the campaign against wife abuse and a hopeful sign of changing public attitudes towards domestic violence. Maybe the decision would prompt other women to speak out about their abuse. Maybe the case confirmed that the legal system was finally prepared to protect women from violence in their own homes. But others were not so quick to see the verdict as setting any legal precedent or even as a victory in the pursuit of justice. Jane's own lawyer, Alan

Ferrier, said he did not see the verdict as having any consequences for other similar cases. "Battered women do not have a licence to blow the heads off the men who abuse them just because Jane Stafford got off," he told the Halifax press. "You simply won't find many situations in which a jury will say it is okay for a person to kill someone," he added. "This was a special case."

Wayne MacKay, a distinguished professor of criminology at Dalhousie University, asked, "Is it the moral of the Stafford case that an abused wife can kill her husband without engaging in the crime of murder?" And while he agreed that it was hard to find much sympathy for Billy Stafford, was a man like Stafford a fair target for vigilante justice? In his opinion, Jane Stafford had been the person on trial, but it was Billy Stafford who had been found guilty.

And it looked as though the Nova Scotia attorney general's office agreed. Less than a month after her acquittal, the Crown appealed and requested a new trial. In its application, the Crown contended that Jane had been in no immediate danger from her husband, who was passed out and unarmed at the time of his death, and therefore she should have been found guilty of first-degree murder or at least manslaughter.

Ten months later, in October 1983, the Crown's appeal was granted. The verdict of the jury was set aside, and a new trial was ordered for Jane Stafford.


Jane's second trial was set to commence in February 1984, nearly two years after Billy Stafford's death. And while a conviction and possible lengthy jail sentence were still hanging over her head, Jane had gotten on with her life after her first trial. She had returned to school and was training to become a nurse's aide. Her youngest son, Darren, was doing well in school and no longer lived in fear. They were both in therapy, and Jane was hopeful about their future.

The courtroom was packed on the opening day of Jane's retrial. Her many vocal supporters had lined up early that morning to make sure they got seats inside. The case was being watched closely by women's groups across the country. But if Jane's supporters were hoping for a contentious and highly emotional courtroom drama, they were out of luck. On the advice of her lawyer, Jane decided to plead guilty to manslaughter and hope for a lenient sentence. Jane's guilty plea was quickly accepted by the Crown, which requested a jail term to discourage others in similar situations from taking the law into their own hands.

Jane's lawyer, Alan Ferrier, called only one witness: Marie Joudrey, Darren Stafford's long-time babysitter. The young woman recounted seeing bruises on Jane and Darren often. She said the little boy was terrified of his father and would run and hide when it was time for him to go home. Ferrier then reviewed some of the sexual humiliations Jane had endured at the hands of her husband. "This was not a man. He was an animal," he said. He also reminded the court what a local RCMP sergeant admitted to saying after learning that Jane had killed Billy Stafford: "That woman deserves a medal." Ferrier asked for a suspended sentence, arguing that Jane would carry the mental scars of Billy's abuse for the rest of her life.

In his remarks, the presiding judge said that Jane had lived a tragic life with a man who clearly showed little humanity. But regardless, battered wives did not have the right to take the lives of their abusers. And while Jane was not a threat to society and was doing well in rehabilitating her life, there must be a deterrence in law. The judge sentenced Jane Stafford to six months in jail and two years' probation, with a recommendation that she be allowed to commute from jail to attend her classes and complete her nursing program.

Two months later, on April 14, 1984, Jane Stafford was released from prison after serving one-third of her sentence. "Good luck

Jane, be happy," said the guard at the prison gate as it closed behind her. Jane had paid her debt to society and could now finally move forward without the threat of any further legal punishment. She was finally free.

Not long after her release from prison, Jane changed back to her maiden name, Hurshman, and graduated as a fully qualified nursing assistant. She also agreed to cooperate on a book about her life. She wanted to share her experience of domestic violence in the hopes of helping other women in similar circumstances. "I want this story to be written, not for myself but for all those others out there who are living the same hell as I did," said Jane. "If even one person picks up the book and is helped by it, that will be reward enough." In 1986, *Life with Billy* was published. Author Brian Vallée retold Jane's harrowing story of abuse in chilling detail. And while many found the book very difficult to read, its publication further generated much-needed attention to the issue of domestic violence in Canada.

After the book's release, Jane became a popular spokesperson for women's organizations and domestic violence support groups. She attended workshops and conferences across the country. The once shy, frail woman had gradually gained her self-esteem and confidence back. Her strength and passion were inspiring to many who heard her story. She was a survivor, and she wanted to help other women.

But not everyone was happy that Jane Stafford had been given a light sentence after her manslaughter plea deal. Some thought she had gotten away with murder. While touring shelters for abused women in Nova Scotia, Jane had to be put under twenty-four-hour surveillance by the RCMP because of threats against her life. Jane tried not to worry. But friends and family were concerned for her safety, and they were also worried that Jane's work with other abused women was exacting too large an emotional toll on her.

She still had a lot of healing of her own to do, and she admitted to feelings of darkness and depression. Those closest to Jane urged her to take a break.

Jane recognized she was still dealing with her own scars, but she didn't want to stop the important work she was doing to help other women. She saw a psychiatrist regularly and worked nights at her nursing job. She told colleagues that she preferred the night shift because she had trouble sleeping. She didn't tell anyone about her nightmares. That's when everything would come back: the images, the sounds, even the smells of her former life. And in her dreams, Billy Stafford was still alive, still terrorizing her.

But eventually, some of those difficult memories were replaced by something much more hopeful. On October 10, 1991, Jane married Joel Corkum, a man she had been quietly dating for over a year. Finally, Jane had everything she had ever hoped for in a partner. He was a compassionate and caring man. They bought a house in Cole Harbour, where they lived with Darren, who was now fourteen.

In the days and weeks that followed her wedding and honeymoon, Jane was on cloud nine. Friends said they had never seen her happier. Then, as their daily lives returned to normal—Joel working days and Jane working nights—the newlyweds fell into a regular routine. Jane was still doing speaking engagements, and Joel could see how those events seemed to trigger a depression in her, but he knew the work was important to her. Joel wanted to support Jane and never pressured her to talk about her past. He had read *Life with Billy* and felt he knew everything about his new wife and the traumatic life she had lived. But there was still one issue in Jane's past that she had never discussed with him.

In February 1989, three years after the publication of *Life with Billy*, Jane was arrested for shoplifting. This wasn't something new for Jane. She already had five other convictions dating back to

1975. She was charged and convicted, even though a new psychiatrist diagnosed her with a dissociative disorder caused by the childhood trauma and subsequent abuse at the hands of Billy Stafford. The psychiatrist explained that Jane's depression, mood swings and shoplifting were all related to her illness, and stealing for her was a symptom, just as overeating, anorexia or compulsive gambling might be for others. She had a disease. "She is a kleptomaniac," he told the court. "But she is not a thief." Jane was placed on probation and instructed to continue to seek psychiatric care for her illness.

On June 9, 1991, Jane was arrested again for stealing greeting cards and cologne from a pharmacy. She pleaded guilty and was fined $375. "Hurshman fined for theft," read the headlines the next day. Jane was humiliated. The stories in the press about her shoplifting referred to her past and the death of Billy Stafford. But she had fought back against him, and she wasn't going to let her name be dragged through the mud again without speaking out. Jane lambasted the *Halifax Chronicle-Herald* for using her name to sell newspapers. "People like me have no idea what normal is," she wrote. "I must spend the rest of my life learning one day at a time. And when I mess up, as in shoplifting, it is because I cannot believe that I deserve to be happy or that I am worthy of good things or good people around me."

A week later, the newspaper agreed to do an interview with Jane about her shoplifting. "It's a disease," said Jane, "just like alcoholism and drug abuse." She said it was a constant struggle for her, and she wanted it brought out into the open so that she could help others. In November 1991, Jane was arrested again for shoplifting, at an IGA store in Dartmouth. This time, nothing appeared in the paper, and she kept it a secret from Joel and Darren. She was to appear in court on March 4, 1992.

|||||||||

In the early morning of February 22, 1992, a worker with East Coast Towing, a tugboat company on the Halifax waterfront, noticed a blue Ford Tempo in an adjacent parking lot. He knew the area well, and he had never seen that car before. Judging by the snow covering it, it looked like it had been there for a few days. And it was still there the next afternoon when an older couple, Roy and Yvonne Kline, drove into the same parking area and parked nearby. Walking past the blue Ford, Roy Kline looked in and noticed a woman slumped over in the front seat. The snow-covered ground showed no footprints near the car. Was she asleep? Passed-out drunk? Kline got closer and noticed the woman's face had no colour. He ran back to his car. "There is a woman in that car," he told his wife. "And I think she's dead."

It was shortly after 3 p.m. when the Halifax police arrived at the waterfront parking lot. Inside the car, they found a woman sitting in the driver's seat, slumped towards the passenger side. It appeared that she had been dead for a few days.

When the police moved the woman's partially frozen body, they discovered a handgun and a small gunshot wound to the middle of her chest. A single .38-calibre slug was later found lodged in the seat behind the steering wheel. Three more bullets were discovered in a plastic zip-lock sandwich bag on the floor of the car, along with a folded flannel blanket. Only the driver's-side door was locked. There was no purse or identification in the car, but a check on the licence plate revealed that the car was registered to a Joel Corkum. The police soon realized who the dead woman was. They had been looking for her for two days after she failed to show up for her Friday night shift at the Halifax County Regional Rehabilitation Centre. Her name was Jane Hurshman Corkum. She was forty-three years old.

When the police discovered Jane's body, they weren't exactly sure what they were dealing with. But given her history and the previous threats against her, they knew that everything had to be thoroughly investigated. Had someone killed Jane because of Billy Stafford's murder ten years earlier?

Jane's death was eventually ruled a suicide, a reality that her family and friends had a hard time accepting. Why would she give up now, after everything she had been through? But, in a strange twist to the case, the police later stated that they believed Jane had intended to kill herself and make it look like a murder. They believed she had paid someone to remove the gun, the bullets and the flannel sheet from the car, but that person failed to follow through with the plan. The police also discovered that, prior to her disappearance, her husband, Joel, had been asking around about buying a handgun. Under questioning after her death, Joel admitted to the police that Jane had obtained a gun. The weapon he described matched the antique gun found with Jane's body. He also described the bag the bullets were in. But he was adamant that Jane was not suicidal. She was scared, he told the police. According to Joel, Jane told him she had recently received threats in the mail and on the phone, and that's why he helped her get the gun. Police theorized that Jane had used the flannel blanket found in the car to protect her hands from gunpowder residue and to muffle the sound of the shot. Subsequent tests revealed gunshot residue on the blanket and on both of Jane's hands between the thumb and forefingers.

Alan Ferrier, the lawyer who had defended Jane during her murder trial and plea deal, hadn't seen her in years but told the press that he wasn't surprised to learn of her death. "I saw her as a lifelong victim," he said. Her kleptomania was out of control, and it was a symptom of much deeper issues. It was just too overwhelming for her. He also said that he believed Jane had tried to make her suicide look like a murder to save her family further embarrassment, and to not disappoint the many women's groups she had been involved with. "Jane never wanted to let people down," he said. "Some people's lives are destined to be tragic," he added. "And Jane was just one of those people."

Before she died, Jane recorded a message to her family. On the tape, she said she was sorry for the pain and humiliation she had caused them due to her ongoing battle with kleptomania. She then specified what she wanted done with her possessions and urged her sons to stay in school. She thanked her family for all their love and support and said she was at peace.

In 1990, the Supreme Court of Canada ruled that battered women are entitled to the defence of self-defence (a "justification"), even if the threat posed by the man is not "imminent." Justice Bertha Wilson explained that if we required battered women to wait for the "uplifted knife," we would be condemning them to "murder by instalment."

Today in Canada, domestic violence is still a terrifying reality that many families deal with in silence. According to a 2021 report from Statistics Canada, approximately every six days, a woman in Canada is killed by her intimate partner.

In her many impassioned interviews and speeches, Jane urged women not to be "silent screamers behind closed doors." "You are worthy of being heard," she told her audiences. She urged women to leave the first time they were assaulted. "Pack your bags and leave. Get out, because it will never get better."

# ACKNOWLEDGEMENTS

To write true crime is to expose someone else's darkest hour. The many names in these twelve stories are the people who have been most affected by a single act of violence. I hope that in retelling these stories I have honoured victims' memories and respected the dedication and commitment of the many family members, police officers and prosecutors who have worked tirelessly in achieving justice. I am thankful to all those who work every day to keep us safe.

My deepest gratitude goes to my editor, Janice Zawerbny, who has been steadfast in her support. Thank you for believing in the importance of these stories and giving me the opportunity to tell them. I value your continued guidance and insight.

To the team at HarperCollins Canada: it is an honour to be working with such a dedicated and talented group of storytellers. Thank you to HarperCollins executive publisher Iris Tupholme and editor-in-chief Jennifer Lambert. And thank you to Noelle Zitzer and Lloyd Davis for your keen attention to detail.

My introduction to the stories in this anthology began on *Story Hunter Podcasts*. I wanted to tell important, impactful Canadian true crime stories. But I will admit I often found myself unable to get through a recording without my voice wavering at times. It's hard not to get emotional in retelling events that have been so painful to others. Thankfully, I have the help and guidance of Daniel Borgers, an amazing audio producer who I know has become equally invested in many of the lives represented in these stories.

As a Canadian, I believe it is important to know our history, including the stories and events that are often difficult to relive. I am very grateful to all our podcast listeners, and I look forward to bringing you many more episodes.

I am also grateful for the continued support of my MFA family at the University of King's College in Halifax, Nova Scotia, and the monthly words of encouragement from my Toronto writing group—Catherine Fitton, Katherine McCall, Margaret Lynch and Marsha Faubert.

I would also like to thank my own family, near and far—in particular, Elisabeth and Armin Borgers, who have shown me unconditional love, kindness and support throughout the years and who always kindly ask, "Have you finished writing your book yet?"

To my husband, Oliver, thank you for your enduring love and unwavering encouragement! I am so lucky to have you in my corner, cheering me on when the writing gets tough and the nights get long. Thanks for waiting up for me.

And to my four-legged companions, who keep me sane and help me appreciate the simple pleasures in life—Roxy, Lily, Maya and Cooper. Treats all around!

# SOURCES

## 1. MURDER IN THE MORGUE: The Two Faces of Stephen Toussaint

Brazao, Dale. "Murder suspect remains identified." *Toronto Star*. July 23, 1999.

———. "What ever happened to Steve Toussaint?" *Toronto Star*. October 18, 1998.

Blatchford, Christie. "Suspect's family not treated as victims by police." *National Post*. August 12, 1999.

Broomer, Stephen. "The chance of resurrection." *Stephen Broomer* (blog). April 16, 2014. https://stephenbroomer-blog.tumblr.com/post/82928527255/the-chance-of-resurrection.

Brown, Barry. "Three church fires, slaying prompt search for Toronto man." *Buffalo News*. April 19, 1998. https://buffalonews.com/news/three-church-fires-slaying-prompt-search-for-toronto-man/article_dc8914ab-1723-593b-8a95-653e43ebc81b.html.

Brown, Desmond. "Family stands by Toussaint." *National Post*. July 23, 1999.

———. "Remains found of man at centre of murder case." *National Post*. July 23, 1999.

"Decomposing body helps solve an old Toronto crime." *CBC News*. July 23, 1999. https://www.cbc.ca/news/canada/decomposing-body-helps-solve-a-old-toronto-crime-1.188944.

Foot, Richard. "The mysteries at St. James." *Ottawa Citizen.*
    May 18, 1998.

Mahone, Jill, and John Saunders. "Police confounded by church
    fire, killing." *Globe and Mail.* April 18, 1998.

"Morgue colleague killed, suspect nowhere to be found." *Toronto
    Star.* January 2, 1999.

Palmer, Karen. "Bones are of U of T slaying suspect." *Globe and
    Mail.* July 23, 1999.

Shephard, Michelle, and Jim Rankin. "Friend was with hunted
    man morning after church blaze." *Toronto Star.* April 20, 1998.

———. "Hundreds mourn lab worker while hunt for colleague
    continues." *Toronto Star.* April 21, 1998.

## 2. DEADLY SECRETS: The Murder of Gladys Wakabayashi

Bolan, Kim. "Accused sought details of victim's death, court told."
    *Vancouver Sun.* October 14, 2011.

———. "Elderly killer too high risk for private family visits."
    *Vancouver Sun.* June 8, 2015.

———. "Appeal of murder conviction challenges confession."
    *Vancouver Sun.* December 6, 2011.

———. "Woman killed rival for sleeping with her husband, court
    told." *Vancouver Sun.* October 13, 2011.

Fraser, Keith. "Richmond woman loses murder appeal." *Vancouver
    Province.* January 13, 2013.

Keenan, Kouri T., and Joan Brockman. *Mr. Big: Exposing Under-
    cover Investigations in Canada.* Halifax: Fernwood Publishing,
    2010.

Middleton, Greg. "Slain mom had secret life and love." *Vancouver
    Province.* July 12, 1992.

"'Mr. Big' sting helps convict senior." *Winnipeg Free Press*.
  November 5, 2011. https://www.winnipegfreepress
  .com/canada/2011/11/05/mr-big-sting-helps-convict
  -senior.
Proctor, Jason. "'Volatile' elderly killer Jean Ann James loses
  bid for private visits with unfaithful husband." CBC News.
  August 20, 2015. https://www.cbc.ca/news/canada/british
  -columbia/elderly-killer-jean-ann-james-loses-bid-for-private
  -visits-with-unfaithful-husband-1.3198433.
Sin, Lena. "Murder suspect described as friendly animal-lover."
  *Vancouver Province*. March 6, 2009.
"Women who kill." *Vancouver Province*. December 11, 2011.

## 3. LOST BOY: The Murder of Nancy Eaton

Claridge, Thomas. "Accused in Eaton slaying admitted guilt in jail,
  court told." *Globe and Mail*. September 18, 1986.
Darroch, Wendy. "Eaton a 'doomed target,' psychiatrist tells trial."
  *Toronto Star*. September 25, 1986.
Denley, Randall. "Relaxing rules for young killer poses risks."
  *Ottawa Citizen*. February 16, 2001.
Dimmock, Gary. "Killer a valuable member of college staff."
  *Ottawa Citizen*. March 30, 2001.
Downey, Donn. "Suspect insane when he killed Eaton, psychia-
  trist testifies." *Globe and Mail*. September 23, 1986.
Evenson, Brad. "Nancy Eaton's killer may soon walk the streets."
  *National Post*. March 10, 2000.
"Freedom weighed for killing of heiress." CBC News. February 13,
  2001. https://www.cbc.ca/news/canada/freedom-weighed
  -for-killer-of-heiress-1.274901.

Freeze, Colin. "Leniency urged for killer of Timothy Eaton descendant." *Globe and Mail*. February 14, 2001. https://www.theglobeandmail.com/news/national/leniency-urged-for-killer-of-timothy-eaton-descendant/article1030207/.

French, William. "A curious coda to murder." *Toronto Star*. February 4, 1989.

Montrose, Margaret. "Fatal friendship evades justice." *Windsor Star*. March 25, 1989.

Plews, Philip. "Dangerous Acquaintances." *Globe and Mail*. January 30, 1987.

Scanlon, Kevin. "Death of a Samaritan." *Maclean's*. October 6, 1986.

Scoular, William, and Vivian Green. *A Question of Guilt: The Murder of Nancy Eaton*. Toronto: Stoddart, 1989.

## 4. SINS OF THE SON: The Disappearance of Minnie Ford

Danese, Roseann. "Paroled lifer begs public to give others a second chance." *Windsor Star*. April 12, 1990.

Fogarty, Catherine. *Murder on the Inside: The True Story of the Deadly Kingston Penitentiary Riot* (Windsor, ON: Biblioasis, 2021).

"Ford says he hit mother after she wielded icepick." *Globe and Mail*. May 27, 1967.

"Ford found guilty of murdering mother, gets life term." *Globe and Mail*. May 31, 1967.

"Friend of Ford tells of plan to smash teeth." *Globe and Mail*. May 19, 1967.

Goldenberg, Susan. "Teen Wayne Ford was convicted of his mom's 1963 murder." *North York Mirror*, November 4, 2022. https://www.toronto.com/opinion/teen-wayne-ford-was-convicted-for-his-moms-1963-murder/article_2b18ff24-467d-5b89-aa7d-c1fc71a14910.html.

Hunter, Paul. "Life after life." *Toronto Star*. May 4, 2013.

"OPP question Minnie Ford's son as disappearance probe reopens." *Globe and Mail*. October 19, 1966.

"Plaster wrapped body of woman found in lake may be Minnie Ford." *Globe and Mail*. October 17, 1966.

"Police continue metro search for Ford woman." *Globe and Mail*. August 12, 1963.

"Prosecutor: He can't prove Ford intended to kill." *Toronto Star*. May 17, 1967.

"Wayne Ford admits killing his mother." *Toronto Star*. May 27, 1967.

## 5. A MOTHER'S LOVE: The Ma Duncan Case

Allen, Tom. "She hired hoodlums to kill her son's bride." *Ottawa Citizen*. July 4, 1959.

Ames, Walter. "Transcript tells of slaying plan." *Los Angeles Times*. December 31, 1958.

Barrett, Jim. *Ma Duncan*. Raleigh, NC: Pentland Press/Ivy House, 2004.

Blake, Jean. "Mrs. Duncan held sane, face death." *Los Angeles Times*. March 25, 1959.

Hulse, Jane. "A tale worth telling." *Los Angeles Times*. June 5, 1997.

Larkin, Deborah Holt. *A Lovely Girl: The Tragedy of Olga Duncan and the Trial of One of California's Most Notorious Killers*. New York: Pegasus Crime, 2022.

"Mamma's Boy." *Time*. January 5, 1959.

Mount, Bob. "Gas Chamber for Mrs. Duncan." *Oxnard Press Courier*. March 21, 1959.

"People v. Elizabeth Duncan." Ventura County District Attorney's Office. https://www.vcdistrictattorney.com/mediacenter/notable/people-v-elizabeth-duncan/.

Rasmussen, Cecilia. "A mother's love was the death of her daughter-in-law." *Los Angeles Times*. January 20, 2002.

Supreme Court of California. *People v Duncan*. 53 Cal.2d 803. Stanford Law School, Robert Crown Law Library.

## 6. ENEMY WITHIN: The Murder of Glen Davis

Alcorba, Natalie. "Murder may be tied to beating in 2005." *National Post*. May 22, 2007.

Cheney, Peter. "Philanthropist's death still a mystery." *Globe and Mail*. December 27, 2007.

Coutts, Matthew. "Killing was obviously planned out by someone." *National Post*. May 23, 2007.

El Akkad, Omar. "Family feuded over fortune, source says." *Globe and Mail*. May 27, 2007.

Goldenberg, Susan. "Next to Casa Loma in Toronto, there was Graydon Hall." North York Historical Society. March 31, 2020. https://nyhs.ca/next-to-casa-loma-in-toronto-there-was-graydon-hall/.

Kuitenbrouwer, Peter. "Glen Davis godson admits hit on patron of wilderness." *National Post*. October 13, 2011.

Leong, Melissa. "A Most Unlikely Murder Suspect." *National Post*. March 4, 2009.

Newman, Peter C. *Titans: How the New Canadian Establishment Seized Power*. Toronto: Viking, 1998.

———. "The hundred-million dollar club." *Maclean's*. October 6, 1975.

Powell, Betsy. "Davis godson writes murderous end to family saga." *Toronto Star*. December 19, 2011.

———. "He ordered Toronto philanthropist Glen Davis's murder. He's on trial for seeking to kill Davis's widow and three others from a prison cell." *Toronto Star*. July 18, 2022.

———. "Did Marshall Ross think a quadruple murder would clear a $3.2 million debt? His alleged plot is fantastic, but consistent, Crown says." *Toronto Star*. July 30, 2022.

O'Toole, Megan. "Glen Davis shooter guilty of first-degree murder." *National Post*. December 21, 2011.

## 7. BEHIND THE LAUGHTER: The Phil Hartman Story

Allis, Tim. "Taking a Bite out of Bill." *People*. January 25, 1993.

Blankstein, Andrew, and Solomon Moore. "Mix of alcohol, cocaine, medicine found in Brynn's blood:" *Los Angeles Times*. June 9, 1998.

Carter, Bill. "A hard job to accept: A slain buddy's show." *New York Times*. October 7, 1998.

Gates, Brandon. "'90s Crime Flashback: The Life and Tragic Death of Phil Hartman." *CrimeFeed*. https://www .investigationdiscovery.com/crimefeed/celebrity/90s-crime -flashback-the-life-and-tragic-death-of-phil-hartman.

*The Last Days of Phil Hartman*. ABC News Special, 80:53. September 19, 2019. https://abc.com/movies-and-specials/ the-last-days-of-phil-hartman.

Lowry, Brian. "NewsRadio to account for loss of Phil Hartman." *Los Angeles Times*. July 20, 1998.

Moore, Solomon, Greg Braxton and T. Christian Miller. "Murder-suicide claims actor, wife." *Los Angeles Times*. May 29, 1998.

Newton, Jim, T. Christian Miller and Solomon Moore. "Hartman puzzle begins to unravel." *Los Angeles Times*. May 30, 1998.

O'Neill, Ann W., and Andrew Blankstein. "Police release 911 tape in Phil Hartman case." *Los Angeles Times*. June 3, 1998.

Thomas, Mike. *You Might Remember Me: The Life and Times of Phil Hartman*. New York: St. Martin's Press, 2014.

Silverman, Steven, "Hartman's death: the police version." *Time*. June 3, 1998.

Stein, Joel. "The most happy fella." *Time*. June 8, 1998.

Sterngold, James. "Comedian Phil Hartman is shot to death in his home." *New York Times*. May 29, 1998.

Tresniowski, Alex. "Beneath the Surface." *People*. June 15, 1998.

Tucker, Ken. "Phil Hartman remembered." *Entertainment Weekly*. May 29, 1998.

## 8. BACK TO REALITY: The Murder of Jasmine Fiore

Banks, Sandy. "Can justice be done right?" *Los Angeles Times*. September 5, 2009.

Carter, Bill. "Fox network will end 'Multimillionaire' marriage specials." *New York Times*. February 22, 2000.

Fong, Petti. "Fugitive looked worn out." *Toronto Star*. August 25, 2009.

"Hunted reality show contestant lived high-flying life before apparent suicide," CITY-TV. August 25, 2009. https://toronto.citynews.ca/2009/08/25/hunted-reality-show-contestant-lived-high-flying-life-before-apparent-suicide.

Kohler, Nicholas, and Rachel Mendelson, "Millionaire Murder." *Maclean's*. September 3, 2009.

Massinon, Stephane. "Model met with ex-husband before murder." *National Post*. August 27, 2002.

Oh, Eunice. "Inside story: Jasmine Fiore's life and tragic death." *People*. August 25, 2009.

O'Neill, Katherine. "Fugitive from murder charges found dead, RCMP says." *Globe and Mail*. August 24, 2009.

Richards, Gwendolyn, and Jorge Barrere. "Murdered model's husband lead police on a high-speed police chase." *Edmonton Journal*. August 22, 2009.

Richards, Gwendolyn, and Sherri Zickefoose. "If my son was guilty, he was crazy." *Calgary Herald*. August 25, 2009.

"Ryan Jenkins' dad—My son is innocent." *TMZ*. August 31, 2009. https://www.tmz.com/2009/08/31/ryan-jenkins-dad-my-son-is-innocent.

Tebrake, Rebecca. "Accused killer found hanged in BC motel room." *Vancouver Sun*. August 23, 2009.

Vallis, Mary. "Not quite famous." *National Post*. August 29, 2009.

Wingrove, Josh. "Reality star sought in model's death." *Globe and Mail*. August 20, 2009.

Zerbisias, Antonia. "It's Donna Reed meets Pamela Anderson." *Toronto Star*. February 6, 2011.

———. "World knows dead model only as body." *Toronto Star*. August 26, 2009. https://www.thestar.com/amp/opinion/2009/08/26/world_knows_dead_model_only_as_a_body.html.

## 9. HOLLYWOOD HORROR STORY: The Murder of Iana Kasian

"Canadian sentenced to life without parole." Global News. June 30, 2018. https://globalnews.ca/video/4307095/canadian-sentenced-to-life-without-parole/.

Edminson, Jake. "Leibel sentenced to life, no chance of parole." *National Post*. June 27, 2018.

———. "Odd handprint highlighted at murder trial." *National Post*. June 14, 2018.

*48 Hours*. "Hollywood Horror Story." CBS News, 43:34.
    October 6, 2018. https://www.cbs.com/shows/video/
    pLUPCX2d9r0j6agM8MAgEOWibpRHvx27/.

Gerber, Marissa. "Graphic novelist sentenced to life in prison for
    2016 torture and murder of his fiancé." *Los Angeles Times*.
    June 26, 2018.

Hamilton, Matt. "Her blood was 'drained' from her: Canadian
    heir charged with torture killing of girlfriend in WeHo."
    *Los Angeles Times*. May 31, 2016.

———. "Man suspected of killing his girlfriend in West Holly-
    wood apartment." *Los Angeles Times*. May 26, 2016.

Hunter, Brad. "How do you treat evil?" *Vancouver Sun*.
    June 20, 2018.

———. "Toronto trust-funder Blake Leibel accused of torture
    killing." *Toronto Sun*. September 24, 2017.

Johnson, Scott. "Filmmaker Blake Leibel found guilty of grisly
    first-degree murder." *Hollywood Reporter*. June 20, 2018.

———. "'Murder, mayhem and torture' off the Sunset Strip:
    The tragic story of the budding director and his dead girl-
    friend." *Hollywood Reporter*. December 18, 2017.

Leibel v. Leibel. 2014 ONSC 4516 (CanLii). https://www.canlii.org/
    en/on/onsc/doc/2014/2014onsc4516/2014onsc4516.html.

Melley, Brian. "Hollywood Horror has Canadian Connection."
    *Globe and Mail*. June 14, 2016.

Miller, Michael. "Depravity intrigued heir of Toronto developer."
    *Toronto Star*. June 2, 2016.

Taekema, Dan. "Leibel could face the death penalty." *Toronto Star*.
    June 1, 2016.

Tchekmedyian, Alene. "Graphic novelist ordered to pay nearly
    $42 million in fiancé's torture murder." *Los Angeles Times*.
    March 1, 2019.

Warnica, Richard, and Jake Edmiston. "Toronto scion held in L.A.
    murder case." *Vancouver Sun*. May 30, 2016.

## 10. MURDER IN THE SUBURBS: The Case of Lucille Miller

California Court of Appeal, Fourth District, Division 1. *People v Miller*. Crim. No. 2512.

Didion, Joan. *Slouching towards Bethlehem*. New York: Farrar, Straus and Giroux, 1968.

Hartsfield, Jack. "Hayton denies Miller romance." *San Bernardino County (CA) Sun*. December 7, 1964.

Hertel, Howard. "Mrs. Miller's fate rests with jury." *Los Angeles Times*. March 3, 1965.

Kissinger, Jessie. "The California Room." *Paris Review*. July 23, 2013.

Klinkenborg, Verlyn. "Rereading the Landscape of an Essay by Joan Didion." *New York Times*. June 29, 2005.

MacNamara, Joseph. "Fire and Vice." *New York Daily News*. July 7, 1991.

Miller, Debra. "A Mother's Crime." *Los Angeles Times*. April 2, 2006.

Pasik, Herb. "Miller jury deliberating fourth day." *Redlands (CA) Daily Facts*. March 5, 1965.

Straight, Susan. "My people aren't Joan Didion's true Californians, and I have felt this so keenly." *Los Angeles Times*. December 21, 2021.

United States Supreme Court. *Miller v State of California*. 392 US 616. Cornell Law School Legal Information Institute.

## 11. BLACK WIDOW: The Many Lies of Evelyn Dick

Butts, Edward. "Evelyn Dick." *Canadian Encyclopedia*. January 24, 2008. https://www.thecanadianencyclopedia.ca/en/article/evelyn-dick.

"The Dick Affair." *Time*. October 28, 1946.

"The disappearing Mrs. Dick." *Globe and Mail*. September 8, 2001.

Edwards, Peter. "Evelyn vanished after serving time for killing her infant son. Did she also kill her husband?" *Toronto Star*. November 14, 2001. https://www.thestar.com/news/gta/ 2021/11/14/evelyn-dick-vanished-after-serving-time-for -killing-her-infant-son-did-she-also-murder-her-husband .html.

"Evelyn Dick." *Murderpedia*. https://murderpedia.org/ female.D/d/dick-evelyn.htm.

"Evelyn Dick and Bill Bohozuk jointly charged with two murders." *Globe and Mail*. March 30, 1946.

Freeman-Campbell, Marjorie. *Torso: The Evelyn Dick Case*. Toronto: Macmillan of Canada, 1974.

Hyman, Ralph. "Jury will hear four statements by Evelyn Dick." *Globe and Mail*. October 14, 1946.

"Jury out in Evelyn Dick case." *Toronto Star*. March 6, 1947.

"A killer vanishes." *Maclean's*. March 21, 2005.

"Life sentence given to Mrs. Dick." *Toronto Star*. March 26, 1946.

List, Wilfred. "Questioning: Dick trial raise point on methods." *Globe and Mail*. March 10, 1947.

"March 16, 1946: Grisly discovery leads to murder trials of Evelyn Dick." *Hamilton Spectator*. September 23, 2016. https://www.thespec.com/news/hamilton-region/2016/09/ 23/march-16-1946-grisly-discover-leads-to-murder-trials-of -evelyn-dick.html.

McNeil, Mark. "The strange and compelling story of Evelyn Dick." *Hamilton Spectator*. April 2, 2016. https://www .thespec.com/news/crime/2016/04/02/the-strange-and -compelling-story-of-evelyn-dick.html.

Rendon, Paul-Mark. "The black widow of Hamilton." *Maclean's*. September 10, 2001.

Schrag, Lex, "Bohozuk denies Evelyn's claim he throttled child: Not father of the baby, oarsman says on stand; secret testimony read." *Globe and Mail.* March 29, 1947.

"Story of murderer Evelyn Dick enthralled and enraged Hamilton." *Hamilton Spectator.* June 26, 2001. https://www.thespec .com/life/local-history/spec175/2021/06/26/story-of-murderer -evelyn-dick-enthralled-and-enraged-hamilton.html.

Vallée, Brian. *The Torso Murder: The Untold Story of Evelyn Dick.* Toronto: Key Porter, 2001.

Wuorio, Eva-Lis. "Evelyn Dick Acquitted." *Globe and Mail.* March 7, 1947.

"'Yes, John Dick is dead' mother quotes Evelyn." *Toronto Star.* October 9, 1946.

## 12. NO WAY OUT: The Jane Stafford Story

Canada. Statistics Canada. Armstrong, Amelia, and Brianna Jaffray. *Homicide in Canada, 2020.* "Table 9: Homicides, by closest accused to victim relationship and gender, Canada, 2020." Ottawa: Statistics Canada, 2021. https://www150 .statcan.gc.ca/n1/pub/85-002-x/2021001/article/00017/tbl/ tbl09-eng.htm.

Canada. Statistics Canada. Conroy, Shana. *Spousal Violence in Canada, 2019.* Ottawa: Statistics Canada, 2021. https:// www150.statcan.gc.ca/n1/pub/85-002-x/2021001/ article/00016-eng.pdf.

Cudworth, Laura. "Inaction, indifference enable abuse." *Stratford (ON) Beacon-Herald.* November 24, 2010.

Hurst, Lynda. "One wife's tale of life of terror." *Toronto Star,* July 19, 1986.

Jones, Deborah. "A violent end to a life of abuse." *Globe and Mail*. March 2, 1992.

Pearson, Patricia. "Life (and death) after brutality." *Globe and Mail*. December 4, 1993.

Shaw, Ted. "Jane's story." *Calgary Herald*. November 7, 1993.

Sheehy, Elizabeth. *Defending Battered Women on Trial: Lessons from the Transcripts*. Vancouver: UBC Press, 2014.

———. "The law and history speak for themselves." *National Post*. December 17, 2013.

Steed, Judy. "Will battered wife face new murder trial?" *Globe and Mail*. February 4, 1983.

Story, Allan. "Cheers for woman's acquittal." *Winnipeg Sun*. January 9, 1982.

Sweet, Lois. "Drunken sadist slain by woman he degraded." *Toronto Star*. July 13, 1996.

———. "Few avenging wives." *Edmonton Journal*. March 23, 1986.

Turbide, Diane. "Pushed to the limit." *Maclean's*. November 8, 1998.

Vallée, Brian. *Life after Billy*. Toronto: Seal, 1993.

———. *Life with Billy*. Toronto: McClelland & Stewart/Bantam, 1986.

Winston, Iris. "Compassionate look at abused wife." *Saskatoon Star-Phoenix*. September 13, 1986.

Young, Pamela. "Revenge of a beaten wife." *Maclean's*. July 21, 1986.